PORTFOLIO
DARE TO DREAM

Bachi Karkaria is a pioneer in Indian journalism, and the creator of path-breaking brands for the Times Group. She is also a popular columnist, bestselling author, literature festival curator and international media trainer. She was the first Indian board member of the Paris-based World Editors Forum, a Jefferson Fellow from Hawaii's East-West Center, and the recipient of the Mary Morgan-Hewitt Award for Lifetime Achievement. Karkaria's books include the critically acclaimed bestseller *In Hot Blood: The Nanavati Case That Shook India*; *Mills, Molls and Moolah*; *Behind the Times*; *Mumbai Masti*; *The Cake That Walked*; and collected editions of her columns in various publications.

DARE
TO
DREAM

A Life of
Rai Bahadur
Mohan Singh Oberoi

BACHI KARKARIA

PORTFOLIO
PENGUIN

An imprint of Penguin Random House

PORTFOLIO

USA | Canada | UK | Ireland | Australia
New Zealand | India | South Africa | China

Portfolio is part of the Penguin Random House group of companies
whose addresses can be found at global.penguinrandomhouse.com

Published by Penguin Random House India Pvt. Ltd
7th Floor, Infinity Tower C, DLF Cyber City,
Gurgaon 122 002, Haryana, India

Penguin
Random House
India

First published in Viking by Penguin Books India 1992
Published in Penguin Books 1993
Published in Portfolio by Penguin Random House India 2020

The views and opinions expressed in this book are the author's own and the facts
are as reported by her which have been verified to the extent possible, and the
publishers are not in any way liable for the same.

ISBN 9780143452034

Typeset in Times Roman by dTech, New Delhi
Printed at Replika Press Pvt. Ltd, India

www.penguin.co.in

MIX
Paper from
responsible sources
FSC® C016779

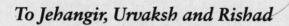

To Jehangir, Urvaksh and Rishad

Contents

Acknowledgements

The piecing together of a legend perforce involves a cast of hundreds, if only because it covers over nine decades, if only because one can't understand the man without grasping the orchestration and nuances of a highly social and people-intensive business.

My gratitude, therefore, to the family linked by blood and, as warmly, by profession, for Rai Bahadur is *paterfamilias* equally to the bell-hop as to the blue-eyed grandsons.

Among them special thanks to:

Rajrani Kapur, Swaraj Khanna and Prem Mehra as well as Rajni Rana, Kavita Mehra, Ashok Khanna and Arjun Oberoi for helping to erode the myth that ambition trampled over caring.

P.R.S. Oberoi (Biki) for a marathon three-day session on every detail of the industry, stoked by Lama's tea amidst the chestnut elegance of Chester Row.

Goodie, Leela and Jutta for the drama attendant on being married to the Oberois.

Gautam Khanna and K.K. Mehra for patiently unravelling the grand design and minuscule detail that go into the building of empire.

Satish Kumar, without whose perseverance, I'd never have taken on the project.

So many others: Among them 'Lord Harry' Kapur for a reconstruction of the old Punjab aristrocracy and Khushwant Singh for that of Delhi. Dr B.R. Nanda, Raja Bhasin, Prem Raj Mahajan and Billy Malhans for a recreation of the Simla ambience. Also, Partap Singh Dhall and Ripu Bhagat for rare insights and leads. Pearson Surita, Ellis Joshua and Irene Harris who plumped up research on the beautiful people of Raj Calcutta and the early years of the Grand.

Everyone in government and in the industry who has shaped hoteliering and been touched by its master builder. More so, all those in the Oberoi hotels in India and abroad who put aside imperative guest concerns and uncomplainingly subjected themselves to grilling. They are all, though unnamed, thanked nevertheless from the heart.

And, of course, the subject of this biography. Yes, for an indefatigable ninety-one-year-long rewind of people, events, influences, disappointments, triumphs; for an unfolding of philosophy, a laying bare of the soul. But, more than that, a deeper gratitude for patience, for the placing of faith, and the inspiration.

Bombay   *Bachi J. Karkaria*
July 1992

CHAPTER I

Daybreak

The clock behind the bell-captain stands sliced exactly down the middle, the line of its hands as straight as the back of the Sikh commissionaire at the door, as unbending as the rose of the breakfast tray being readied in the kitchen. It is six in the morning in New Delhi. Time stands in different, less rigid, postures on the row of other clocks behind the counter. Their quartz crystals measure out the hour on the continents which the empire has annexed.

Unaffected by the world beyond, the glass and granite cocoon in Delhi follows its own rhythm. The guest rises, bestirred by wake-up call and bed-tea, the voice on the telephone, the cheeriness of the butler ever mindful of the line between friendliness and familiarity. 'Should I pull back the drapes, sir?' asks the young man who has brought in the Lopchu and the morning's papers.

The guest surveys the vista presented. The shadow of a hawk darkens the tree cover of Delhi's golf course, the glint of a No 8 iron slices through the green. A parrot with a fiery tail plunges into the camouflage, and two doves sweep down in tandem to a tryst beside the swimming pool, which men in blue boiler suits drag with the meticulousness of mine-sweepers. There is nothing more deadly than a dry leaf. The landscape stretches unmarred, only the horizon is rimmed with commercial concrete. Edwin Lutyens' masterpiece is a roseate blur on Raisina Hill. Closer, a sandstone mausoleum thrusts its dome through the foliage to find counterpoint, light years away, in the dish antenna atop the country's meteorological headquarters. The neem tree rains down its yellowed confetti. The guest turns the knob on the bedside console, and Vivaldi fills the room.

There is quite another orchestration in the kitchens down below. At 6 a.m. the tea, coffee, breakfast paraphernalia are assembled. Hollow and flat-ware stands in neat stacks, the place settings of silver

1

are laid out on trays, everything is systematized so that service can knock off the precious seconds like a hundred-metre sprinter.

As Delhi prepares for breakfast, the belly-dancer has just finished setting Mena House on fire. It is 2.30 a.m. in Cairo, and the hedonistic Egyptians disappear into the scented darkness in a flash of cream shoulder against lacy black; the pyramids stand in timeless silhouette just beyond the hotel's boundary wall. Further up the country, the crew of the *Shahryar* have just finished scrubbing the decks as the boat bobs languidly on the Nile, half-way through its cruise between the pharaohs' temples at Luxor and Gamal Abdel Nasser's high dam at Aswan.

Saudi Arabia is an hour ahead of Egypt. At the Dammam hotel, the flight crews have come in through the night, signed their advance check-in forms, and, in a jumble of intercontinental accents, slid the computerized keycard into the room door, hung up their uniforms and readied themselves for bed as Delhi prepares to rise from it. The muezzin's *tajud* call has already reverberated from Medina's sacred minarets, waking, from the very fount of Islam, the faithful to bow in the special sixth *namaaz*. The staff has already commenced the cleaning of the lobby and restaurants. The coffee shop savours its single hour of solitude.

Time-zones, cultures, indeed an entire hemisphere away, the coffee toffs collide with the brunch bunch at another 24-hour café. At 11 a.m in Melbourne, the first round of beer cans has been opened with a vacuumed *puckk* as swanky swagmen pour into The Windsor.

Back on the other side of the antipodes, the Iron Curtain has lifted and a plush one is to part, revealing yet another historic property, this time in Hungary. Here, the clock has struck 1.30 a.m. and a brief halt has been called by those knocking together a mock-up suite in Gresham Palace. Budapest is the latest colony in a sway spread across four continents.

The rule encompasses a dozen cultures, ranges in architecture from the Victorian to the futuristic, covers every geographical location, mountain and sea, urban sprawl and what is derisively labelled least-developed land-locked country. Corporate czars, members of the Concorde set and connoisseurs shuffling credit cards ask for its stylish brand by name.

The high-voltage activity criss-crosses the world and converges on the epicentre, a farm tucked between two sleepy villages, a forty-minute drive out of Delhi. For all its languid tranquillity, it is the seat of power. Peacocks, as flamboyant as the industry, mewl and strut through rolling acres half as gold as green. A modest house squats at the end of the gravelled pathway. Listen carefully, and you will hear the heartbeat of a hotel empire.

Bathed, cologned, as cuddly as a teddy bear, the man emerges, flanked by two bearers in blue serge trimmed with gold. He shuns their supporting ministrations. He has risen well before our chosen hour of 6 a.m. Indian Standard Time (IST), inspected his herd of Hereford and Haryana milch cows, paused to examine his peach trees, dealt with a stack of guest comments and added his own for action, perused the daily room occupancy figures from Melbourne to Madras, and answered all his letters.

Mohan Singh Oberoi is as old as the century, but the meld of Savile Row and savvy remains. The footsteps falter, but not the memory as he lowers himself into an armchair. In soft and measured tones, the chronicle begins.

Delhi's honeyed winter light fills the room. It pours in through the French windows; more of it filters through the extra pane ingeniously fitted above them. Like all those in his kingdom, it is a room with a view, lavished with cascading bougainvillaea, climbing monstera, variegated croton and ascetic Japanese palm. The lawn is velvet underfoot. A mynah-bird takes up its position on the ledge, and taps out its tattoo on the supplementary pane, a staccato accompaniment to the march of hours that record the triumphs and the trivia of nine decades.

The season turns to searing summer, but a pirouetting sprinkler slakes the thirsty grass. The livery changes from blue serge to white terrycotton. So does the attire of our protagonist, who has replaced cashmere with linen. He dispensed with the felt hat and suspenders some years ago, but the Bally Swiss shoes are still always correct, brown with the cream trousers, black with the dark. Rai Bahadur, *paterfamilias,* who created the Indian hospitality industry and took it to its super-deluxe culmination, sits with his hands folded across his stomach. Smiling inscrutably, he says, 'I often wonder how I did it.'

The story-teller and the chronicler mesh in a time capsule. The present is kept at bay by the Gurkha at the iron gate. Only memories make their exits and their entrances. Memories, and Muniruddin with the tea.

Mohan Singh Oberoi talks without drama; the tale needs no embellishment. The adventure unfolds. Battles across the chequerboard of power. The hushed swish of antique carpets pulled from under adversaries' feet. Patience and perseverance, stodgy attitudes, but indispensable to the long-distance runner.

Mohan Singh Oberoi tells the incredible story of the boy from unknown Bhaun who became the country's first and best-known multinational, the charity student who threw India's begging-bowl image in the face of condescending international aid, the village lad who gave the top-flight global business traveller a new standard of style. Mohan Singh Oberoi talks of wine, women and song. And, the mynah-bird, tapping out its refrain on the window-pane, cocks its head and listens curiously.

CHAPTER II

The Boy From Bhaun

No one, really, had heard of Bhaun, and Bhaun returned the compliment. In this dusty hamlet of the Punjab (now in Pakistan), no one knew of Hilton or Forte, or perhaps even the Tata, who, smarting under the rebuff at the all-white Watson Hotel on Bombay's Esplanade, had built his own splendid and non-discriminating one by the sea.

As clansmen huddled round the winter fires or mothers rocked their little wards to sleep, the tales were of more conventional warfare and more standardized heroes, their exploits sanitized for the protection of tiny ears that stayed up to listen.

They heard of Prophet Mohammed's flight to Medina, of Ranjit Singh's spirited defence of the Punjab. They heard stories from ancient epics that had preceded time but were yet to find a telegenic immortality. The children awed to the tales of the first of the ten Sikh gurus, Nanak, who was saved as a babe from a cobra, distributed to the poor his father's gift of trading capital, and showed the bathing pilgrims at holy Hardwar how absurd it was to think they could propitiate ancestors by flinging the Ganga's water sunward. They thrilled equally to the exploits of the last of the Gurus, Gobind Singh, he of the roan stallion and the white hawk, *neela ghoda, chitteyan bajan,* whose courage was matched only by his wisdom.

There was a catholicity to the story-telling, for Bhaun may have been remote, but it harboured in fraternity three of the faiths of India; two-third of its population of 8,000 was Muslim, the rest Hindu and Sikh in more or less equal proportion. The British had ruled the country for a century-and-a-half, but one barely ever saw a white man in Bhaun.

In 1839, Jamsetji Tata was born in Navsari, grew up in Bombay through the riches and then rags of his father's failing business. Just as J.N. Tata had begun leaving his mark on history, Conrad Hilton was born, in 1887, in San Antonio in the middle of the New Mexican desert. As Hilton wandered between taking a degree in mining and working as a bank cashier, a sickly Charles Forte whimpered his way into the world in 1908 in Italy's Monforte, as remote an outpost as Bhaun. In time, these men would become more than just names to Oberoi.

Even if impulsiveness would never be his style, an impulsive act shaped Mohan Singh Oberoi's life. The decisive act was his mother's. Sardar Attar Singh, a strapping twenty-year-old Sikh had gone to Peshawar in search of a track-laying job, had fallen to an influenza epidemic instead, and died before he could say good-bye to his eighteen-year-old bride, and their six-month-old son. Not unlike Tata in distant Bombay—and at roughly the same time—the widowed Bhagwanti refused to reconcile herself to second-class status and was as determined to regain lost dignity. One night she simply picked up her sleeping infant and walked out of her barb-stung marital house in Chakwal to her father's welcoming one in Bhaun, twelve kilometres away.

His father's heart-breakingly premature death was the first of the many tragedies which, in Mohan Singh's birth chart, would play catalyst to fortune. If Bhagwanti had not been widowed, she might never have had to return forever to Bhaun. Without a need to build upon her father's position, she would never have acquired the influential friends who would later set her son on course to success.

Bhai Garbarah Singh kept an eye on the earnings of his fellow villagers as much as he did on the progress of his little grandson. Bhaun, like so many of the sturdy hamlets of the Punjab, sent most of its sons to the army. Bhai Garbarah acted as savings bank for retired soldiers and for those still active; he methodically portioned out to their families the remittances sent home. Bhaun's was largely a money-order economy.

Mohan Singh's grandfather was also pawnbroker and lender to farmers awaiting their harvest. He kept seed grain which he loaned out in return for kind when the waving fields ripened. He handled all this with such fairness that the first branch of a modern bank to open in Bhaun soon closed down. The villagers had continued to place their faith in their old banker.

Bhai Garbarah Singh built independent quarters for his daughter, but she virtually ran the main house and, it appears, the lives of her brother's family as well. Not that Sardar Bhagat Singh minded. The older Mohan was a good role model for his own son, Partap, and the two cousins would work for long years together later. Strong-willed, capable and tireless, Bhagwanti helped her father in his business, taking over his place as local moneylender. But in the early years she concentrated on her little boy.

Hacking through nine decades, the man on the farm plucks out the cameos of his childhood. Mohan Singh Oberoi talks of Bhagwanti nursing him till he was two, and never eating anything spicier than *dal* and *roti* for all those months so as not to upset the fragile infant's digestion. Of his mother getting him ready for school when he was six, dropping and picking him up each day. She made the three-kilometre journey once more every afternoon, carrying hot lunch and *lassi* as well as a separate pitcher of water—Bhaun could get terribly hot and dusty in summer, and her boy would face the afternoon session better if he were refreshed with a good wash.

He remembers his mother's magic touch that transfigured the simplest meal, recalls festive days replete with specialities saturated with aromatic, home-made ghee; the cloying *boondi laddoo* and *sooji ka halwa* and the flaky, savoury *matthi*. Winter afternoons still stir up the taste of cornmeal *rotis* with spiced *dal* and of *kanji* made from the black carrots of the Punjab. The mother urged the child to eat as well as they could possibly afford, but turned stern disciplinarian on the question of waste. One evening, the boy refused to finish the butter on his plate and, in a tantrum, smeared it on the wall instead. The wilful act triggered a hammering that the nonagenarian still has not forgotten.

He remembers cajoling his grandfather into letting him ride the family horse, which soon became a close companion in a lonely childhood. He brushed the chestnut every evening after school, chopped its hay, watered it, and, on weekends, roamed about on it, as free as the wind in its mane. Or at least as free as his protective mother would allow him.

More flashbacks. The day the first bicycle was pedalled in. The day the railway line at Mandhra was extended up to the village. The day the first newspaper arrived from Rawalpindi. And the day a travelling salesman first brought tea to Bhaun. The celebration of the spring festival of Baisakhi by Hindu, Sikh and Muslim alike. Every one lighting the myriad earthen lamps of Diwali, every one partaking of the sacrificial *qurbani* on Baqr-e-id.

Oberoi recalls the school where he was not allowed to play with other boys lest he get hurt, where there were five classes but only one teacher; and yet where a great deal was learnt. His first English lessons. The occasion when the visiting inspector asked all the 'free' boys to stand up. Mohan Singh, burning with humiliation, rushed to his mother after school and insisted that, henceforth and forthwith, she should find whatever way she could to pay for his education. Bhagwanti, recalling her own pride, managed to do so. On another occasion, the boy told his mother that he was no longer going to wear the coarse clothes he did. 'I always wanted the best,' says Mohan Singh.

CHAPTER III

By A Hair's Breadth

By the time he was fourteen, Bhaun's village school had taught Mohan Singh everything it could. Bhagwanti decided that, however painful the parting, her son would have to leave if he wanted to study further. She chose Rawalpindi and the Dayanand Anglo Vedic (DAV) school, run by the followers of the nineteenth century social reformer and educationist, Swami Dayanand Saraswati. Profound changes were taking place in India at the time, and the DAV school was eminently suited to provide a young man with a balanced mix of tradition and modernity. Bhagwanti had chosen wisely.

In Rawalpindi, Mohan Singh encountered two objects with which his future was linked. He saw his first Englishman. And he saw his first hotel. Flashmans. The boy could be forgiven if, in his wildest fantasy, he did not imagine that one day he would own it.

Returning home on vacation twice a year, he noticed with pride that Bhagwanti was becoming as influential as his grandfather. By now she had come in contact with the landed families of the region, chief among them Rai Bahadur Kahnchand Kapur. The imposing gentleman, whose ancestral *mohalla* or locality lay in the Jhelum district, was a member of the old Indian Provincial Service. His forte was revenue, and several of the princely states of the Punjab vied for his services as their Dewan or Prime Minister. He moved among the kind of power that Mohan Singh, despite his new exposure, could barely comprehend—governors, political agents, commanders-in-chief of the British armed forces. Kahnchand told Bhagwanti that her son was clearly a cut above the rest. During one of his holidays, the teenager also met a boy somewhat younger than him, a lad whose father had died of tuberculosis believed to have been contracted from his sister-in-law. Bhagwanti, not having forgotten her own struggles, had befriended his mother who had to live on the kindness of a rich relative, Vikramajit Singh. Mohan Singh's new companion was named Shiv Nath Singh, and the two would meet again. And again.

One morning in 1916, Bhagwanti had reason to make mounds of her coveted *laddoos* to distribute to every household in Bhaun. Her son had passed his matriculation exam. Now, Mohan Singh made a third move, from Rawalpindi to Lahore and the college run by the same DAV missionaries. Lahore was, for the Punjabis, a state of mind. Smitten by its beauty, the Armenians who had come through the passes to settle here, had written, 'Isfahan is half the world/Provided there is no Lahore.' Its commercial success found counterpoint in a cultural cornucopia. Its law college had honed the sharpest legal minds of the subcontinent. Unlike Varanasi, hoary seat of Hindu learning, or Lucknow, custodian of all the elaborate arabesques of Muslim culture, or Amritsar, home to the Sikhs' most venerated gurdwara, Lahore was not the exclusive domain of any one denomination; it was eclectic, elegant, intellectual—and great fun to live in.

By all accounts, Mohan Singh made the most of the city's varied offerings. He may not have been a coffee-house radical, but he was certainly to be found of an evening in bustling Anarkali or in the Shalimar Gardens, soaking up the fresh air and the atmosphere, and watching more than the gulmohur in bloom.

It was also in Lahore that Mohan Singh, after sixteen years, caught up with his father's side of the family. Attar Singh's brother, Sardar Sunder Singh, lived a lavish lifestyle here, and when he discovered that his nephew had come to study, he would hear nothing of this 'hostel-*shostel* business'; Mohan Singh simply had to move in with him, his wife and daughter. Not surprisingly, Bhagwanti did not approve. But her maternal instincts triumphed over egotistic pulls. After all, her walk-out from Chakwal was now ancient history, and she could be certain that this way someone was there to ensure that the young man was not seduced entirely by the allurements of Lahore.

Mohan Singh's move exposed him to the world of production and business. His uncle owned a flourishing shoe factory, and he soon discovered that his nephew had quite an eye for detail and design. Besides, he could be relied upon to help out with maintaining discipline, especially during the boisterous aftermath of pay-day when the Chinese workers swapped inscrutability for intoxication. The Sardar asked the young man to supervise the factory when he got back from college, and generously supplemented his pocket-money in return.

By the time he had completed the half-way mark to his Bachelor's degree, and passed the Intermediate examination, Mohan Singh decided he would much rather start earning and spend all his time not just at the factory, but also at the sales outlet, interacting with customers. Making a unilateral declaration of independence from academe, he informed the principal of the DAV college that he would not be attending any more classes. He presented the accomplished fact to his guardian, and with considerably greater trepidation, to his mother. Both were furious. Despite a flurry of letters and family conclaves, neither managed to make the boy retract his decision. It did not take too long after that for Sardar Sunder Singh to realize that his nephew's dropping out of college could result in raising his business. He gave him a full-time managerial job.

He was now good and proper *Mr* Mohan Singh Oberoi, and the eighteen-year-old loved it; interfacing, grappling with problems, sussing out client needs, responding to them through innovation and modification in shoe design. Succumbing, in short, to the magic of the marketplace.

But he couldn't continue in his uncle's Punjab Boot & Shoe factory business for long. There was too much upheaval as the country stirred itself to a traumatic awakening. India had expected that the service and sacrifice of its soldiers during the First World War would be rewarded by a corresponding end to colonial oppression. Britain, instead, doled out only the token freedoms of the Montagu – Chelmsford reforms, measures which Annie Besant, echoing larger sentiment, spurned as 'ungenerous for England to offer and unworthy for India to accept'.

Mohan Singh's early career fell victim to the protest that spread across the country, making a panicked administration bring in the draconian Rowlatt Act that gave arbitrary powers to arrest and imprison without trial. It only fanned the flames. The teenager stood with the tense groups in Lahore as the tragedy at Amritsar flashed through the Punjab and then the world. General Dyer's knee-jerk reaction of clamping a ban on all public gatherings; the defiant, perhaps unknowing, populace collecting on 13 April 1919, in an enclosed compound to express its opposition; the arrogant General ordering in fifty troops with instructions to fire at the peaceful meeting—and shaming history at Jallianwalla Bagh.

The massacre tempered the steel of the Non-Cooperation Movement, and the resolve was presented to the Nagpur session of Congress the following year. 'Plassey laid the foundation of the British empire,' declared Mahatma Gandhi. 'Amritsar has shaken it.' The tremors also shook the country. Sardar Sunder Singh's shoe factory could hardly remain immune; it closed down. Despondent, Mohan Singh returned to Bhaun. There, his mother in her wisdom decided that his current 'jobless, penniless and virtually friendless' state was the ideal mix for marriage. She chose the girl next door.

'She was young, charming and very pretty.' The memory of his bride still brings back the gleam to the eye, seventy-one years on. The depression dissipated, Bhagwanti's decision no longer seemed as irrational. They were married, the fifteen-year-old girl, blushing without the help of a later ersatz blush-on. The groom still a callow youth at twenty. But Mohan Singh Oberoi recalls that it took him only a few months to discover how perfectly his mother had plumbed the depths of his heart, and found exactly what it had so soundlessly yearned for.

The couple went round in the ritual seven circumambulations in Sikh ceremony—the *Guru Granth Saheb* replacing the fire of Hinduism, The celebration was very much the same. Baskets of flowers were brought in from Peshawar. A band from Lahore in all its tinsel splendour led the *baraat*. For four days, the dancing and the full-throated singing never stopped. Neither did the feasting.

Great brass platters were lavished with hearty frontier food. Spit-roasted lamb flavoured with the herbs of mountain meadows; chickens pulled out of white hot tandoors; cottage cheese simmered in yoghurt; leafy vegetables smothered in cream; lentils tempered with spices and afloat in home-made peasant butter. All the food, in fact, that later would be found within the hand-tooled morocco binding of a five-star menu, the food that would for many years remain pretender to the throne of Indian cuisine, till the same five-star restaurants learnt to give tongue to the aspirations of other regional specialities. It might be trite to say that the marriage was talked about in Bhaun for years after, but it was none the less true.

Mohan Singh decided he should go back to Lahore since the shoe factory had begun to hum again. But before he could throw himself into the business once more, he took a momentous decision. He resented the fact that his beard was only a scraggly one, he couldn't

12

pamper it with wax and roll it with authority like so many of his peers already could. One day, again refusing to settle for second-best, he simply shaved it off. Not as innocuous a decision as it might seem, considering that the family was Sikh.

His uncle was livid. A staunch believer, he considered this a highly offensive act. Mohan Singh walked out—and escaped a future as a seller of shoes by a hair's breadth. His grandfather back in Bhaun was equally shocked, though his mother took it in her stride, perhaps to dilute the all-round rejection of her son. Mohan Singh, however, had his bride, and, soon, their baby daughter. She may not have been the Queen Empress of India, but to them she was still 'Rajrani'.

Before he could settle down to another limited rural existence, fate intervened with the second of its path-turning calamities, another epidemic, this one of bubonic plague, this time in Bhaun itself. Bhagwanti, fearing for the baby, insisted that they simply leave town. Thus, as though in some biblical replay, the young couple fled their native home and into the unknown to save the life of their first-born child.

They went to the hill-station of Murree, now in Pakistan, where Bhagwanti had some cousins. The odd jobs Mohan Singh could find there were simply not enough to support the family. Murree may have been on the Raj map, but it was only a poor cousin of the glittering summer capital of Simla (now Shimla). The classical push-pull factor came into play, Mohan Singh would have to go and look for employment there. He wrote to a friend in the Public Works Department (PWD), spelt out his present straitened circumstances, told him that he had taught himself shorthand and typing, and asked if he could come up and try his luck in the soulless but secure catacombs of government service.

The friend replied saying that the floor of his tenement was his bed, but he was welcome to share it. So, in 1922, leaving behind his wife and daughter and changing several buses, he arrived in Simla. Luckily, interviews were being held just that week. Mohan Singh Oberoi sat for the test.

And failed.

CHAPTER IV

Corset And Steel Frame

Young Mohan flunked the first interview he appeared for. He did not know it then, but he had escaped 'babudom' by a shorthand squiggle. Head bent, the lad walked despondently down the Mall, but he soon found much more clamouring for his attention than the shine of his well-buffed shoes.

Simla without the 'h', like 'Poonah' with one, is today such a staple of nostalgia fantasia that the uninitiated might be surprised to learn that such a place actually exists. It seems more a metaphor, like Ruritania or Malgudi. The sensitive European Community was not unaware of its temerity—to say nothing of the incongruity—of imposing itself on a 7,000-foot-high spur of the lower Himalaya, and commandeering a hamlet that was almost as old as the hills.

Emily Eden, the intrepid diarist and Lord Auckland's sister says it all in *Up the Country:*

> Twenty years ago no European had ever been here, and there we were, with the band playing the 'Puritani' and 'Masaniello', and eating salmon from Scotland, and sardines from the Mediterranean, and observing that the chef's *potage á la julienne* was perhaps better than his other soups. . . and all this in the face of those high hills, some of which have remained untrodden since the Creation, and we 105 Europeans being surrounded by at least 3,000 mountaineers, who, wrapped up in their hill-blankets, looked on at what we call our polite amusements, and bowed to the ground if a European came near them. I sometimes wonder they do not cut all our heads off and say nothing more about it.

The village boy from Bhaun quite matched this audacity as he proceeded to carve out an empire in the footprints of the Raj. Mohan Singh, however, went in reverse, beginning at Lord Lawrence's summer capital and then proceeding to Calcutta, Job Charnock's city, which the Crown, like a corporate raider, had seized from John Company.

Mohan Singh Oberoi came to Simla exactly a hundred years after the first European set foot in the place. In 1822, Captain Charles Pratt Kennedy had been dispatched to establish a rudimentary order on the hill states, and proved to be a trailblazer in other ways as well. Monsieur Victor Jacquemont, adventurous member of the Natural History Museum of Paris, who had stayed in Pratt's rough-hewn house amidst the deodars, had written home that the artillery captain was as hospitable as the surrounding terrain was not. He served elegant breakfasts and magnificent dinners, the latter stretching over a full four hours. The French naturalist, who pre-empted Emily Eden by roughly a decade, added his own comment on the incongruity. In a letter to his father in Paris, he wrote:

> Isn't it strange to dine in silk stockings in such a place, to drink a bottle of hock and another of champagne each evening, to have delicious Moccha coffee and receive the Calcutta papers every morning?

It might be recalled that the Hon. Miss Eden arrived in Simla sixty years before the mountain railway did. Not that its lack deterred the well-heeled gentry who made the annual trip every summer. Today, you can fly into the hill-station, but there is no guarantee that the experience of travelling in a Vayudoot Dornier in a high wind will not be akin to a ride in a 'dhoolie' *(doli)* which was described as 'sitting in a half-reefed top-sail in a storm'. This canvas and bamboo litter was the main mode of travel for those who could not do it astride a stomping chestnut mare. Besides, even the most sturdy steed was known to turn skittish and leap over the precipice on being suddenly confronted by a mountain goat or monkey.

Once up, however, it was little short of paradise for the 'heaven born service', and minor functionaries. Lord Curzon may have bought the Retreat in nearby Mashobra to escape the 'despotism of the despatch boxes', but, by all accounts, an officer had difficulty remaining a gentleman in that rarefied atmosphere.

It was very early in its imperial existence that Simla acquired the reputation of being the haunt of flirt, philanderer and fortune- hunter, of match-maker and maiden-chaser, and, by Gad! the cad. It was only a kill-joy like Honoria Lawrence who primly pursed her lips and dismissed Simla society as 'a bundle of tinsel, rags and dirt', its conversation the 'contents of a dustpan, a many-sided buzz of scandal, and vanity, hasty censure, mutilated praise and insincere profession'.

While the Punjab Government also moved up to Simla and the Indian Army was headquartered there, it was the annual migration of the Government of India that gave Simla its airs. There is, of course, sufficient record of affairs of the State and serious decision-making, not all of it as florid as George Abereigh-Mackay's in *Twenty-one Days in India*:

> How Mysterious and delicious are the cool penetralia of the Viceregal office. It is the sensorium of the Empire, it is the seat of thought; it is the abode of moral respon- sibility! What famines, what battles, what excursions of pleasure, what banquets and pageants, what concepts of change have sprung into life here? Every pigeon-hole contains a potential revolution, every office box cradles the embryo of a war or death. What shocks and vibrations, what deadly thrills does this little thunder-cloud office transmit to far away provinces lying beyond rising and setting suns.

Simla had indeed come a long way since the time it had been merely a sanatorium for English men, women and children, pallid and plagued by an assortment of unknown tropical fevers, who had sought permission from the joint owners of the 'pergannah', the Maharaja of Patiala and the Rana of Keonthal, to build their houses there. Per- mission had been given and rent not demanded, only the stipulation that 'they should refrain from the slaughter of kine or the felling of trees, unless with the previous permission of the owners of the land' (Colonel E.G Wace's Settlement Report on Simla District). In 1930, the Political Agent, Major Kennedy, had, on behalf of the govern- ment, negotiated the buying of a tract deemed sufficient for a settle- ment. And, if ownership came, could imperial summer capital be far behind?

Young Oberoi quite forgot his failed test as he gazed upon the purposeful stride of power, the glide of furred and ostrich-feathered creatures from a world very far from Bhaun, or even Lahore. The Mall had lost none of its impeccable turn-out, even if the empire had lost some of its innocence since the Prince of Prussia's physician, Doctor Hoffmeister, noted during a visit a dozen years before the Revolt of 1857:

> No-one ventures to make his appearance there who is not mounted on a handsome horse, or who cannot sport the whitest linen, the most stylish cut of coat or showy uniform and white kid gloves, for one must make special toilette here in order to enjoy the open air.

Mohan Singh saw the flamboyant princes of the Punjab in their crested rickshaws drawn by liveried coolies, but didn't dream that he would be supervising their passage in a short while. Even less, as he stared in wonder at the baronial proportions of the Viceregal Lodge, did he imagine that, decades later, his line of destiny would meet it at a tangent. Mohan Singh walked as if in a daze and found himself outside a grand doorway that seemed to attract the most beautiful and the best. 'Faletti's Cecil Hotel', said the wrought iron tracery on its awning.

Like Charles Forte before the sleek file of restaurants in London town, like the callow Lee Iacocca outside the Ford Motor Car Company in Detroit, the twenty-two-year-old Mohan Singh Oberoi stood dreaming before the soaring nine-storeyed facade of Simla's Cecil Hotel. With a hundred rooms, it was the glittering station's most scintillating hostelry. The only other that could be mentioned in the same breath was Simla's Grand Hotel housed in what had once been Bentinck Castle, summer home of the Governor-General who had banished *sati* and *thuggee* from the land. While the Cecil was owned by John Faletti, its competitor belonged to his Italian compatriot, Signor Peliti, whose delectations in butter and sugar had so entranced Lord Lytton that he had brought him to Delhi as Viceregal confectioner.

17

Faletti and Peliti, their similarly lilting syllables were not the only coincidence. Cecil's rival bore the same name as the Calcutta hotel where, a quarter century later, Oberoi would hurtle into the big league. But the young man could not have grasped the irony that crisp summer morning high up in the hills. He could not have known the game-plan that fate had begun charting out for him as it turned him away from the secretariat, and drew his footsteps towards the Cecil, and his destiny towards a future far removed from clerkdom.

Mohan Singh stood riveted to the kaleidoscope of power and style moving before his eyes, and made his decision. He was not leaving Simla till he had got a job at the Cecil. Flicking away an invisible piece of fluff from his best worsted trousers, he pulled himself up to his full height, ordered his pounding heart to calm down, and, taking courage in both hands, strode confidently through the front door. The hall porter threw him out.

'No vacancies,' he said. Famous first words. Words that spur some, deter some. The young man did some game-planning of his own. The Manager was sure to go home for lunch, and the customary afternoon lie-down. He befriended a nearby shopkeeper, persuading him to point out the quarry. As soon as Mr Grove, for that was his name, strode into sight, Mohan Singh walked smartly up to him and said, 'I am looking for job, sir. Do you have a vacancy at the Cecil?'

D.W. Grove's eye took in the youth. The perfect knot of his tie did not escape his notice nor did the shine on his shoes. The suit was not expensive, but it was well pressed. The Manager did have an opening, but did not think it would measure up to the expectations of this smartly turned out chap. He said so. Trying to keep the excitement out of his voice, Mohan Singh said, 'I'll be glad to take any job you offer, sir.'

'See me at three this afternoon,' said the Manager, and walked away. It was some time later that Mohan Singh Oberoi realized, to his consternation, that he had not told Grove his name.

The error of omission was indeed a hurdle. One as big as the snooty hall porter. 'How can you have an appointment with the Manager if you say your name won't mean anything to him?' he demanded. But Mohan Singh's charm had got him out of tricky situations in the past and would do so often enough in the future. The porter let him through.

Mohan Singh Oberoi, host to the world, began his career as a clerk at the Cecil at fifty rupees a month, staying in a one-room tenement called Band Quarter 4, ten feet by nine feet, at the bottom of the hill.

CHAPTER V

Formidable Gertie

Mohan Singh Oberoi's main duties seemed to be confined to keeping track of the hotel's coal supplies. But he displayed his celebrated initiative virtually from day one. Ramchand's shop in the lower bazaar supplied fuel to Cecil Hotel, and the new clerk conscientiously insisted on every consignment being weighed again on delivery. This practice was maintained with all supplies as he rose through the ranks and became his own master.

One day, he figured out that he could effect a considerable saving for his employers by ordering the infinitely cheaper coal-dust balls. He could light the boilers with them at night, they would burn slowly while the hotel slept, and the next morning all it would take would be a scuttle or so of rock coal to get the fire crackling and the water on the gallop. Cheaper coal, but hotter water; happier guests, higher profits. The pattern had begun to take shape.

It was not long before D.W. Grove decided that the talents of the man from the Mall should not remain hidden under a bushel. He summoned him to his office, and said, 'Mr Oberoi, didn't you type out your application letter? So may I presume that you are familiar with the machine?' 'Yes, sir,' said young Mohan Singh eagerly, and promptly volunteered the information that he knew shorthand as well. Grove said, 'In that case would you please take a letter.' He dictated,

> Dear Mr Johnson,
> We are in receipt of your letter of the 8th. We have
> reserved a room for you from September 19 to September
> 25, 1922. The reservation consists of a room facing the
> valley. A bathroom is attached. The charges are Rs 15 per
> day, inclusive of meals.
> Assuring you of our best services, I remain,

Yours truly,
Sd. D.W.Grove.

Young Oberoi took it down in shorthand, typed out the letter without an error and handed it to his boss. He was elevated to Guest Clerk and his salary upped. After some months D.W. Grove acquired Simla's fashionable Davico's Tea Rooms, and left Cecil Hotel. The Manager and his 'find' would meet again, in a considerably altered equation, at the Grand in distant Calcutta. Strangely, its namesake in Simla, the erstwhile Bentinck Castle, burnt down the same year that Mohan Singh began his career down the Mall. Contemporary records describe it as a spectacular conflagration, visible for miles around 'and there were several bad cases of looting'.

Signor Peliti may have been the empire's greatest pastry cook, but his perspicacity didn't quite match his *petit fours*. He had not insured the property. Since the tragedy occurred at the time of an economic recession, the great hotel remained, for over a decade, nothing more than charred rubble. It was only in the mid-Thirties that it was taken over by the industrialist, Ganga Bishen, who, in a few years, had to surrender it to the imperial government under the Defence of India Rules. Military and civil officers used Peliti's former hostelry with pleasure since the catering was by Davico's and, later, Wenger's, two of the most scrumptious names of the North. Today, barely a sepia shadow of its past splendour, Simla's Grand Hotel is an assembly-line holiday home for government employees.

Ernest Clarke took D.W. Grove's place as Manager of the Cecil Hotel, and an enduring relationship began to cement between the middle-aged Englishman and the young shaven Sikh, one impressed by the lad's diligence, enthusiasm and initiative, the other by the Briton's meticulousness, decency and sense of fair play. Clarke and his clerk worked together to keep up the hotel's formidable reputation. With not a little help from Gertie.

Gertrude Clarke was the terror of the bearers, and the sound of her sensible shoes clacking across the linoleum had the immediate effect of accelerating the speed of sweeping, dusting, polishing. She could spot a speck at twenty paces. Indeed, Ernest Clarke was in the habit of getting work accomplished by using the magic words, 'Memsahib wants it done'.

Hotel-keeping in Simla had progressed not a little since the time the Prince of Prussia's physician had, in addition to his observations about the Mall during his 1845 tour, commented on the fact that a hotel had recently been 'set up for the accommodation of strangers, a thing utterly unheard of in the plains of Hindustan. A Frenchman is at the head of the establishment and we find ourselves very well off in his house.' The good doctor was thus spared the inconvenience of 'sleeping on moist ground', the all-too-uncomfortable hazard of travelling in such godless parts.

Incidentally, the same missive revealed that he had even unearthed a couple of old pianofortes. 'I have,' wrote Dr Hoffmeister with ill-disguised anticipation, 'selected the best of the two, and tuned it for the sake of playing some old favourite now and then in the evening, or accompanying a duet.'

Its shorter-lived rival may have had the grand antecedents of a castle but the Cecil had started life in 1868 as the modest, one-storeyed Tendril Cottage. It changed several hands, sometimes ig-nominiously by public auction. It was rebuilt, and then had to be torn down almost immediately because of poor construction and raised again. Tendril Cottage became a hotel only after it was bought by the hill-station's well-known Hotz family, some of them photographers, others crack electricians who had brought light to the Maharaja of Patiala's palace at Chail and his house in Simla as well as to several PWD buildings.

Mrs Hotz nurtured Cecil Hotel to glory, and then sold it to John Faletti, some say in a fit of pique against the constant needling of the Simla Municipal Corporation. She went off to look after Wildflower Hall in neighbouring Mahasu.

CHAPTER VI

Inns And Outs

Mrs Hotz's huff was Mr Faletti's fortune. The suave Italian had not only turned around Simla's United Services Club, he was little short of a royal favourite. John Faletti had won a place in the heart of the Prince of Wales through the traditional route of his stomach. His Royal Highness was well pleased with the catering arrangements made during the vastly successful tour of 1905-1906, so when King George arrived to survey the brightest jewel in his crown it was naturally Faletti who, by command, laid the splendid table of the royal shooting camp in Nepal.

By the time Edward, as Prince of Wales, came out in 1921-22, the Italian was entrusted with the catering for the entire tour, both in India and Burma (now Myanmar), picking up honours for his services to the Crown.

With testimonials from no less than His Imperial Majesty it was not difficult for John Faletti to enter hoteliering, and, like Oberoi, he did it through the Cecil, albeit at a more exalted level. Even before he laid his soft, stubby and sure hands on it, Mrs Hotz's enterprise was established enough to command a buying price of Rs 250,000 way back in the first decade of this century. Faletti, realizing its even greater potential, spent almost another Rs 600,000 on renovating the main building. Oberoi is currently engaged in a similar exercise, though at considerably greater expense.

John Faletti ran the Cecil and the hotel in Lahore that bore his own name as private enterprises till 1916, when he decided to go public, floating the Associated Hotels of India (AHI) Company with a capital of six million rupees. It was India's largest—and first—chain, and comprised, apart from these two hotels, Maidens in Delhi, Flashmans in Rawalpindi, Deans in Peshawar, Corstophons and Longwood also in Simla, as well as another Cecil, this one at Murree, the other balmy hill-station on the western side of the still undivided Punjab.

By the time Ernest Clarke and Mohan Singh began polishing its plaque, a chronicler, in 1925, had unequivocally labelled Simla's Cecil the hotel of the East 'par excellence'. The Cecil did its bit to give the Twenties their roaring adjective, laying out the red carpet every Saturday when the Viceroy himself might grace the occasion and place the crown on the voguish 'bobbed' hair of the Miss Cecil Queen. Flapper fashions from Europe had taken only the length of a P & O voyage to arrive at this trendy centre of empire, and the wild gyrations of the Charleston, in a flourish of patent leather pumps, kicked the staider dances off the varnished ballroom floor.

Mohan Singh closely observed the panoply and pageantry that passed by his desk all day. He was a quick learner, grasping the social nuances as well as the nitty-gritty of hotel management and he could not have found better role models than the privileged guests of the Cecil: British officers, Indian royalty, black knights, upholders of justice, the sterling company boxwallahs. Not restricting his efforts to the job description of Desk Clerk, he took on several responsibilities, including those of cashier. For the princes, he became a sort of strong room and the occasion often arose when he would discreetly suggest a better way of putting to use the sums of money entrusted to his safe keeping. Always very subtly, never overstepping the limits of decorum, but usually with success. Mohan Singh quite clearly had inherited his mother's unfailing instinct for handling finance. It won him many friends and future patrons.

One night, after stormy parleys with the still obdurate upholders of the Raj, Motilal Nehru came to Mohan Singh, manning the reception desk, and asked if there was someone who could type out a document. The young man volunteered to do it himself, retyping to ensure completely clean copy. He then delivered the six, neat, long pages to the formidable barrister. Motilal read it through, and handed him a hundred rupee note in quiet appreciation. Mohan Singh's salary then was sixty rupees a month. He used the unexpected windfall to buy himself and his wife their first watches. There was enough left over for a blanket to replace their threadbare one, as well as new clothes for the children.

Mohan Singh was busy and happy, synonyms in his lexicon. By five in the morning he would have made the steep, nearly vertical, climb up the hill from his cramped Band Quarter 4 to ensure that the boilers were ready to hiss and the room bearers were sufficiently awake to answer the bells for morning tea. He made the difficult climb again to and from lunch at home. His young wife would wait to hear the crunch of his shoes coming down the incline before she started rolling out the *chapatis* for lunch. He took a little time off for the simple Punjabi fare in preference to the stews and roasts.

Besides, he wanted those few minutes with the family that gave him the reserves to take up his second shift and work late into the night. In the evenings, he would take his wife and children for a stroll on the Mall, proud of the fact that, despite his lowly station, they were all well turned out enough to walk the smart avenue which still demanded the standards of *toilette* that had so impressed Dr Hoffmeister some eighty years ago.

Perhaps Ishran and he would laugh together in remembrance of the first night of her arrival in Simla from Murree. 'I had subjected Band Quarter 4 to a thorough cleaning in excited anticipation, but an army of bedbugs marched out of the mattress and up the wall.' Or they would recall how he had ordered satin slippers as a surprise for his little bride: 'They were in all the colours of the rainbow, but they were all a size too small.' Perhaps Ishran would tell him of their daughter Rajrani's latest prattle or, more likely, complain about little Tikki. 'He took perverse pleasure in throwing all her kitchen paraphernalia into the *khud*. Our first son had arrived in 1924, and we'd named him Tilak Raj, the anointed one.'

Tikki, as every one soon began to call the little terror, had a mind of his own, often in conflict with his mother's notions of a child's behaviour. But the father only smiled indulgently. In his eyes, his 'little rajah' could do no wrong. And surely the boy had the makings of a businessman? Whenever someone gave him a gift of cash he would run out into the garden and bury it: 'I'm planting a money tree,' he would say.

Their second son, Prithvi Raj Singh, was born in 1929; like his Rajput namesake, he would stamp the Oberoi dynasty with his own distinctive imprimatur. Since Tilak Raj was Tikki, Prithvi Raj soon became Biki. Next came another daughter whom they named Swaraj in anticipation of a still distant independence, and, finally, the baby of the family, chubby little Prem.

Rajrani grew up with Bhagwanti in quiet Bhaun, being the only girl in the boys' school which she attended specially for the English classes.

As far as her grandmother was concerned, the value of knowing the language elbowed out any dangers that might lurk in co-educational corners. She had taken Tikki as well, but the boy proved a handful even for her.

For many years, during the long winter vacations and the shorter summer breaks of their hill schools, Rajrani, Tikki, Swaraj, Biki and little Prem, ran wild and free amidst the wheat-fields of Bhaun, or in their grand-uncle's orchard, a few miles away where they gorged themselves on bunches of juicy pink *lokart* and the magenta, caterpillar-like Indian mulberry, known locally as *shatut*.

In many ways, the Gibraltar-like Bhagwanti never faltered in her support to her son and his family.

CHAPTER VII

Hotel Number One

One morning in 1927, while Mohan Singh sat filling up the guest ledger, Ernest Clarke entered the office and asked, 'I've been given a year's contract to run the Delhi Club. Would you care to come down and join me there?' The young assistant hesitated only for a fraction. Then he said, 'With pleasure.' He did not forget to add the 'sir'. It was a reckless decision, leaving an established chain for an uncertain future. The decisive factor was faith. No salaries, terms or designations were discussed. Mohan Singh questioned very little about his boss, least of all his sense of fair play. At the end of the month, Clarke gave him an envelope containing seventy-five rupees.

Ernest Clarke made quite a killing on that contract. Enough, in fact, to think of taking on a hotel of his own. Where else, but back in his old haunt. Mohan Singh followed him to the Carlton, a small hotel at the other end of the Simla Mall. Clarke leased it from the Bank of Upper India Limited in 1929, which, in turn, had taken it over in 1925 from its original owner, P.W. Fitzholmes of nearby Kasauli, for Rs 150,000. Ernest Clarke renamed the hotel after himself, though one can still see 'Carlton' spelt out in mosaic under the carpet of the reception area.

Clarkes Hotel came nowhere near the style of the Cecil. With fifty rooms, it was only half its size. The Cecil, being a close neighbour of the Viceregal Lodge, had basked in its glory, and had many of the same amenities built into it. Clarkes had a less well-heeled clientele and worse plumbing.

Messrs Hotz & Brandon, Associated Chartered Architects, Delhi and Simla, who had been asked by Clarke to evaluate the property had pronounced in their letter of 29 January 1929:

. . . the Main Building has sunk considerably towards the

27

south west corner and the floors of all the rooms need to be jacked up and levelled. Almost all the bathrooms are abnormally dark and therefore insanitary. The access to the bathrooms for the servants is scarcely short of scandalous as the staircases are narrow, steep and there is insufficient headroom provided. . . Taking into account the above features, and the fact that there is no modem sanitation in the building, I would not recommend you to acquire it for a sum exceeding Rs 175,000.

In short, it provided just the sort of challenge to someone determined to learn everything about hotel-keeping, brick by brick. Clarke took it on lease from the bank at Rs 9,000 a year. The hotel started as a one-man show. Within a year it became a two-man show. Under an indenture dated 17 March 1930 Mohan Singh Oberoi was made partner. Now, with a stake in its future, he convinced Clarke that they should buy it over mortgaging the property against the loan; they would have to pay just marginally more than the rent as interest and repayment.

Clarke certainly did not have access to the kind of money needed to make the down-payment, so Mohan Singh decided to tap the wealthy associates of his mother. The first name that sprang to mind was that of the distinguished Rai Bahadur Kahnchand Kapur who had so impressed him years ago. Mohan Singh went to see him in Sirmoor state, where he was Dewan. The young, shrewd hotelier's negotiations had helped beat down the figure to Rs 40,000 lower than the valuers' estimate but Kahnchand could not muster the Rs 135,000 that was still needed. However, he got in touch with the affluent Delhi contractor, Sardar Bahadur Narain Singh, who agreed to loan the money, provided the property was mortgaged in the name of his son, Jagjit. Once again the irony. Narain Singh had built, among other capital landmarks, the Imperial Hotel, which his other son, Ranjit, would inherit, and which later would figure decisively in the life of our principal protagonist.

Ernest Clarke and, more than him, his wife, the domineering Gertie, yearned to see the home country. Young Oberoi could be relied upon to look after the hotel. They went on a long-deserved vacation. When they returned after six months, they could not believe the difference Mohan Singh had made to the property. For the first time in its history, he had advertised, proclaiming 'under European Management', which was not technically untrue. He had persuaded the army to patronize his hotel; and having livened up the Clarkes' bar, he drew the younger government set as well. Occupancy doubled to eighty per cent. Ishran Devi had worked shoulder to shoulder with her husband to achieve the miracle, going herself to the bazaar to ensure the right quality, measure and price. Yet, at the end of her long day's journey into night, Ishran Devi sat and caringly removed the wrinkles in her husband's suit the old-fashioned way, with a heated brass pot, a *garhvi:* a proper iron was beyond their budget.

Ernest Clarke was impressed. And his faith in his own abilities was not a little shaken. He would soon have greater reason for self- doubt. Simla's distance was some protection against the effects of the Depression that had sunk the globe into a similar state of mind but the financial situation was not reassuring. Apart from the loan, the duo had paid Rs 7,000 on registration and other fees and Rs 34,000 on repairs, mainly to introduce some light and air into the dingy bathrooms at which the valuer had turned up his nose. They had even replaced the old thunder-boxes with more sanitary conveniences.

The Delhi Club contract had brought in a lot of money, but not enough. Expenses, interest and insurance on the Simla hotel had mounted. There were also heavy liabilities for the Grand Hotel on Delhi's Underhill Road that had been leased along with the Carlton, and also renamed Clarkes Hotel. Ernest and Gertie usually spent the winter in Delhi, going up to the hill hotel once during those months to see the snow. Oberoi and his cousin, Partap Singh Dhall, were left entirely in charge of the Simla Clarkes. From Delhi, on 24 November 1933, Ernest wrote a panicked letter to his young partner.

For the first time, and certainly not the last, Mohan Singh was confronted by a severe financial problem. For the first time, and certainly not the last, the clear-headed approach came into play. Within four days of the date on his partner's letter, in fact, just one day after he received it, he sent a reply and a solution.

He wrote, 'Personally I do not think the solving of our difficulties lies in disposing of the property. (It) will not be in any way advantageous to us, but on the other hand it will be disastrous to the business and to us all.' He explained how Jagjit Singh would never give them a worthwhile option, 'considering the time the country is passing through'. There was no hope of his charging them a reasonable rent, and they might end up 'paying Rs 3,600 over and above the Rs 11,400 we pay as interest/rent, taxes and insurance and ultimately lose the property as well'.

But he found a loophole. Instead of paying Rs 20,000 a year towards capital that they were committed to, they should pay only half that amount since under the agreement, 'We are hurt only if two instalments of Rs 10,000 are not paid one after another.' He also pointed out that, should they be unable to meet even the one instalment, they should try to persuade Jagjit Singh to settle only for interest and no return of capital till their financial situation eased. His plan was to pay just as much as was necessary to keep the creditors happy and just as little as was needed to keep their own heads above water. More important, he explained to Clarke, on account of a short-term setback, they should not act impulsively to destroy what they had built up. 'It is more than possible that with the New Delhi hotel things may turn better and then we will be sorry to have lost a property which we have set up with great pains to our taste and requirements.'

The gambit paid off, the hotel was saved, a month-long conference of ICS officers at Metcalfe House as well as the horse shows of the season filled all the rooms of the Delhi Clarkes and the money began to flow in again. However, a situation soon arose that was analogous to the warrior chieftain Shivaji's lament on hearing that his militia had wrested the Simhagarh Fort but that his General had been killed, '*Garh ala, par simh gela*', the play on the citadel's name translating as, 'we've won the fort, but lost the lion'. Clarkes Hotels, from the year after, would be without its namesake. Not that the other lion, Mohan Singh, really minded.

Gertie Clarke was keeping indifferent health and prevailed upon her husband to return home for good. Mohan Singh was only too ready to take over the whole show, goodwill as well as liabilities. Ernest Clarke's shares were worth Rs 20,000, at today's prices, a modest sum, but near unaffordable in those difficult days.

Ishran Devi saw her husband's inner struggle as he stood so near his ambition, and yet so distanced from it. Quietly she took out the modest store of jewellery she had received at the time of her marriage, and placed it before him, keeping only the ring he had given her from his own earnings. Mohan Singh refused. She held her ground. This was no time to allow macho notions to come in the way of their future, she said. With finality. Mohan Singh fought the lump in his throat, and went to the jeweller on the lower Mall. At the fifteen rupees a *tola* price of those days, it simply was not enough. The jeweller gave him only five hundred rupees for his wife's entire trove.

Husband and wife did not sleep that night, but by morning they had worked out another option. They would ask Rai Bahadur Kahnchand Kapur to help out. Mohan Singh again took the first bus to Nahan, the capital of Sirmoor. The elderly gentleman was, again, pleased to see how well Bhagwanti's boy was shaping. Touching his mentor's feet, Mohan Singh made some small talk, and then came to the point. Kahnchand knew how much hinged on this figure. He made a quick calculation. This time it was a request modest enough for him to manage.

The cash was bundled up in a cloth bag and put into the family Model T Ford. Mrs Kapur said she would go too, and Kahnchand's son, Hari, also decided to join the expedition. Mohan Singh took the wheel, and they set off for Simla via Kalka. With trepidation they drove through the forests and the sparsely inhabited countryside.

Mrs Kapur saw a dacoit behind every bush. Hari was caught in the vortex of adventure, but Oberoi kept his mind only on the road ahead of him. They were afraid of getting waylaid and robbed at blunderbuss point, instead they ended up stuck in the shallows of the Narkanda which they thought the Ford could ford. Finally, they extricated themselves, and got to Simla. Years later, Mohan Singh would tease his 'aunt', 'Bhaboji, remember how you sat tight on top of the bundle in the middle of the river?'

Under the deed of dissolution dated 14 August 1934, Mohan Singh Oberoi became the 'sole, absolute and exclusive owner of the business known as Clarkes Hotel, Simla and Delhi'. It came a day in advance, but Oberoi could not have hoped for a better—or more portentous—thirty-fourth birthday present. As his first-born child, Rajrani, gave him a birthday kiss that nippy autumn morning, he whispered softly, 'Just wait, *bitti*, when you grow up, wherever you go, there'll be an Oberoi hotel.'

CHAPTER VIII

Cockscomb With Bare Feet

At thirty-three, when he did not even have a company, Mohan Singh Oberoi had laid down what would remain corporate policy into the next generation, namely, that to make anything of a hotel you have to own it, and that you should not let a lack of finances stand in the way. Three decades later, when he asked Claude Feninger, President of ITT-Sheraton International how they had managed to build up such a chain, the expansionist secret disclosed to him had a sense of *dejà vu* about it. Feninger said, 'We take a loan, giving the property as collateral.'

This is exactly what Mohan Singh had done in the case of Clarkes. He had raised the money from Sardar Bahadur Narain Singh, even if at a staggeringly high twelve per cent rate of interest. Convinced that the brash young man would never be able to repay, the Sardar had presumed that this prime property on the Simla Mall would fall into the lap of his son. However, slogging, scraping, Mohan Singh, now the sole owner of Clarkes, did not ever again default on his schedule of repayment. He had not forgotten how close a call it had been in the winter of 1933.

After he had cleared about half the loan, the Chairman of the Punjab National Bank (PNB), Dr Maharaj Krishen Kapur, happened to check into Clarkes, Simla. Mohan Singh knew about opportunity's inconvenient habit of knocking just once. He spent a lot of time with Dr Kapur, arranged to bring the finer points of his managerial skills to his notice, and then, one evening, he said, 'Sir do you think your bank could advance me Rs 60,000?' 'No problem,' said the man from the bank, adding, 'would an interest rate of three per cent suit you?' Mohan Singh could hardly stop himself from impolitely dashing off to tell his wife the news. Or tell Sardar Narain Singh he did not need his money any longer.

Ishran Devi and Mohan Singh worked even harder now that the hotel was their's alone. Ishran supervised the kitchens. The eagle eye she kept on housekeeping gave serious competition to the optical acrobatics her husband exerted on everything else. She got up early to ensure that the bearers did not dawdle over their cups of tea and got on with the job of attending to guests. Abdul the room bearer in his elaborate head-dress and unshod feet, was still the great totem of hotels. Answering the call-bell with a *'Ji huzoor'*, bringing up the tea and the *chhota hazari,* or obliging with a trayload of soda and ice were the outer limits of room service. All other meals were had during set timing in the cavernous dining rooms, complete with curls of butter, Melba toast, proper fish knives and, most correctly, soup in plates. The upstart Chinese bowls were yet to invade civilized luncheons.

Mohan Singh planned out the day's fare with the head cook. There was no such indulgence *as Á la Carte,* and the *Menu Fixée* was nothing too fancy either. It featured the great staples of the Raj, mulligatawny soup or consomme, fried fish, pot roast, *kofta* curry. And a 'savoury' after the bread-and-butter pudding without which, surely, the sun could never set on the remotest outpost of Empire. If the *baba-log* of the Raj also came along on the trips to Simla, they ate at 6 p.m. and were in bed before the parents came down. Dressed for dinner.

Mohan Singh's children went to local schools, but Tikki continued to be as wayward as ever. His parents felt that the boy would have the best future in government service, or the army would do nicely, thank you. To this end, Master Tilak Raj Oberoi was sent off to the Royal Indian Military Academy, a few ranges away, in Dehra Dun. At the entrance test, the formidable panel of interviewers asked him why he wanted to join the august institution. Unawed by the stony visages, the lad answered with candour if not with tact, 'Only because I like the uniform.'

Discipline far less demanding than a military school's was anathema to Tikki. Used to getting his way without too much fuss the school was not the most compatible of environments for the high-spirited adolescent. One day he decided to borrow a car. He forgot the minor courtesy of asking for it, overlooked the insignificant fact that it belonged to the headmaster. He was rusticated. He returned to Simla.

Mohan Singh, of course, bestowed none of the indulgence he showered on his elder son on himself. In the sixteen years he spent in

Simla he did not once find time to see a film or even step into the station's fabled Gaiety Theatre, built in 1838, where Hermione Montagu had held court in the green room, and where the Amateur Dramatic Club wrested the most coveted membership. The Gaiety laid claim to posterity because its was the first curtain to be raised in the Himalaya over a proscenium arch, but there was also the fact that Lord Lytton had directed several of its productions, some said, merely with an imperious wave of the hand as he reclined languidly in front of the stage.

The Viceroy's interest, however, can hardly be questioned since he renovated the theatre and added three gilded boxes, bringing it as close to London's Royal Albert Hall as was possible with Simla's constraints. Commenting on the opening of the spruced up new auditorium in 1887, a cub reporter of the *Civil and Military Gazette,* Mr R. Kipling by name, penned a couplet reminding all those who fret and strut their hour about the stage of the transience of their act:

Time, the grim destroyer,
Already blurs the photos in your foyer. . . .

Perhaps with his tongue firmly in his cheek, precocious Rudyard dismissed the tales of moral turpitude associated with the actors and actresses:

Praise most yourselves-the Perfect and the Chaste
Why 'chaste' amusement? Do our morals fail
Amid the deodars of Annandale ?
Into what vicious vortex do they plunge
Who dine on Jakko or in Boileaugunge ?
Of course it's 'chaste'. Despite the artless paint
And Pimm's best wig. Who dares to say it ain't?
Great Grundy! does a sober matron sink
To infamy through rouge and Indian ink?
Avaunt the thought. As tribute to your taste,
WE CERTIFY THE SIMLA STAGE IS CHASTE.

Even fifty years later, the productions at the Gaiety were impressive, but Mohan Singh was too busy. All work and no plays did not make for dull evenings as far as he was concerned. And it paid off.

The Punjab National Bank loan, for instance. Thanks to the Clarkes' enhanced reputation, Mohan Singh and his wife could double their room rates without dropping occupancy, and the second part of the liability was cleared at twice the speed as the first.

Mohan Singh, thirty-six, was now his own master. The tantalizing dream that had first danced before his eyes in 1922 had ensnared him completely. He was hooked on a paradise where the rooms are always full and the waiters never drop their trays. Such ambition could never be circumscribed by a fifty-room hotel. He felt a strange sensation in his upper back. Perhaps, it was the wings itching to sprout.

CHAPTER IX

The Colonel And The Monk

Four years had passed since Mohan Singh acquired Clarkes. Things were running smoothly, everything was in control, the guests and money were coming in. In short, life was too dull for the man who hoped to have a hotel in every part of India. The world would have to wait a little longer.

About this time Mohan Singh just happened to have gone to Delhi to clear up some matters with suppliers. Waiting to take the train back to Kalka, he just happened to meet an old friend from the Bhaun days who mentioned that there was a hotel up for grabs in Calcutta. 'Can we swing the deal?' asked Mohan Singh. 'Yes,' said the friend, 'if you hurry.' 'Is it worth it?' asked Mohan Singh. 'Yes,' said the friend, 'if we play our cards right.'

'I'm coming with you,' said Mohan Singh, rushing off to cancel his ticket to Kalka and buy one in the opposite direction. There was just about time to send a telegram to Clarkes to tell his wife about his change of plan.

It was only as the Lahore-Calcutta Mail steamed out of Delhi that Mohan Singh realized that he had not even asked the name of the hotel. The friend raised one eyebrow, smiled sardonically, paused dramatically, and said, 'The Grand.' Oberoi nearly jumped off. He had always aimed high, but not that high. The Grand was legend. The Cecil, which, to him, had been the ultimate, had a hundred rooms. The Grand had five times the number. Its reputation was formidable. He stared at his friend. Only Shiv Nath Singh could have dragged him into this. Shiv Nath, who had manoeuvred his way up the world from being a poor relation in the house of his uncle, Vikramajit Singh, near Bhaun. He now was in virtual control of the great outfitting and furnishing establishment in Calcutta, Samuel Fitze & Co., having, like the cuckoo nesting, edged out the English partners who had taken him in.

In the early years of Oberoi empire-building, Mohan Singh and Shiv Nath Singh would become classical protagonists, like the Kauravas and Pandavas of earlier mythology, like Kane and Abel of the later Jeffrey Archer novel. Mohan Singh, the cool calculator; Shiv Nath, the Machiavellian manipulator. But, patience. Now, as the Mail hurtled across the country hurling Mohan Singh towards a new horizon, Shiv Nath merely told him the story of the Grand and how this once-magnificent institution came to be forgotten under a shroud.

The Grand had started out as the mansion of a Colonel of the same name, who, having come by a piece of land in a lottery, proceeded to build for himself a home patterned on a country seat that he had wistfully coveted as a young man back home in England. This seemed to be something of a habit in colonial Calcutta, for, hadn't the Marquis of Wellesley done the same, ordaining Government House to be a facsimile copy of his beloved Keddersfield?

Colonel Grand's home seems to have set the mode for the debate and dalliance that would mark the mansion in its later incarnation as a hotel. While the Colonel was part of Calcutta's cerebral landscape, his daughter-in-law was engaged in less high-minded pursuits. A fragile-featured, full-figured beauty, judging by her portrait, she ensured that the city's scandal sheets never ran out of material. Having trod her satin-slippered way through a field of broken hearts, she abandoned her swains and the city. Some years later she surfaced in Paris—as nothing less than the Princess Talleyrand.

A little renunciation was, therefore, in order, and Colonel Grand's home entered, at least in name, a more ascetic phase. It became Mrs Monk's Boarding House. But as this establishment, too, it did its share of trail-blazing. Annie Monk was Irish, fifteen-stone, and was once married to a sailor, exactly the combination needed to handle unruly patrons. So, she set about setting up the new kind of accommodation devised at the end of the previous century by another intrepid woman, Mrs Box: the boarding house, answer to the prayer of all those who had come east to find gold in Charnock's mud flats but were not ready, willing, or able, to set up home.

Annie Monk began from 13, Chowringhee Road, and soon became the talk of the town. Whether her patrons struck gold or not, she did, and she was soon able to acquire and expand to Nos. 14, 15, 16 and 17. A contemporary account of her place, considering its success, is surprising: 'The furniture was half covered and half exposed, the room half swept, many of the wine glasses had no legs and so stood upside down. . . the glass in the picture frames had cracks and the spider had festooned every nook and cranny with giant webs.' Yet she lured gentlemen from government circles, the Board of Revenue, the Bengal secretariat and the Customs. One is not certain whether such upright citizens could lay low a place with such devastation.

Annie Monk flourished for twenty-five years, and, having made her pile, sailed back home to the Emerald Isle. But her fledgling efforts at hoteliering were to be vastly bettered by an adventurer who would come from far-off Armenia to raise it to a grandeur that matched the name of the Colonel who had first built upon that site.

Stephen Arathoon had come to Calcutta as a wide-eyed twenty-year-old from his native New Julfa in Armenia. He came with less than a hundred rupees in his pocket, and began his career as a hawker, peddling his wares from a wheelbarrow, but with an astuteness that we will encounter later in his successor. By the time Arathoon died, he had built up a real estate empire, and become part of the triumvirate of Armenians who owned Calcutta's toniest properties.

His first move was to J. Boseck & Co., Jewellers and Silversmiths, engaged in the traditional craft of his own family. Undeterred by the plush trappings of the establishment, he had walked in, asked for a job, answered his potential employer's questions with a quiet confidence. He learnt more tricks of the trade than Boseck taught him, and had soon built up a private clientele and income.

When the Theatre Royal was put up for sale, in 1894, he had the capital to buy it. It was part of Annie Monk's estate, and apparently as grotty as her boarding house, for we hear from an early chronicler, that, during a performance, a somewhat discerning horse thundered its protest, fell through the worm-eaten stage and played the devil's tattoo with its hooves on the corrugated iron walls below for the rest of the evening. Mercifully, in 1911, the whole structure burnt down. Of course, Arathoon collected the hefty insurance, and began the building of his Grand Hotel.

Like dominoes, one by one, slabs of the old estate fell into his hands, till Arathoon controlled the whole block on fashionable Chowringhee. In front of it stretched the green sward of the Maidan. Behind it was the famed Sir Stuart Hogg Market. To its right stood that pillar of empire, the department store, Whiteaway and Laidlaw, known as the Harrods of India. There could be no finer location for a hotel, and Stephen proceeded to make his better than its two rivals, Spence's, established by John Spence before 1830, when there is the first recorded allusion to it, making it perhaps the oldest Western-style hotel outside Europe, and the Great Eastern Hotel, built by David Wilson in 1841.

The Grand thrived under Stephen, but, after his death, the iron control of its management had rusted. So had the pipes. Illness raced swiftly and silently through the hotel, first typhoid and then enteric fever. Some say the sewage leaked into the drinking water; others pinned its cause on a cat putrefying in an overhead tank. Six people died, several were laid low, including Stephen's widow.

With reputation lost, room occupancy soon followed suit. In 1937, Stephen's son-in-law, Gregory Arathoon, ordered the massive iron gates shut and the staff retrenched. The giant chandeliers and furniture were covered in white, but the shroud of gloom that encased the once majestic hotel was more palpable.

CHAPTER X

500 Rooms, One Cockroach

Mohan Singh Oberoi, thirty-eight, had reasons to gape as he stood before the magnificent pile on Chowringhee Road, Calcutta. Indeed he could not get over his wonder over all three, the mansion, the avenue and the city. Two generations later, they would name the experience culture shock. Delhi may have been the seat of seven empires, but the Raj had arrived there a scant twenty-seven years earlier; Simla may have been winter capital, but it was ultimately only a Himalayan hamlet. On the other hand, John Company had presided over Calcutta for two-and-a-half centuries. However scathing young Rudyard Kipling had chosen to be about a city 'chance-detected, chance-erected', there was no denying that Job Charnock's muddy boot-print had left a monumental imprimatur on posterity. The pagoda tree had been well shaken, and the pleasure domes of merchant prince and company nabob rose to make Chowringhee the promenade of lithograph and legend. The Grand Hotel was still among its most fabled buildings, distinctive and imposing, despite the overhanging pall of death.

Once again, Mohan Singh marvelled at his own temerity. Surely he was pushing his luck too far. Just the other day, possession of the fifty-room Clarkes had seemed the pinnacle of ambition, and here he was hoping to take over 500. It might have stilled the butterflies in his stomach to have known that the hotel's builder, Arathoon Stephen, had started life pushing his wheelbarrow down this very stretch.

Indeed, in one of history's neater coincidences, Arathoon Stephen had come from his native New Julfa through the passes of the North-West Frontier just a decade or so before Mohan Singh's birth in the shadow of this same rugged geography. Like Oberoi, failing the PWD test in Simla but still striding confidently into the Cecil Hotel, the Armenian had walked into the plush interior of J. Boseck & Co.

At about the same time that the Grand Hotel had begun to live up to its name, Mohan Singh entered the hotel business, albeit as a lowly clerk, half a subcontinental breadth away.

Arathoon Stephen was, in many ways, the perfect predecessor of Mohan Singh Oberoi. Both shared an unflappable self-confidence, an unshakeable ambition. Both made their fortunes as much by counting pennies as by investing pounds well. Even when he was a millionaire and more, Arathoon Stephen continued to sell the piled-up newspapers and empty bottles to the *bikriwalla*, his favourite daughter, Anna, keeping a hawk's eye on the man's hand-held weighing scales.

Like Mohan Singh, Arathoon was also a gentleman gifted with the ability to turn even the most adverse situation to advantage, to get on top of the trickiest turn of events. Major H. Hobbs, in his delightful chronicle of the great hotels of the Orient, *John Barleycorn Bahadur,* tells the story of an angry guest who swept into Stephen's office one morning brandishing his teapot apoplectically, crying, 'Cockroach! Cockroach!' Stephen did nothing more than raise his monocle to his eye, peer inside to examine the offending insect lying comatose on the bed of perfect Darjeeling, let the monocle drop, sit back and pronounce, '500 rooms, 500 teapots, one cockroach. Very good average.'

It is from Stephen Wilkinson, A.F.C., F.R.I.B.A, who built a chateau-like hotel for Stephen in Darjeeling, and possibly also had a hand in the flawless design of the Grand, that we get another story highlighting the Armenian's astuteness. On 14 June 1936 he wrote a letter to the Editor of the *Observer* of London:

> Apropos of Mr Arthur Hodge's book, *Lord Kitchener,* I should like to relate a true story about the late War Lord. As is well known, the late 'K-of-K' was a great collector of china, and when Commander-in-Chief in India, used to visit the house of a friend of mine in Calcutta (I refer to the late Arathoon Stephen, well-known millionaire Armenian) who possessed a remarkably fine collection of Oriental china.
>
> During one of my visits, 'K-of-K' called and as usual we all proceeded to the room containing the collection. Among the exhibits was a small vase having a tubular stem

and a bulbous base which 'K-of-K' greatly coveted, but the owner would not part with it at any price.

While examining the piece, the stem unfortunately came in two, and the great 'K' was left standing aghast with a piece in each hand, apologizing for the accident and offering to make good, as far as possible, the damage. Of course, Stephen made light of the matter until after the departure of 'K' when there was much lamentation and not a little blaspheming during which he asked me what was to be done about his most precious piece.

I suggested that it would be a good idea to have the stem joined and the fracture covered with a gold band, stating that this vase was accidentally broken by His Excellency Lord Kitchener of Khartoum, etc., giving the date of the occurrence. This was done by a local jeweller, and so effectively that the vase was given a more prominent place in the collection than before, and for all I know, still occupies this position at No. 2 Camac Street, Calcutta to this day.

Arathoon Stephen's granddaughter, Irene Harris, vouches for this story. But the vase is no longer at 2, Camac Street, the old house having been taken over by the asphalt jungle that has overgrown this once leisurely avenue. It is in England, in the home of one of Stephen's five daughters, Burma.

Arathoon's Grand was one of the first buildings in Calcutta to install a hydraulic lift, an event that brought in droves of adventurous citizens lining up for a ride, not unlike the curious Bombayites who would come half-a-century later to gawk at the lobby and escalators of Bombay's Oberoi Sheraton. The enterprising Armenian once again turned nuisance-value to profit, selling soda and refreshments to those waiting their turn. When someone complained that the prices were scalping, Stephen, without losing either cool or courtesy, informed the angry gent that he was welcome to go out and consume his sodas at a fairer price but the management could not guarantee the reservation of his place in the queue.

Calcutta challenged Schweppe in 1814 when Messrs Tulloh Co. announced 'respectfully' that they were appointed Sole Agents for the sale of Soda Water, made at the Bengal Soda Water Manufactory.

As always, the irrepressible Major Hobbs offers a delicious footnote:

> A friend in Mozufferpore complained about the local soda
> being flat and received the following explanation:
> 'Honoured Enormity, this is to inform you that my father
> he has been ill and unable to make water but in a few days
> he will be better when he will make plenty of water with
> lots of gas.'

When the initial tour groups of Americans arrived in the 1920s, Indian hoteliers expected them to be the first of the big spenders scattering fistfuls of dollars. Stephen slapped a charge of an anna per glass of iced water, and a visitor, losing her cool, collared the first available Englishman to complain, 'We never pay for it in Sioux Maw or Medicine Gulch, and even in London, England, or Athens, Greece, we got it for nothing.' They marched to the American Consul in protest.

Stephen, of course, refused to be browbeaten by a bunch of people who, in Hobbs' memorable phrase, 'two days later would have vanished as completely as Shakespeare's shoelaces', but he did not repeat his error. He did not charge the next batch of Americans for iced water, though he still made his profit. He managed to get the tourists to drink only soda at two annas a bottle by posting a notice in every room saying that the 'purity of the water cannot be guaranteed'.

The tourists, however, would have the last laugh. It was precisely because the management could not guarantee the quality of the water that Stephen's son-in-law, Gregory, a decade later, had to close down the hotel, and ultimately sell out to Mohan Singh Oberoi.

CHAPTER XI

The Grand Vision

Mohan Singh strolled up the length of the block that the Grand occupied. Surveyed its noble facade. Sized up the wide first floor balcony that ran from end to end, and under which W.B. MacCabe, once Chief Engineer of the Calcutta Corporation, had always refused to walk, declaring it unsafe. He stood humbled before this magnificent structure. This was the challenge that the fledgling wings were waiting for. Mohan Singh forgot the apprehension he had felt on the train, and went up to the chowkidar who sat outside the barred gate rubbing a wad of the addictive *khaini* with thumb on palm. 'Could I have a look inside ?' The watchman gave him the address of the Mercantile Bank, liquidators to the estate of Arathoon Stephen, Esq.

Mohan Singh put on his smartest three-piece, and had himself driven up to the bank on Clive Street. The Manager was more than willing to offload the liability, and it was apparent that this gentleman's credentials were as impeccable as his suit. The Manager said rent for the lease was Rs 12,000 a month. The Simla hotel would do nicely as security, he said, his alacrity prompted by Mohan Singh's oblique reference to the fact that, unlike the Grand, it was flourishing, and had not lain barred and bolted for a year.

When the Bank Manager, pushing his luck, asked for good-will, the shrewd hotelier put on his most miffed look and said, 'What good-will? It is bad-will!' The Manager ruefully conceded the point, and it was Oberoi's turn to push his luck, 'In fact, in view of the circumstances, you should reduce the rent.' The banker agreed, and the deal was made at Rs 8,000. Mohan Singh was more than willing to carry out the sole condition that a European be appointed Manager. He'd had enough experience of their superior talents in hoteliering; besides he recognized that nothing less would restore public confidence in the 'bugged' establishment. By the time he returned to the Grand Eastern Hotel where he had checked in, he already knew whom he wanted: D.W. Grove, who had first employed him at the Cecil.

He also knew he could not go it alone. Three thousand equity shares worth Rs 300,000 were issued on 14 December 1938, of which 1,001 were allotted to Mohan Singh Oberoi, with the remainder equally divided between Rai Bahadur Kahnchand Kapur, Shiv Nath Singh, Rai Bahadur Hari Ram and D.W. Grove. The last named gentleman had tired of selling Danish pastry at Davico's and yearned to get back to the glamour of hotels. Mr Grove also signed a five-year contract as manager on what was then a generous stipend of Rs 1,000 a month, plus room and board.

Hotel (1938) Pvt. Ltd. was formed to take the management lease for Stephen's Chowringhee Properties from the Mercantile Bank. Kahnchand Kapur's eminence made him the natural choice as Chairman of the Board. Mohan Singh would be Managing Director and would run the show, keeping a ten per cent extra of the profits for his efforts. He was the only one of them with experience; even though Shiv Nath owned Palace Hotel in Karachi, his business was, in the main, pleasure.

It was, however, somewhat premature to think of profits. The immediate and compelling reality was the one-year accumulation of filth inside the Grand. Armed with the documents and the keys, Mohan Singh Oberoi drove up grandly to the huge, wrought-iron gates. The chowkidar smirked quietly behind his *salaam* for he knew the shock that awaited the new boss inside. Asphyxiating dust, nauseating garbage, the putrefaction in the overhead tanks, the patina of decay. But Mohan Singh saw much more than that.

It was pitch dark and he involuntarily dropped his voice to a whisper inside the ghostly vault. The chowkidar struck a match, and Oberoi beheld a magnificence beyond his wildest imagining. Rich tapestries, gilt mirrors, marble pillars, exquisite carpets and massive chandeliers. Silver neatly stacked in the kitchens. Shelves full of crystal, albeit encrusted with grime.

He sat for hours alone in the cavernous pitch of the lobby. The only sound was that of the scurrying of the rats—and the clacking of his brain. By the time he left, the darkness outside had matched the one inside, but he knew exactly what he was going to do to restore the hotel to a grandeur that would make Arathoon Stephen sit up in his grave in gratitude.

Continuity, not change, would be the basic tenet. Oberoi conceded that it would be difficult to match Stephen's ambitious and perfect design: the unique four-sided hotel boxing in a 67,000-square-yard court centred with a garden that exuded coolness and fragrance to each one of its 500 rooms. To say nothing of the view. The concentration instead should be on Operation Clean-up, backed by Operation Retrieval.

Oberoi realized that the missing asset in the ghost hotel was invaluable. He established a communications network that would bring the old staff back. As the news spread that the Grand would once again hum, they returned, first in ones and then in armies. Cooks, bearers, *masalchis, dhobis* and *durwans*; the furniture duster, the silver polisher and the washer-of-china-with-care.

Every single item of the inventory that ran into a hundred thousand was scraped, scoured, scrubbed. Everything from the tiniest peg measure to deep-piled carpets fifty feet across. Oberoi stood in attendance, advising, supervising, often rolling up the sleeves himself. Anything that needed replacement had to get his okay. Every task deemed finished had to get his nod. He was on hand from six in the morning through the sweltering summer afternoon, the evening's southerly breeze. It was only very late at night that he walked past the pavement sleepers back to his room at the Great Eastern.

Continuity, not change, except in the matter of the fatal flaw: the germ embedded in the hotel's gut that had found its way to that of its guests. Oberoi ordered every single pipe torn out, every overhead tank thrown away, and the most modern plumbing that money could then buy, put in. To cut corners here would be to send every other effort down the drain.

The silver, the glass, the gilt, the marble, the porcelain, the wood—all shone. Everything was back in place, including the same clerks at their ledgers, the same *durwans* at the doors, the same cooks and bearers at their respective posts at range or rooms. The massive gates opened again on 21 December 1938 and the hotel sprang to life as though at the press of a button. Or the kiss of a prince. But the happily-ever-after ending would have to await another upheaval.

CHAPTER XII

Soda For Your Bath

D.W. Grove and Mohan Singh Oberoi opted for a soft opening rather than an ostentatious one. But a few select guests were invited, including *The Statesman*. The Lady of Chowringhee Square reported the new look of the Lady of Chowringhee Road:

> The Grand Hotel, Calcutta, reopened its doors last night for the first time after nearly a year, when the hotel was closed for extensive realterations and redecoration. Those few months have not been wasted and the decorative scheme is now very pleasing to the eye. To celebrate the opening a cabaret, given by Erwin Klein and his orchestra and other well-known artists, was presented in Casanova, which is decorated in a shade of delicate pink with the stage a pale blue in contrast.
>
> Erwin Klein's Viennese orchestra gave a good performance and were ably supported by the other artists. They will continue to appear at the hotel every evening with the exception of Sunday, for some months. Laura Shorthand, who appears with the band, sings well, and the Wilhelmine Quartet, Tereza, Gabrielle, Elizabeth and Wilhelmine, gave fine performances. Outstanding in the cabaret was Gabrielle Franz, a charming French artiste, who gave several outstanding dances.

But mud has the habit of sticking. While a lot of people dropped in at the bar, very few checked in. An unpalatable situation for a hotelier who later would declare that all the money is to be made from the rooms, and very little from the public areas. It would have given little consolation to Oberoi to have been told of the warning of an early soldier of fortune against Calcutta's eating places, however upmarket their offerings:

'You're quite all right inside the bar,
But khubburdar the caviare!'

One day, Mohan Singh met the father of Bobby Kooka, who would later create Air-India's delightful maharajah mascot. Kooka Senior often came to Calcutta to oversee his cinema halls. Spotting him in the Casanova Bar, Oberoi asked him to shift to the Grand from his customary Great Eastern Hotel; he would give him a discounted rate. 'I'll die of cholera,' said Kooka. Oberoi ordered him a Scotch on the house, and told him of all the plumbing and work they had put into the hotel. When Kooka still looked sceptical, he said, 'Look, you needn't drink any water at all, you can have all the soda you want free of charge. You can even use it to brush your teeth if you are that worried about typhoid on tap.' Kooka checked in. And became a regular.

The word spread, not surprisingly much of it exaggerated. That a very rich Punjabi had taken over the Grand Hotel, that whisky flowed like water, and the bath tubs were filled with soda. Mohan Singh did nothing to scotch the rumours, knowing that the hotel could do with less-than-adverse publicity. Business began to look up. At first there was only a trickle of permanent residents. But the Christmas season and the stylish entertainment laid on gave the hotel a boost.

Clarkes back in Simla was doing well enough to underwrite some of the Grand's losses. When the family moved, in this great cultural leap forward, half-way across the country to Calcutta, Mohan Singh left behind a Manager there. He also asked his mother to come over to Simla from Bhaun. Nothing escaped her eye either. Not that she had mere observer status. Rajrani, serving the perfect flaky *matthis* her grandmother taught her to make, recalled Bhagwanti going to the fruit market, organizing a huge cellophane-covered gift basket and marching off to a British officer, with an interpreter-relative in tow. 'You'll have to get my work done,' she said in Punjabi, with the right mix of obsequiousness and authority. It was. Mohan Singh, clearly, owed not a little of his future success to his genes.

At the Grand, another strong, very efficient woman exerted her influence on the nitty-gritty of running a hotel. Savitri Khanna soon rose to become Controller of Household, a position less mundane than the name suggests, for in Mohan Singh's manuals, the housekeepers held the master key to a hotel's success. Savitri Khanna worked almost on par with Mohan Singh and Ishran Devi, with them bringing new hotels up to their standards.

It was Savitri Khanna's son, Gautam, with whom the willowy Swaraj Oberoi fell in love in 1950 as they glided across the floor one night at Firpo's, the equally tony dining place on the block adjacent to Oberoi's hotel, with its deep-pile staircase, its mirrored banquet hall, its Viennese string quartets. It was not a little awkward for Savitri Khanna, but she knew the family closely enough to broach the subject to Rai Bahadur herself. Even without a mother's forgivable hype, even if he did not have a fortune to match that of the post-war Oberoi's, young Gautam was no mean catch. He had shone in the railway job that had come his way on his father's premature death. Rai Bahadur could spot a human being's potential as surely as he could a hotel's. He asked him to join his family, and soon after, his business. It was the jackpot, for Gautam Khanna charted much of the Oberoi destiny all the way to the dizzying heights. Today, he is Biki's right-hand man.

Older family associations had also been cemented by marriage ten years earlier, in 1940, when Rajrani, the eldest daughter, wedded Colonel J.C. Kapur, nephew of Rai Bahadur Kahnchand Kapur. Kahnchand had brought up 'JC' along with his own sons, all like the princes of the states where he had been Dewan. They were married at the Grand, in a style that matched the venue. They made the most elegant couple of the season, the striking nineteen-year-old bride and the handsome army officer, as skilful on the playing field as the one of battle.

Prem, the third daughter, would also marry into the services, in 1957, choosing Captain K.K. Mehra. Rai Bahadur agreed less readily to the match. Prem was his 'baby' and, as he said later with the laughter spilling out of his eyes, it was only too evident that 'she loved her army-man more than me'.

It was in the early years of the Grand that a young lad called Muniruddin ran away from his native Bihar village, and, like thousands of others, landed up with a relative who had a job in Calcutta. His uncle worked at the Grand, and the boy was soon slipped into service. One morning, as Mohan Singh conducted the daily inspection of finger-nails, continuing Arathoon Stephen's practice, he spotted the new face, told him to step aside, and to see him in his office. Young Munir's heart sank. It looked like his urban adventure was going to end almost as soon as it had begun. The Burra Sahib grilled him for ten, aeon-long moments. Then he told him to join his personal staff. Muniruddin is still there, the first of the faithful servants, and now the major domo at the farm, in gold braid and brass buttons.

Mohan Singh's office at the Grand was no less modest than the one he'd had at Clarkes but the hands-on style which had already become his trade-mark quickly asserted itself. He was everywhere. Weighing everything to remind suppliers that he knew his onions—and asparagus. Ruling the roast in the kitchen—and tasting it. Ensuring that waiters did not think their job was to make guests wait. At night, he burned the midnight oil which, too, he must have acquired on the most competitive terms. 'I knew I had to check every single payment, tally all orders placed against all supplies drawn, and calculate right down to the nearest anna. I knew I couldn't cut corners, so I had to cut costs.'

However, the Grand's balance-sheet at the end of the first year did not reflect the untiring effort. The other partners began to doubt the wisdom of their investment, and threatened a pull-out.Oberoi pleaded, cajoled, persuaded. It was only a matter of time, he said. It was only teething troubles, he said. 'All right,' he offered, 'all profits will be shared, all losses will be borne singly by me; just give me three more months, and then break up the partnership if you must.' Clarkes was doing well enough for the partners to take him at his word.

Things got worse. But in the very factor that kept guests away lay the hotel's salvation. Calamity appeared like the *deus ex machina* of Greek tragedy to save the day for Mohan Singh Oberoi. This time it was not a virus; it was war.

In 1938, when the Grand changed hands, Europe had become restive, still suffering from the fall-out of 'the war to end all wars'. In 1939, just as the hotel had been given the kiss of life, the juggernaut of the Third Reich had rumbled into Poland. In 1940, no one deemed it politic to launch upon a grand tour of the East; besides, even British officials who patronized the hotel were called up to service, as the stiff upper lip showed definite signs of cracking despite the valiant Battle of Britain. Then came the attack on Pearl Harbour and America fissioned into the war, changing its face even as it wiped Hiroshima off the map.

Ironically, it was the war coming closer to Calcutta that rescued the Grand's—and Mohan Singh's—future instead of torpedoing it.

Calcutta was overrun by the men in khaki. Together with Kandy in Ceylon, it became the eastern theatre's centre for rest and recuperation as well as the base for flying out troops and supplies to the battle zones of Burma, the Philippines, Singapore. The soldiers went down the road to Mandalay that had already achieved poetic celebrity in the earlier war, up the River Kwai that was still to attain a cinematic one. The men arrived in tens of thousands, and every inch of space was commandeered. A requisition order was posted on the Grand for the billeting of officers, signed by the representative of the Allied Command.

Oberoi had to think on his feet, and as soon as they could carry him, he went to the British Quartermaster General. Shrewdly, he took his English General Manager along. 'You can have the hotel, sir,' he told the Commandant, 'but how will you feed your officers?' The man snapped, 'That's my business.' Oberoi was determined to save his. 'How much do you reckon it will cost you, sir?' he asked. The crusty army-man could have thrown the persistent chap out on his ear, but chose to say, 'Rs 12 per man.' 'If you allow me, I'll do it for 10,' said Mohan Singh, and did not forget to add the 'sir'. The Quartermaster narrowed his eyes, sized up the man, observed the white Manager at his side, and barked, 'Done!'

CHAPTER XIII

Never A Night Without A Fight

Mohan Singh knew vaguely what he was getting into. He had some inkling, too, of what he would get out of it. But he could never have imagined the magnitude of either. Or the change it would bring.

First, he had to plan the strategy. Plan a mobilization and then a demob. In reverse order. Mohan Singh and his Managers proceeded to disband all the trappings of luxury, especially the fragile ones. The crystal and fine china were carefully packed away. Precious carpets rolled up, silver cellophaned. They next commandeered the sturdier, the more expendable—and the more appropriate. Even the king-size beds were dismantled and replaced with camp-cots. Four to a double room. The hotel's hallmark of elegance was replaced with the rubber stamp of expediency. It was a long way to tip a rare hostelry, but now the Grand was no longer afraid of the Colonel's bogey.

The men came marching in. If they were no saints, you could hardly blame them. And war-time Calcutta laid it all on. Never did red lights blaze so invitingly. Never were amber eyes gazed into so longingly. Never was the green signal on the go with such impunity. The notorious Karaya Road with its curving balustrades, was filled with raving beauties. In any colour, from pure White Russian to red-blooded Latin to Mongolian far from yellow. And if it was a mixed bag you fancied, you could get a Eurasian in any blend of your flavour.

Many of the exotic inmates of Sensuality Street were soon interned in foreigners' camps; spies were known to come in from warm beds. But pleasure did not get rationed with this withdrawal of well-stacked supplies. With commendable dispatch, armies of Anglo-Indian girls now moved in to face the troops.

As usual, everyone else blamed the Americans. They always had more of everything to throw around for a better fling: money, perfume, silk stockings and the parachute material that became the great fashion for frocks. In and out of the Grand they breezed, each solider's arm festooned with a beauty or two. Or three or more. The Duchess of Chowringhee Road had never known anything so rumbustious before, but she had to admit that she rather enjoyed cavorting with the corporals.

Her Managers were in the thick of it. Ellis Joshua, not unlike his boss, had entered hoteliering with nothing to recommend him other than his brash self-confidence and, similarly, had risen from the ranks with his eagerness to learn. 'Josh' played bouncer. He had his strategy well worked out. When he saw the first bubbles of trouble rising, he would approach the stroppiest soldier of the group, tap him on the shoulder and say, 'Excuse me, sir, one of your friends seems to need your help in the Gents.' When Charlie went to the post to check, 'Josh' followed, and knocked him out cold with a left upper-cut. Then, dusting his hands and nonchalantly stepping over him, he went back, all baby-faced innocence, to look out for the next man asking for it.

The Casanova Bar changed out of its stuffed-shirt image into that of a Wild West saloon. Joshua had a motto for it, 'Never a night without a fight'. It had two entrances, one through the lobby, the other through the street. Enforced exits were naturally through the latter.

Mohan Singh kept his iron hand on the operations to ensure that His Majesty's billet was not confined to the barracks. He had promised a clean bed and wholesome food, and he provided both. But he could not always guarantee the quality of the booze for demand far outstripped supply, even though Oberoi's men had fanned out all over the country to corner the market at any price. However, if the soldiers were 'drinking poison', it was not because this was the hotel's way of sabotaging the Raj. As for other pleasures, Oberoi had an open-mind, open-door and open-palm policy. If the Major wanted Barbara he could have her without the Grand playing Salvation Army. With no small gain to itself. Every morning, the Manager, and often the boss himself, did a head count. The soldiers had to pay for both bed and broad.

At one time there were some 4,000 officers (and friends) staying here instead of the quota of 1,400. Camp-cots overflowed from the corridors, and on occasion, even the open courtyard became a dormitory. The lobby was always a sea of khaki waiting for the British billeting officers to assign them their 'quarters'.

The staid dining room underwent an equal metamorphosis, but, to their credit, the twelve elderly permanent residents stuck to their guns, and their customary tables. Jacob Ezekiel, Rachel David, and the two jewellers who had their shops in the arcade, Mr Boseck and Mr Walters, sat and gaped, anachronistic old-world islands in a tumultuous sea. Long buffet tables were laid out with stands devised by Mohan Singh to keep the food hot inside the massive tureens placed atop them. Forget about gloved service from the left, the officers helped themselves and sat at folding tables for four, crammed into the cavernous room.

And oh, how they danced on the nights 'ere they bled. More sedately at Prince's. Wildly on the open-air dance floor that had once been Stephen's skating-rink. Heady with the whisky, the stars above, the girls below, the maddening scent of frangipani and the danger on the morrow.

Sonny Lobo's band played as it had never played before. Teddy Wetherford, the dreamy-eyed crooner, sang as he had never sung before, sometimes in counterpoint to Kitty Walker just tripping out of her teens. 'One more number, Teddy-boy!' 'One last song, Kitty-baby!' the soldiers roared, delaying with their catcalls the sun already setting on the empire. If they drank, danced, loved, laughed, sang, spent as if there were no tomorrow, for many of them there wasn't.

For Oberoi, however, today took care of tomorrow and many days thereafter. His may not have been the only fortune made in the war, but it was certainly the one made most entertainingly. It was as if a giant children's-party *khoi*-bag had been prodded open, and a vast treasure tumbled out, instead of the usual puffed rice and plastic whistles.

The cash flow turned into a deluge. Stories are told of cashiers unable to count the money and, bleary-eyed, shoving it under the carpet to resume the task next morning. Of notes being weighed since they were too numerous to count. Of Ishran Devi going to sleep on a mattress stuffed with the blue-backs. Of someone unwittingly opening the door to an annexe and being submerged in the stuff that fell out. But then, rumours of money always gain currency at such time.

The partners thanked their stars that they had not pulled out their stakes. Rai Bahadur Kahnchand Kapur was pleased to see his faith in his protégé vindicated, at no small gain to himself. Dr Hari Ram remained his quiet, unobtrusive self. Shiv Nath Singh, of course, complained that though Mohan Singh's skills at multiplication of assets could not be faulted, he tended to be careless about division. But there were such vast sums going around that mathematics was largely an academic question. While Mohan Singh, as usual, was everywhere, Shiv Nath's equally high visibility was confined to the bar and the boudoir.

Tikki, who had just entered the business, got the chance to prove that abandoned studies were no great loss. He began a laundry business of his own, servicing all the sprawling American bases in Calcutta. He was at hand at the Grand to handle the money and turn it to advantage. Here he first showed the financial acumen that he could have done so much with. But that story comes later.

Mohan Singh not only made money, he got honoured for it. One afternoon in 1943, the Governor invited him to tea. And informed him that, in return for services rendered to the British Army and other contributions made, His Majesty would be pleased to confer on him the title of Rai Bahadur. Would he accept? Of course he would.

Honours without number would follow in the next fifty years, but this is the one he still values the most. Why? 'Because it became part of my name.' Few, henceforth, would call him Mohan Singh. It would always be Rai Bahadur.

1943, however, was not a year for celebration. Bengal reeled under the Great Famine, and it was the British *Statesman* that informed the world at large about Britain's policies that had, first, impoverished the countryside and, then, imposed war-time restrictions on the shallow boats which would have allowed some food to trickle in from the other rice bowl, Burma, now under Japanese Occupation. Starving peasants swarmed into Calcutta—and virtually dropped dead in the streets. Ishran Devi, far more sensitive to these things, organized a huge soup kitchen, mobilized her own army of helpers, and fed thousands. She persuaded her husband to decrease the portions in the dining room to prevent waste, and divert whatever was possible to the poor.

Each day the city supped only on loss and grieving. Then, the communal Great Calcutta killings decimated almost as many as hunger had, in a far less silent tragedy. Mahatma Gandhi arrived in Calcutta with his potent moral weapon, refusing to abandon his fast till the people of Noakhali abandoned their fratricidal madness. It was a time of hatred and anguish, but it sealed the fate of the Raj. And it was at this time that Oberoi worked out the details of the coup that would win him an empire of his own.

CHAPTER XIV

Chained At Last

Mohan Singh's success at the Grand had dissipated any apprehensions he may have had about vaulting ambition overreaching itself. He took his cue from another poet, believing that a man's reach must extend his grasp or what's a heaven for?

The ultimate hoteliering prize on the subcontinent was the Associated Hotels of India(AHI), a chain not unfamiliar to Rai Bahadur for he had started life in what had once been its most scintillating link, the Cecil at Simla. Now, he prepared to take a sentimental journey— and a lucrative one.

The AHI was ripe for plucking. John Faletti felt it was time to say *'arrivederci'* to his eight luxury hotels and retire to evenings in Rome. He had said his goodbyes, at greatest length to N.V. Smith, the secretary whom he had loved, warty face and all, much to the resentment of his son, Manuel, who used to vent his spleen on another hotel in the chain; every time he was outraged by Papa Faletti's indiscretions, he would go and chop down a tree at Delhi's Maidens.

All that was history. Faletti sold out his thirty per cent share holding to Spencer & Co, that great British institution which gave railway meals their distinctive taste, managing the spotless dining cars as well as the station restaurants with their trade-mark, wire-netted swing-doors.

By the time Mohan Singh won his war booty at the Grand, Spencer & Co had lost interest in AHI. Dividends had been swallowed by interest on a Rs 1,200,000 annexe to Cecil built by Faletti, indifference had eroded management, and the smaller holders were only too keen to get rid of shares which had dropped to three rupees from their face value of ten. The real estate, however, remained impressive, holding aloft the most prestigious hotels in the country: apart from the Cecil, these included Longwood and Corstophons also in Simla, Maidens in

Old Delhi, Faletti's in Lahore, Flashmans in Rawalpindi, Deans in Peshawar and another Cecil, this one in the salubrious hills of Murree. Besides, they had recently taken over the lease of the Imperial Hotel, Sardar Bahadur Narain Singh's showpiece in the heart of Delhi.

Mohan Singh began mopping up the shares. But he had to do it in stealth and silence, without alerting the Directors of Spencer & Co. to the imminence of a corporate decapitation. He bought only through the banks. The name of Oberoi wasn't so much as whispered. Thus, even when the Directors heard about a transfer, they dismissed it as the folly of some eccentric. He bought only in small lots. It would be counter-productive if too strident an interest pushed up the value. The nascent hotelier moved in unhurried, measured steps.

As each lot fell, he smiled his quiet smile, raised a glass of White Label to himself, and permitted himself a pat on the back. What he did not know was that Shiv Nath Singh, having predictably got a whiff of his partner's carefully orchestrated scheme, had begun an operation mop-up of his own. Soon, however, each realized what the other was doing, but continued to feign innocence, nothing in their daily interaction at the Grand giving away either their moves or their espionage network.

Mohan Singh maintained his lead, pocketing the pawns. But Shiv Nath beat him to the knight, G.V. Pike, nothing less than a Director of Spencer's who owned the last slab of shares that Oberoi needed to wrest complete control. Shiv Nath had travelled up to Pike's house in Tara Devi on the outskirts of Simla, and broached the subject of the shares as discreetly as it was possible to do while remaining a gentleman. The Englishman was all but persuaded. He told Shiv Nath to return in a week's time.

Oberoi had also been angling for this critical block, and knew that for as large a fish as Pike, he would have to forgo proxy, and go in person. But when he arrived at Tara Devi, he heard about his partner's visit just the previous day. The Englishman had slept over the matter, and made up his mind to sell. Since Shiv Nath had made the first offer, he would give him first option. Oberoi would have to wait till a week and a day.

Mohan Singh sat cooling his heels at Clarkes. But once again the famous bug came to his rescue. This time it was Shiv Nath's daughter who fell ill in Mussourie, and he was summoned to her side. He did not take the precaution of informing Pike for Shiv Nath Singh revelled in stratagem for its own sake, and lacked the meticulousness of the serious strategist. Besides, he did not know that, for Oberoi, Pike's block of shares was the *coup de grace*.

Mohan Singh presented himself to the Englishman on the dot. He knew that Shiv Nath had been far away from Tara Devi, and kept his fingers crossed that he had been as careless as usual. He uncrossed them as soon as he saw the shares on the table. After many years, he once again found it necessary to calm the pounding of his heart.

Pike, however, hesitated. He felt he should give Shiv Nath some extra time since it was his idea. Mohan Singh once again thought on his feet. 'How much has he offered?' he asked. The other Singh had told Pike that he would buy at double the market price, at six rupees. As swift as he had been with the British Commandant, Oberoi said, 'Allow me to make my bid at Rs 8.' Once again he did not forget to add the 'sir'. Pike asked him to return the next day. This time Oberoi knew that he had checkmated his rival.

But there was still a hitch. With as much assurance as he could muster, he asked the Englishman to trust him, and hand over the shares. Pike wanted to know why he was in such a hurry, surely his word was good enough? Oberoi said, 'I can't pay you till I have possession. I have to use them as collateral to get a bank loan.' The precious documents changed hands. A few days later, Oberoi handed Pike a cheque for Rs 80,000. Over a celebratory sherry.

Just as the 1944 annual general meeting of the AHI was about to commence at Simla's Cecil Hotel, a dapper native gentleman in a three-piece suit and felt hat arrived together with his cousin and a canvas hold-all. He presented himself to the redoubtable N.V. Smith, who was regulating entry into the meeting, and sought admittance. The secretary did not bounce him out as a hall porter had done in the same place twenty-two years ago, but as coldly told him that she did not see any Mohan Singh Oberoi on her list of shareholders.

With impeccable aplomb the gentleman drew out a large envelope from the bag. N.V. Smith saw it was stuffed with AHI shares. The cousin, Partap Singh Dhall, added that there were several more where these had come from. The flabbergasted secretary hurried inside to inform the Chairman. Sir Edward Buck came out, and Mohan Singh Oberoi repeated what he had said. Requesting Dhall to open the hold-all, and without unnecessary flamboyance, he proceeded to bring out bunches of certificates. 'Would you be so good as to ask someone to count them?' he said. It was already obvious that they were well over the majority.

Sir Edward Buck adjourned to an adjoining room and confabulated with his Board. In a short while he emerged, and said, 'Mr Oberoi, you clearly hold the controlling interest. Allow me to offer you my congratulations and my place at the head of the Board.' The transfer of power was as simple—and as graceful—as that. Mohan Singh was back where he started. At the Cecil Hotel, Simla. This time as owner. The tiny Band Quarter 4 was left far below in the *khud;* the boy from Bhaun had climbed to the top of the hill.

CHAPTER XV

Shiv Nath's Revenge

Mohan Singh did not take up Sir Edward Buck's offer. Instead he told him that he would be pleased to have him continue as Chairman while he would be content to be Managing Director. It was a move both shrewd and gracious. For a long time yet, an Englishman at the corporate helm would continue to be a value-added status symbol.

Sir Edward was a 'big shot' in more ways than one. His passion was hunting and everything he bagged was recorded in a game book in his crumbling mansion in Mashobra, which naturally also overflowed with trophies. Every winter, he moved to Delhi where he owned a piece of land, but no house. The lack did not worry him since he set up tents on his property, one as bedroom, another as study, a third as sitting room, all fully furnished.

The Englishman loved his Scotch, and the case sent over with regularity no doubt contributed to the friendship that grew between old Chairman and young Managing Director. The latter, never a man to waste an asset, even put the former to work, requesting him to be in charge of outstandings. If the dog-eared files at the Maidens Hotel are any indication, Sir Edward enjoyed his job vastly, for there are several memos from him to Managers of the different hotels of the chain demanding to know why 'Mr Milliston of Room 72 was allowed to leave without settling the bill of Rs 906 that he had incurred?' Or 'What action was intended to be taken to collect the Rs 476 owed by the Nawab of Mamdot?' To say nothing of a prolonged correspondence on the case of a certain M. Johnson who slipped on the floor of her room at Faletti's and demanded damages.

Since he held a number of Associated Hotels India (AHI) shares, Mohan Singh appointed Shiv Nath to its Board. However, he soon regretted not having learnt from his experience at the Grand, for Shiv Nath began trying to edge him out boasting that he could 'pluck

Mohan Singh out of Associated Hotels like a strand of hair from a block of butter'. Finally Oberoi decided he'd had enough. Working all night with his lawyer, Ved Vyas, and a trusted team, he formulated a way to dismiss him from the Board. All loopholes plugged, Partap Singh Dhall was sent at four in the morning to get the evidence and signature of the Chairman, Sir Edward Buck, who was then lying ill in Simla's Ripon Hospital. By next morning the name had been struck off the list of Directors. Shiv Nath reacted as he always did to an unfavourable turn of events. He filed a case. He claimed that, as a partner of Hotel (1938) Pvt. Ltd., he had equal right to Mohan Singh's shares. A more litigious man would be difficult to find and this time he filed suit with a vengeance, instituting proceedings in Lahore, Kanpur, Lucknow and Simla.

Finally, however, Mohan Singh decided it would be simpler to pay out a large sum of money than continue this enforced sightseeing tour of the interiors of the High Courts of India. Besides, he did not put it past his tormentor to use the shares he still had as a launching pad for another take-over bid. He offered to buy him out. Shiv Nath went smirking all the way to the bank for he creamed Rs 20 lakh* off his rival.

Mohan Singh had lost a great deal of money but with the shrug that would also mark later setbacks, he set about looking for the next challenge.

_____

One lakh is equivalent to one hundred thousand.

CHAPTER XVI

No Pall On The Mall

Rai Bahadur Mohan Singh Oberoi borrowed the twenty lakh rupees to pay off Shiv Nath from Ram Kishen Dalmia, giving him the shares as collateral. Six months later, Dalmia, facing his own problems, demanded repayment of the loan in ten days failing which he would sell off the shares. For the first, and perhaps only time in his life, Mohan Singh lost sleep. Had the Associated Hotels of India (AHI) prize dropped into his lap merely to be mockingly whisked away? He went almost in tears, to Lala Yudh Raj, who was now Chairman of the Punjab National Bank (PNB). 'I've just five days left of the notice period; I'll lose the company I've put in so much to gain. Please help me,' he pleaded. The Lala obliged.

That settled, Oberoi, went about picking up the pieces. He may have inherited an empire but, like all grand old edifices, it tended to leak. The effects of Spencer & Co's neglect of AHI had to be reversed. Flashmans at Rawalpindi required a new wing. Maidens in Delhi needed funds to get back its former glory. Its predicament was not unlike that of the three young women who decades earlier, had come out East, stayed in the hotel and, caught up in Delhi's blandishments, overshot their budget. They were forced to send a telegram to their parents: 'Send money or can remain maidens no more.'

The Cecil in Simla had to contend with the trickling off of the imperial summer exodus in the face of strident opposition from a Congress increasing its clout by the day. The Burma Government moving its secretariat to the hill-station during 1942-46, after the Japanese bombardment, was hardly any compensation. But the likes of Sir Khizr Hayat Khan, Sir Jogendra Singh, Sir Sunder Singh Majithia and their over-dressed *begums* and *sardarnis* still added to its shine, luring the young Khushwant Singh to walk the six miles from his father, Sir Sobha Singh's, summer-house in Mashobra, to feast on the sights of the Mall, savour the heady perfumes wafting across the Ridge, and eavesdrop on the gossip at Scandal Point.

Rickshaws still plied in the town, curtained for the *begums*. Their varnished panels were buffed to mirror finish, so were the umbrella rack, boot rest and brass lantern. For night hire, you paid eight annas over and above the day-time rate of one rupee four annas for the first hour. The important families, of course, had their own double rickshaws with liveried coolies or *jampanis*. The owner of the Imperial Rickshaw Works, which fabricated most of these vehicles, had letters of appointment from Lord Reading to Lord Mountbatten.

Adjacent to the Cecil's entrance stood the garage for the Chairman, Sir Edward Buck's double rickshaw, though this was not the one used to provide the two free rides into town included in the hotel's tariff. The garage would become Broadway, Partap Chand Mahajan's little store where Pandit Nehru and M.A. Jinnah occasionally may have picked up cigarettes if not peace pipes, on their way to negotiations at the Viceregal Lodge, and where Indira Gandhi may have dropped in with her two little boys years later to buy comics or a bright red rubber ball.

Nursing a brandy at the Clarkes' bar today, B.R. Nanda nostalgically recalls that there was not a bus or truck to be seen till after 1947, when Simla continued to be seasonal capital of the divided Punjab, but the first hooded taxis had begun to carry travellers up from the rail-head in Kalka. There were strict controls on these new-fangled modes of transportation, allowing them just one journey up in the morning, one down in the evening, no night travel. And no speeding. The minimum time given to hairpin round the hills was three-and-a-half hours, and anyone doing it in less was promptly challaned. Barriers along the way ensured that the drivers adhered to their time permits. Today, as monster trucks thunder recklessly up and down, drowning the scent of cedar resin in carbon monoxide, it is not only old-timers like Dr Nanda who yearn for a return to more cautious times. And safer ones.

There were also health posts that covertly doubled as security ones, with their standard catechism of *'Aap ka naam?' 'Baap ka naam' 'Kahan therenge?'* (Your name? Father's name? Where will you stay?) And should the needle of suspicion start flickering, you would be discreetly followed. These were tumultuous times, and one of history's most dramatic sunsets was about to take place.

Rai Bahadur's celebrated eye on the main chance was not restricted to splendiferous hunks of real estate. He seized smaller opportunities with equal speed. In Simla, he could not use the car in which he came up from Delhi every summer since no horse power was allowed on the Mall, so, rather than let it lie around, he converted it temporarily into a taxi. Its uniformed chauffeur, peaked cap and all, made it the most attractive choice for those not wanting to take the slow mountain railway up from Kalka.

Simla continued to have its colourful characters. One of them, not only on account of her bright auburn, later hennaed, hair, was Stella of Kapurthala. The Raja of that state had fallen in love with her as she sang in a London music hall. He had stood moonstruck all night by the piano and told her he would lay the treasures of his kingdom at her feet. This had translated to, among other luxuries, a retinue of seventy-eight servants and weekly visits to Lahore to have her hair conditioned and coiffured. But the fairy-tale ended when the Raja wanted to remarry because, by the law of princely primogeniture, for the son to succeed the father, the mother too would have to be blue-blooded. Stella agreed to an annulment of the marriage after tantrums and a settlement of twelve lakh rupees.

Alas, a confidence trickster did her out of this money, and brought her marginally into the Oberoi story. She began staying in the Cecil annexe allowing herself the sole luxury of a roast chicken for dinner which she cooked herself in the attached kitchenette. At Scandal Point, they dubbed her 'rubber lips', and whispered that she called out to anyone ready, willing and able to help her take off her knee-high boots. As a later song would put it, '*Shake off your silver spurs/And help me pass the time/As I give to you my summer wine.*'

CHAPTER XVII

Wolves In Sharkskin

Not the least of the assets that Rai Bahadur acquired when he cleaned out the AHI chessboard were its Managers. The stocky Teutons, Hahn at Faletti's, Krushandl at Deans, Steiner at Maidens and Bret at Grand, Chico Sibilia at Corstophons and, at the Imperial, his brother, the most legendary of them all. With charm and efficiency in roughly equal parts, his fashionable white linen suits always impeccable, his black moustache always waxed and curled, Senor Italo Sibilia was as much at home among the guests as among the skillets in which he rustled up a superb ante-pasta. Their boss learnt as much from them as the Managers did from him, and still thinks that the Indians who succeeded them cannot match their style and skills.

It was with their help that Mohan Singh maintained the hotels, preserved them as fully furnished bastions of *la dolce vita* through the turbulence of those times, and provided an island for the *bon vivants*. The men in two-toned spats and gold Sheaffer's pens in the breast pockets of their sharkskin suits. The women in strapless 'will-power' taffeta dresses or swathed in chiffon with broad brocade borders. They sat in charmed circles, and if someone had interrupted their stylish revelry to announce that the peasants were revolting, it would scarcely have been surprising if they had arched their eyebrows and said, like Louis XIV, 'Yes, aren't they?'

But no one could roll back the tide or shut off the screams of communal schism as freedom arrived in a bloodied birth. The horrors that followed the line of Partition's unthinking blue crayon were the most chilling, both in Mohan Singh's native Punjab and his new base, Bengal. In the latter, inflamed passions had been somewhat shamed into submission by the Mahatma, but in the western wing, the trains to Pakistan carried only corpses. His beloved Bhaun went to the other side. Scores of his kinsmen poured into Delhi and were given shelter, succour and hope at Maidens.

By fortuitous circumstance, Rai Bahadur had put off the rebuilding of Faletti's in Lahore, and his negotiations for Nedou's in the same city were infructuous. Fortunately, the beautiful, elegant city, calligraphed on every classy Punjabi heart, went over to the other side. Had he bought Nedou's and paid its wealthy timber merchant owner, Lala Jodhamall, the price of seventy lakh rupees, it could well have been money lost forever, perhaps sinking the company as well. Partition also took away Corstophons, Flashmans, Deans and the other Cecil at Murree.

Rai Bahadur had cultivated his contacts well, and he had enough friends who formed the new bureaucracy in Pakistan. Many of the rich and landed escaped with only their lives during the upheaval of Partition including Goodie his daughter-in-law-to-be, but Oberoi was able to run his establishments under the new banner of the Associated Hotels of Pakistan. He even repatriated profits till the Indo-Pakistan war of 1965 sealed the borders implacably. The great hotels were then declared enemy property, with no compensation to be paid for their loss. Years later, in 1983, General Zia-ul-Haq, then the Pakistani President, stayed along with other leaders at Delhi's Oberoi Intercontinental during the Non-Aligned Movement(NAM) conference. Rai Bahadur asked him only half in jest, 'When are you giving me back my hotels?' The effusive General gave him the usual bear hug, but little else. All he said was, 'Be my guest in Pakistan, I'll leave instructions to see that there's no delay in granting you a visa.'

That, at least, would have given Oberoi the opportunity to put his foot in the door, and his ingenuity would have taken care of the rest. But before he found the time to go, the charismatic Zia was dead, his plane blasted out of the skies in 1988.

CHAPTER XVIII

Good-Bye Partners

1947. Freedom. As well as problems in the power house.

In Calcutta, the bureaucracy may have brought down the Union Jack and said its good-byes to the tearful strains of Auld Lang Syne. Rai Bahadur may have mourned the passing of the Brits who had taught him so much and given him more. But he was thankful that they did not take the Season with them. The boxwallah Burra Sahibs continued to mark Burra Din with Burra Khana, the Christmas lunch with all the trimmings. The Jamsaheb still dropped in to commemorate the prizes won by his aristocratic Afghans at the Calcutta 'Kennel Club'. In the Grand's bar, they talked of Burdwan's dahlias stealing the show at the Royal Horticultural Gardens and reminisced over how Keith Miller flogged Mankad out of the Eden Gardens during the first India–Australia match after the war. At Prince's the short, stocky Mongolian-featured Mahabir Shamsher Jung Bahadur Rana celebrated yet another triumph of his filly at the Royal Calcutta Turf Club. And, often enough, Jai of Jaipur would be the guest of his good friend Tikki, lured to Calcutta where he had wooed and won Ayesha, the Dresden beauty of Cooch Behar.

But, behind the scenes at the Grand, it was not quite the fiefdom of 'Cooch Parvah Nahin', the Utopian kingdom of no concerns. The partnership was cracking, partly because Rai Bahadur, so clearly the boss-man, wanted it to. Partly because Shiv Nath Singh needed intrigue like other people need vitamin supplements. The avuncular Kahnchand Kapur and the gentle Hari Ram tried to make him see reason, but he continued to join issue with Mohan Singh at every meeting. He insisted on backseat driving, even though it was Oberoi who, being the only one of the four with any real experience of hotels, had been given sole charge of management. Shiv Nath constantly carped over his day to day decisions, ranted that Mohan Singh was giving too much leeway to the 'good-for-nothing' workers; cavilled that the other partners were not getting their fair share of profits or enough privileges at the hotel; complained that Rai Bahadur was concentrating all the power in his hands. And alleged that he spent far too much time with Freny Cama, a pretty dancing teacher, who had, incidentally, also caught Shiv Nath Singh's eye.

Despite his constant needling of Rai Bahadur, when it suited him, Shiv Nath would ally himself with Oberoi. He played his role in the sidelining of Kahnchand Kapur who had stood by Mohan Singh through the difficult years, and the instating of Sir Ushanath Sen as Chairman in his place. Sir Ushanath, an eminent barrister, would add greater glitter to the Board than Kahnchand, who was now past his prime, murmured Shiv Nath. Mohan Singh succumbed, but only temporarily, for old remembrances and gratitude soon triumphed over corporate expediency. Kahnchand Kapur once again became the titular head.

Finally Rai Bahadur decided he was ready to go it alone. In English idiom, 'possession is nine-tenths of the law'; his mother had taught him its earthy Punjabi equivalent, 'The owner of the stick is the owner of the buffalo.' So, in a one-upmanship move in 1947 not unlike his *coup de grâce* at Clarkes on the same reasoning, Mohan Singh bought over the property of the Grand, paying for the shareholding a little more than Rs 3,452,000. The Associated Hotels of India, now owned by Mohan Singh, advanced whatever loan was needed. Gregory Arathoon's forty-seven-lakh-worth of debentures, mortgaged to the Mercantile Bank when the beauty lapsed into her coma, passed into the hands of the Midas who had applied the magic touch.

Some time later, he presented his partners with a choice: they could either contribute a large sum for the renovation that the Grand needed or they could allow him to buy out their stakes. They had invested Rs 25,000 nine years ago. He would give them two lakh rupees in full and final settlement. He knew Kahnchand was an old man; that his sons were settled in other fields; that he would opt to take rather than give. He knew Dr Hari Ram would follow. He knew Shiv Nath would be difficult. He was.

Not only did he spurn the offer, he worked on the other partners to convince them they were being bought off cheaply. That the two lakh rupees being offered was nothing compared to the killing Mohan

Singh would make on the property. The Grand would become the *grande dame* of Calcutta, wiping out the competition, he said. In that prophesy he would not be wrong, but the two older men did not bite.

Rai Bahadur's strategy would fall flat on its face if he got rid of the cooperative partners and remained saddled with the contentious one. There was only the usual way out: he doubled the offer to Shiv Nath. The Rai Bahadur recalls, seeing the flicker of hesitation, he quickly said, 'All right, take five lakhs, but for God's sake keep your mouth shut.' The chap squeezed one last drop out of Mohan Singh's eagerness to take complete charge. 'Agreed,' he said, 'but I'll stay on with my family at the Grand for another three years.' Mohan Singh did not argue. He was a patient man. The partnership—and Hotel (1938) Pvt. Ltd.—was dissolved in 1952.

Shiv Nath Singh and Mohan Singh Oberoi, despite their great differences in temperament and ethics, were not unlike each other. Both were master strategists, both men of great style. Shiv Nath could charm a bird off a tree, but he reserved his energy for more worthwhile conquests. He could win a woman over in two minutes flat. And he had all kinds of ways to send them into ecstasies. At one of his parties, the *abdar* came in bearing aloft the tray of liqueurs. The host had seen to it that each woman was handed a drink that exactly matched the colour of her sari.

His nephew, Vien, recalls that he always looked as though he'd just stepped out of a powder box, never without his felt hat, often with a silver-topped cane, and usually in a fragrant cloud of Lanvin's 'Arpege'.

Mohan Singh, who was no mean charmer himself, was never a gambler, certainly never on a gaming table. But Shiv Nath was the poker player, the race-goer; he bought horses like Mohan Singh bought hotels. He had a Rolls-Royce that he used only for gliding to the Royal Calcutta Turf Club. It was painted in his racing colours of beige and brown, and his woman companion for the afternoon was also expected to dress in the same hues. Not that he showered her with the necessary silks; one of his stable of girlfriends, says his nephew, Vien, branded him a 'picey bounder' unwilling to spend despite all his flamboyance.

Shiv Nath's standard solution was, 'Let's take him to court,' and in later years, he would teach himself law to appear in the scores of cases he had got entangled in. The family claims that when his brother (and

Vien's father) Vishen Nath Singh, contracted TB and went to Switzerland for treatment, Shiv Nath tried to wheedle his sister-in-law into making over all his shares in the property to his name. Fortunately, she was advised against it. Her husband recovered, and returned.

Probably in resentment over the fact, Shiv Nath, soon after, insisted on a division of assets, the houses in Mussourie and England, the petrol pump in Kanpur, Samuel Fitze in Calcutta. Once again he managed to seize the larger share. At the time of the split, Vishen Nath and his family were staying at Spence's Hotel and he insisted on his brother paying the full rates till he had made alternative arrangements.

At the Grand, Shiv Nath's constant fulminations against the staff had been neutralized by the tactful Mohan Singh; at Spence's he was exposed. He made himself so hated that the workers were all set virtually to kill him. He had to escape in the middle of the night, in disguise, and in ignominy, leaving the hotel, the second oldest in the British Empire, to its fate. The government took it over. And rubber-stamped it with trade-mark dowdiness.

Incidentally, the same lot befell the equally historic Great Eastern Hotel, on the other flank of the Lal Dighi tank. The Grand would have no competition in Calcutta till the late 1980s, when the Taj finally made it to a city which should have been the Tatas' pocket-borough, since not far away, at Sakchi, Sir Dorab had completed, in 1911, the vision of his late father, Jamsetji Tata.

It would be with the Taj, in Delhi, in the Seventies, that Shiv Nath Singh and Mohan Singh Oberoi, the manipulators with impeccable manners, would meet one last time across the square-board of corporate enterprise.

CHAPTER XIX

Raj Exorcized

However far he flung his stake, two places would remain closest to Rai Bahadur. Calcutta, where he began his upward thrust; Simla where he began. In the former, the Raj did not go gently into the good night. Where John Company once straddled Clive Street, like a sola-topied colossus, the mercantile nabobs still held sway and sterling companies continued, unaffected by equity dilution. Even if the white man had unshouldered his burden, brown sahib, black knight and blue-blooded maharajahs willingly defended the bastions of privilege.

Till the early Sixties, an urbane and irreverent Calcutta cocked a snook at the rest of the world as it stepped into the Grand to see what new outrageous pleasure Ellis Joshua, still its Manager, had laid on. Prince's had plenty of show-girls and Scherezade sparkled for much more than a thousand and one nights. The Indian government was lavish with foreign exchange. Along with the crates of John Dewars' White Label and the French and Italian chefs, hotels imported nightclub acts. All life, *Mein Herr*, became a cabaret.

The Great Eastern Hotel and Firpo's were still to run to seed, but the Grand had already established supremacy within the triumvirate, scintillating with such legends as the West Indian singer, the Great Hutch, and such top brass as Duke Ellington. There was also Hermione Gingold, with her wicked, witty patter, and the *doyenne* of the *double entendre*, Betty Anchors, who, together with her piano-thumping partner, Pat Kaye, swivelled her eyes and her hips to sing the ditty of 'Red Riding Hood/ 'Who wasn't very good', drawing big, bad wolf whistles from the genteel crowd. The Sisters Bee snaked in, wearing skin-tight gowns, blew seduction in smoke rings, sat on laps, caressing and caressed; then, to the roll of drums, they gave their final bow letting their wigs fall off to reveal two bald, unmistakably male heads. Not that the genuine article was not laid on. A caravan of Egyptian belly dancers, Margo prancing in on Latin American rhythms, the German artiste whose name has been forgotten by the fading Calcutta 'seasonals', but not her see-through blue blouse. There was even a Japanese troupe, as stylized as *ikebana,* as petite as *haiku,* and getting plenty of yeses for their softly, sensuous variation on a Noh theme.

The grand coup was the Bluebell Girls, toast of Gay Paree, said to comprise the 'world's most beautiful women', stunning, sculpted and nothing under five-feet-ten. Biki Oberoi sweet-talked and silver-crossed the palm of Madame Bluebell to bring eight of them out for one season. The girls ran riot. One of them fell for the English boss of the Britannia Biscuit Co; another for a Czechoslovakian consultant at Bata's and a third for the chef of Prince's. Since the feelings were reciprocated in all three cases, the helpless Madame found her act upstaged by bells of the wedding variety.

Buckling under the foreign-exchange crunch that came in the mid-Sixties, Rai Bahadur teamed up with the impresario, K.C. Sen, to discover and present at Prince's what was, at first disdainfully, called 'local talent'. When the Anglo-Indians, too, went away, taking the last remnants of old Calcutta with them, the Oberois stopped cabarets in all their establishments. Vulgarity had replaced art, and they did not want any part in the prurience that demanded only sleaze, with no patience for style.

Naturally, the Christmas Day buffet and the New Year's Eve Dance were the highlights of The Season that continued spiritedly into Independence. Gilded pine cones, genuine Christmas tree, fake snow, *papier maché* reindeer, a real Santa Claus, plastic mistletoe, proper presents. Since Calcutta's jute barons had originally come from the Hebrides to the Hooghly, there was plenty of Scotch, salmon and the schmaltz of Auld Lang Syne, everyone taking the rather high road, and willingly suspending disbelief as they succumbed to the regulation nostalgia.

Bombay's society swingers, preening today over their patented theme-parties, might care to know that long before they devised the genre of '*Mujra* on Malabar Hill', Joshua had laid on all kinds of 'Nites' where decor, dress and the delectations on the table had to fit the designated subject.

'A Nite in the Nuthouse' is remembered because Ted Taylor, a notorious playboy of those years, arrived pulling a rickshaw in which sat a painted woman of the night, languorously holding a bunch of virgin-white lilies. Alas, both rickshaw and rider were barred at the portals; the theme notwithstanding, it was sheer madness for Taylor to think he could bring either into the Grand.

Nothing in Calcutta has ever been able to take the place of Prince's, perhaps the subcontinent's most scintillating nightclub. Apart from its ambience, it was the city's first public dining establishment to get air-conditioning, the first to introduce the cover charge. Prince's closed down in the Seventies. As swinging a place would be introduced, but the Grand had the sensitivity not to put it where Prince's had been; the ghosts of good times past would have shuddered at the strobe-lights, stomping and synthesizers of a discotheque. They would never have been able to learn that a DJ was now a disc jockey not a dinner jacket, or that the Pink Elephant as it was called, was something more substantial than an alcoholic apparition.

Calcutta changed. The remaining blithe spirits of the Raj were shouted down by the strident cries of revolution. A new dawn broke over West Bengal as the firebrand Jyoti Basu challenged the Congress stronghold in the state towards the end of the 1960s, and later turned it into an indomitable 'red fortress'.

The Grand did not die like Firpo's or succumb to government take-over like the Great Eastern. But it suffered. As much under the weight of its own obsolescence as the power that grew, for Mao's Bengali cadres, from the barrel of a gun. The *salaam huzoor* salutations of the old days gave way to the *lal salaam* of the communists. The air-conditioning simply gave way.

Reviving the hotel was in some ways a greater challenge than setting up one from scratch, because here the old had to be dealt with, in addition to installing the new. But Rai Bahadur was determined not to let his flagship go under. In a masterly psychological move, he invested a vast sum in the Grand in the Seventies, launching massive modernization. The message, loud and lavish, was that the Oberoi group meant to continue to keep Calcutta on the national and global map, even though international airlines had deserted Dum Dum, and a flight of capital further crippled what was once the commercial nucleus of empire.

Tikki had been at the side of Rai Bahadur when he made his war-time fortune from the Grand. Biki took his place when it was time to pull it out of its ennui. Besides, they had the long and varied experience of Satish Kumar, who was appointed General Manager of the hotel and who would grow to be as much of an institution in the next twenty-five years. Together they persuaded the unions with carrot and stick that the alternative to peaceful coexistence was no existence at all. The workers only had to cast their gaze a block away to Firpo's for confirmation.

Almost as a mock-up classroom model, the changes that had revolutionized hoteliering over the past quarter century, were telescoped into six months. Guided by Satish, professional young Managers from the Oberoi School of Hotel Management in Delhi took over from the old-school types whose only textbook had been experience. The 350 overhead tanks were replaced by a modern hydropneumatic system, the air-conditioning overhauled. Charcoal gave way to clean gas, the *babu* and his dog-eared ledger to sleek business systems. Abdul, the superannuated room bearer, gave way to a Mark II model half his age. The *dhobis'* pounding was replaced by an in-house laundry, complete with giant washing machines and area-specific irons that, with a hiss, took the crease out of a collar or put one back on a pair of trousers.

The insecurity that these changes engendered in the older staff was assuaged when it became clear that no one would be thrown on the streets. A retirement policy was introduced to the satisfaction of the union. Those past forty-five were asked to move to less visible—and less strenuous—areas, so that the fresh young image could present itself. By then Biki had learned his father's tactful way of handling workers. As the brash young heir-apparent began grasping the realities, he recognized the benefits of softening the adversary roles of union and management that Calcutta stroppily thrived on. Besides, how could issues become intractable when so many of the bearers still knew him as 'Biki *baba*'—the little boy who had grown up before their eyes when the family had lived in the hotel?

Slowly, the dowager emerged anew, mercifully not as a giggling young debutante, but with grace, dignity and dynamism toned up again; and, seeing her new buoyancy, you would not realize how close a call it had been.

In the 1980s, Biki would order a yet more ambitious face-lift. Even if this were prompted by the fact that the Taj was finally setting up shop here, neither the Grand nor the city complained. Both got the spin-off benefit.

While Calcutta had metamorphosed into a sabre-rattling new persona, Simla slid quietly downhill. The Punjab's princes and bureaucracy still used it as a hot-weather retreat. Army officers had always come over from the Jutogh Cantonment, and social life flared to some of its old brightness when the Western Command marched in to headquarter at the place. The Simla Queen and the Cecil Princess continued to hold court, and get their photographs into the glossy *Onlooker,* then still India's *Tatler.*

But these were just flashes. The state machinery moved to Chandigarh and the High Court followed suit. Rai Bahadur and his friend from the IAS, Prem Raj Mahajan, could not persuade the government to implement their recommendations that would have brought in the tourists and revitalized Simla's economy. Matters both improved and worsened when Himachal Pradesh graduated from union territory to state, with Simla its capital, in 1971. Now it could collect its own taxes but unauthorized buildings proliferated like its famous mushrooms. Water supply and sewerage systems built for a township of 25,000 were now asked to satisfy the needs of 125,000 locals and 50,000 tourists.

And though the tourists poured in, cramming into cheap, crowded, airless, insanitary hostelries called Himalaya View overlooking bazaars piled with garbage, the Cecil's kind of guest fled Simla. They would rather take a Far-East package tour. Clarkes, which was right on the Mall and less expensive, managed to stay open all year, but John Faletti's magnificent hotel, host to the empire's Beautiful People, staggered under its overheads. It tried to cut its losses by remaining open only for six months, then four, then only a pathetic two. Incidentally, Manuel Faletti, son of the owner of the Raj's largest chain, found himself working at a modest hoteliering job in India; Rai Bahadur brought him back, in a position befitting his lost patrimony. But the trees he used to hack in frustration at Maidens were safe.

Rai Bahadur, saddened by the state of the hotel where he had started, hardened his heart, and decided to sell. But the government offered only twenty-five lakh rupees, far below his floor-price of thirty-five. Finally, in the summer of 1984, devastated by the death of Tikki, and unable to bear the seediness of the place where his little rajah had grown up, Rai Bahadur personally put a padlock on the doors of the Cecil. He would not reopen it, he decided, till he had restored it to a style befitting its past, worthy of the Oberois' present.

An ambitious renovation project was launched in the 1980s not only of the hotel, but also its environs, and today, Rai Bahadur, in his nineties, personally supervises its progress by remote control. 'Be sure to see the blueprints of my new plans for Band Quarter,' he told his chronicler who went up to see where it all began. Or rather down. Down the steep gradient of the hill across the road from the Cecil to the ten-foot by nine-foot hovel which will now be something of a monument.

CHAPTER XX

Consolidate, Not Diversify

Rai Bahadur's phenomenal accomplishments would ensure that no one could any longer dismiss the profession with a sneering 'Only a hotelier!' Indeed, this was the essence of his success. His mind was kept off other professional diversions by the same all-exclusive concentration that, like a smart bomb, helped him identify a problem in his hotels and eliminate it with equal speed. He had learnt early that having too many irons in the fire comes in the way of striking the iron when it is hot.

A travel agency, however, is hand-maiden to the hotel industry. So, when Tikki and his friend, Ripu Bhagat, came up with the idea in 1948, Rai Bahadur approvingly endorsed his son's far-sightedness. Mohan Singh had seen the growing network of Thomas Cook & Co. which was founded in 1841 in England, and touched Indian base in 1881. The peripatetic company had taken the first organized groups around the world, and changed the clientele—and configuration—of hotels forever. Jeena & Co., the first Indian travel agency, was established by the perspicacious Pallonji Hormusji Katgara in 1900, the year of Rai Bahadur's birth. It would cash in on this head-start during the next three generations to bifurcate into the Travel Corporation of India and take the tide of tourism at its flood, leaving the parent company to handle packages instead of package tours.

The new venture was called Mercury Travels because Rai Bahadur recalled having heard of a similar agency in Paris with this apt name. Tikki soon lost interest, but, by then, Mohan Singh via his daughter Swaraj, had already found Gautam Khanna, who took over Mercury Travels and spread it round the world. The agency has travelled a long way from 31 March 1948, when it started out with just three office tables on the first-floor balcony of the Grand, occupied by a Mr Ghosh, a Mr Mukherjee and the Managing Director, Mr Ripu Bhagat.

When Cyril Radcliffe had nonchalantly scratched his blue crayon across the subcontinent to cleave it into two, he clearly did not worry too much about dislocation; aside from the other more tragic consequences, Partition also meant that Indians had to continue to cut across what was then East Pakistan if they wanted to travel from the rich tea gardens of north Bengal to those in Assam. To eliminate this inconvenience, the government decided to provide a direct rail link. Someone had to build accommodation for the staff as well as the railway stations. This was Tikki's new diversion. Again with Ripu Bhagat, and two American experts, he floated the Indo-US Investment Company to make hollow-brick prefab housing and won the bid for the Siliguri end of the scheme. The two rich boys, who were more at home on the Riviera than the riverine maze of the north-east, soon realized that these jungles were not their idea of the wild life. Ripu perforce, had to stick it out, but Tikki passed the baby on to his father.

Rai Bahadur not only held the bawling brat, but plunged personally into looking after it. This meant Mohan Singh, already India's leading hotelier, transporting himself to new and mucky terrain. Ripu recalls how the older gentleman gamely hopped on to the self-propelled trolley every morning to go up and down the track to supervise the progress of the housing. How, without fuss, he shared the oil-lamp-lit, one-room, one-bathroom accommodation in Siliguri which, in 1949, was yet to metamorphose from dirty outpost to dirty boomtown, courtesy smuggling across the Bangladesh border.

There were no millions involved, and there was no reason why Rai Bahadur should have stayed a hundred miles from nowhere, but the challenge excited him. He had got where he was by picking up gauntlets, not throwing in the towel, and he continued even after Ripu had withdrawn from the scene. The project ultimately fell through, defeated by circumstance that was long on distance and short on reliable labour. For brief periods, Rai Bahadur also took on schemes as diverse as making beer to making bicycle dynamos. But he soon realized that there was no point fissioning his energies and resources.

On 26 May 1949, Mohan Singh floated The East India Hotels Ltd (EIHL) 'after the East India Company', for, like its historical namesake, Oberoi too had shaken the pagoda tree, and returned from his forays a 'nabob'. Associated Hotels of India (AHI) merged with it. Although it was a public company, the original subscribers were a small group, comprising Oberoi himself, his son, Tilak Raj, Motilal Khaitan, Ripu Bhagat, N. Haksar, E. Brett and Man Singh. It would not go truly public till 1956 when his Delhi Intercontinental dream would demand the sacrifice of exclusive holding on the altar of equity. Hotel (1938) Pvt. Ltd., formed to take over the Grand lease, continued alongside till the dissolution of the partnership in 1952.

Two years before EIHL was registered, Rai Bahadur had entrenched himself deeper in the eastern region, in neighbouring Orissa, the ancient land of Kalinga. On one of his trips to the region, the hotelier had chanced upon a tumbledown property on a forgotten palm-fringed beach. Even the name of the hamlet was redolent of the cockles, mussels and potted shrimp sold along British piers—Gopalpur-on-sea. Its silence was broken only by the breakers and the occasional coconut thudding to the ground. It was like nothing the land-locked Rai Bahadur had ever seen. Moreover, observing the state of disrepair that the bungalow lay in, he immediately sensed that Maglioni, its Italian owner, would not waste too much breath on bargaining. He did not. Oberoi got it for just Rs 300,000.

He thought it would be a good idea to use it as a getaway place for family holidays. But since he never got away for family holidays he had a better idea. The Oberoi Palm Beach opened in 1947, and still stands untouched by the concrete commercialism that has destroyed nearby Puri's once equally pristine beach.

In 1951, his eastern stake climbed higher. He bought the second hotel that Arathoon Stephen had built, this one in spectacular Darjeeling. The turreted structure sprawled high above the Mall, past such evocative institutions as the Planter's Club—each of its sixty-five rooms affording a vista of the mighty Kanchenjunga. Oberoi's conquest of the Everest Hotel came two years before Tenzing Norgay and Edmund Hillary conquered its better-known namesake as a coronation day gift to Queen Elizabeth of England.

Beginning to redeem his promise to little Rajrani, the now not-so-young man had established himself in the East and in the next few years would go West.

CHAPTER XXI

Half-Way To A Century

Fifty is a good time to stop and take stock. The half-way mark to a century is a watershed, a time when the characteristics of a man have been established, the traits that had and would take him to the top are well defined.

At fifty, the nine-to-fivers may crane anxiously at a retirement round the corner; they may have perhaps already crossed professional menopause. But life was just beginning at fifty for Rai Bahadur. He had made a fortune beyond his wildest dreams. It had jumped out at him from nowhere, just when he feared he had overreached himself and that he would go under with the Grand. He had proved to be the master manipulator, and acquired the top-drawer hotels of the subcontinent. He was the first dyed-in-the-wool Indian hotelier, and by the time the century was ready for another turning, he would still remain exclusive in his class.

He pioneered room service in India, establishing a rudimentary one at Clarkes, thus eliminating the cluttering retinue that travellers brought along with their portmanteaus and hold-alls. Apart from giving corridors the appearance of a railway station, these personal servants interfered with the smooth functioning of the kitchens. And probably siphoned off the sugar as well.

It is as difficult today to visualize a hotel without room service as it was to provide it with one in the first place. It was not enough to install a primitive system of coordinated call bells in room and pantry. He had to teach the bearers not to dismiss the sound as the clanging of the tram outside. Like Pavlov's dog salivating at the sound of the bell, the reflex of picking up the salver had to be conditioned. Pavlov probably achieved his objective faster.

Rai Bahadur had his own method of licking a problem. He would pitch camp in the contentious area, quietly observing, and would not move till he had pinpointed the bottleneck, and then devised a way of circumventing it.

Laurels were not meant for resting on, and retirement was something of a joke. When asked three decades later when he planned to retire, he would reply, 'Why, I retire every night!' So, not surprisingly, at fifty, he was ready to make a new quantum leap—into an international standard of hoteliering. A decade later, he would expand his empire into the international arena itself. And, in yet another twenty years, when it would appear impossible to gild the deluxe lily any further, the Oberoi group would unveil an entirely new interpretation of perfection.

Few will disagree with his daughter Rajrani's claim that her father did in one generation what most entrepreneurial families would take at least two to achieve. He did it by daring to think big and never forgetting to think small. No task was too lowly, no ambition too high. He would not have made it, if he had not accounted for every potato at Clarkes any more than if, still penniless, he had not coopted every contact to find the thousands to buy his first hotel. You had to give him credit for this courage, and the banks did so. The scale model would grow larger as the magnitude of his operations increased.

In the beginning was the system, and that is what had to be adhered to till the end. His hoteliering manuals were first written in the Thirties and Forties when the dynamo charged through every department. Actually the style was nothing quite as flamboyant. The cool, calculated moves that had plotted his career graph marked the way he gave efficiency its form.

The system was laid down in the manuals which became thicker as the chain got more and more svelte. The way a bed should be made, a tray arranged, crockery stacked to minimize delays. If the way of cooking scrambled eggs was specified, so was the flourish with which they should be served. The standard was set to eliminate the grey area of personal whim or discretion. If the manual said 'rose on breakfast tray' a carnation, however dewy, would not do. If the manual said 'six lumps of sugar in the bowl', that is what it had to be. Every time. It was the quantifying of that ostensibly abstract concept: perfection. And it was in those early years that Oberoi decided that he would never presume to have achieved it. He could remain a step ahead of the competition only if he recognized that perfection is a commodity whose shelf-life depends on it being kept open at its upper end.

All this wisdom did not arrive in a blinding flash. It grew with experience, another commodity that perforce had to be open ended, ongoing.

Rai Bahadur had kept a close watch on every aspect of the operations when he handled Clarkes in the absence of Ernest and Gertie Clarke. He continued to do so when his hotels stretched across the country. And the grip never loosened when country became continents. Yet, even at the height of his power, if you went to see him with an appointment, he never kept you waiting for more than ten minutes at the most, and he always conveyed the impression that he had all the time in the world, that nothing was more important for him than the problem you had brought him. That, too, was one of the keys to success: his concentration. Nothing was allowed to intrude into the matter he had chosen to grapple with at that particular juncture.

His staff had already begun to worship him, not only for kindnesses great and small, but also because of his easy accessibility, the fact that he cared to remember each one of them. The history of industry is replete with legendary founders who knew each employee by name; it is not as easy to find parallels to Rai Bahadur's one-to-one relationship that continued even when his hotels crossed the international border.

He built up confidence in his people, made them want to perform personally for him. In the early Sixties, he would place his faith in a young and untested lawyer, ignoring the claims of more experienced men. 'I couldn't betray that confidence and had to prove that it was justified,' said Lalit Bhasin, who grew to handle the company's legal matters at the topmost level, go on its Board, become the youngest-ever Chairman of the Bar Council of India, and acquire global standing.

Today they call it 'hands-on' and 'management by walk-through', but the self-made men who also made Indian enterprise had not read about it in a Harvard Business School case-study; *they* were the book. With other pioneering entrepreneurs who knew every nut and bolt of their enterprise simply because they had put it there, Rai Bahadur shared the gift of the simple solution to the seemingly complex problem; with those who have built up their personnel registers from scratch, he shares an infallible knack of picking the right people.

Or learning from them. Inder Jit, the journalist-politician, who knew him from the days his father, Durga Das, had his Indian Press

Association office at the. Cecil where Mohan Singh was still a clerk, will tell you that he closely observed his British bosses, and picked up the discipline and detail, the correct ways of dealing with seniors and subordinates alike. Munir, his major domo, will tell you that when he acquired Associated Hotels of India(AHI) and the gold mine of Managers that came with it, 'He didn't say "I'm the new boss, you do things my way from now on." Instead, acknowledging the superiority of their skills, he learnt from them.' Humility was another trait Rai Bahadur shared with the founders of industrial empires.

By fifty, it was clear that he had a sure grasp on people, the greatest asset of a service industry, an industry where the warmth of a receptionist's smile can determine the health of the bottom-line on the balance sheet, where a slogan shouted in the lobby equals a spanner in the works.

By now it was also evident that his strength lay not in the flamboyant gesture, but in a cool, quiet, calculated working out of strategy. A patient, non-aggressive wait for the kill. It did not make for great drama. But it made for success.

CHAPTER XXII

Learning From The World

As the century and Rai Bahadur both crossed the fifty mark, the hotelier had acquired recognition throughout the country. Now he decided he should get to know the rest of the world and vice versa. Characteristically, his first sortie abroad had to be nothing less than a trip around the globe. Mohan Singh, Ishran Devi, and their daughters embarked on their grand tour in May 1952. Tikki and Biki, already in Europe, joined them in France, their first stop.

Prem, just into her teens, was incredulous that the ticket she held in her hand would carry her to three continents in as many months. Her father was even more excited than her. While the family planned its shopping list and sightseeing gist, he got down to business. He designed—all by himself—a brochure that explained who he was and spelt out the specialities of his empire. He also announced in it that he was going to build a new hotel with seven restaurants, three bars, a swimming pool and 500 rooms. He had to be taken seriously by the world's great hoteliers, or there was no point in indulging in the expense of this trip. The illusion was as important as the fact; reality could wait upon the vision. Having had the brochure printed as glossily as possible at the time, it was the first thing he packed into his suitcase. Next went in all the smart suits. He had known the importance of the first impression from the very first day of his working life.

The trip was prompted by the International Hoteliering Congress in Paris. From there the Oberoi family travelled on to the continent, crossed the Channel and then the Atlantic. For Rai Bahadur it was a fact-finding tour. He had decided that his next hotel was going to be no second-hand one, and by now it should be evident that second-best role models would hold no interest for him. If he was going to build a world-class hotel in India, he had to find out, first-hand, how it should be planned.

They stayed in the classiest. The George V in Paris, the Dorchester in London, the Waldorf-Astoria in New York and Hilton's newest number in Puerto Rico. Phase I of the action plan would swing into operation as soon as they were shown to their rooms. Rai Bahadur would ring for the bell-hop and ask him to be 'good enough to deliver this envelope to the Manager, or, if possible, the Owner'. It contained his brochure and a hand-written note. Naturally, his phone would jangle soon enough, with the Manager informing him that it would be his pleasure if Rai Bahadur Mohan Singh Oberoi would join him for a drink at seven that evening.

This would enable him to put Phase II into gear; being shown around the facilities for the rest of his day. He would ask detailed questions and make copious notes on each department and service, front to back, inside out. He collected every sheet of publicity literature, every menu.

He noticed that, in all the best hotels, the kitchen was the epicentre, and all the restaurants were set on its radial. He incorporated this in his future blueprints. He sized up the merits of rooms on both sides of the corridor instead of the traditional singles. He noted that the most modern hotels had switched to room service orders being placed on the telephone rather than through a call bell. He weighed the pros and cons, and conceded that they had made the right decision. The call bell might provide a more personalized response, but the telephone gave you a faster breakfast; there was enough scope for interfacing in the reception and restaurants. He learnt that each public area should look out on a garden, and every room should have a view.

At one of the hotels, he sat in the lobby to see how the flow of guests was organized. Or should be. This place had a narrow reception desk, and people impatiently waited their turn. Or did not, taking their custom elsewhere. Out came his pad, in went an entry: counters should be long enough to service three or four guests at a time. All this is taken for granted today, but way back then it was ground-breaking. He made a neat—and very large file—of his observations.

He subpoenaed Prem to help in the reconnaissance. The girl found it embarrassing. Besides, billing departments and bathrooms were not her idea of sightseeing. She remembers they added Texas to their itinerary simply 'because Daddy was told that the newly built Shamrock there boasted the first health club in the history of hoteliering'.

He swung through twenty-five hotels, and by the time he was through, the days of Abdul, the doddering room bearer, were well and truly numbered. Four decades later, Rai Bahadur still recalls how much he learnt from the trip that prepared him for his next great leap. He also remembers that most of the hotels insisted on his being their guest.

Yes, he also found time to shop. He bought something for all his staff. Even if it was just a fountain pen. And he did not buy at random. Each item was specifically chosen for its individual recipient. He did not need a list. His 'personnel relations' had already become something of a legend, aided by his phenomenal memory. He not only knew all his employees, he could even tell you the last time their mothers-in-law had been ill. And with what.

CHAPTER XXIII

Maidens No More

The telegram sent by the profligate young Raj ladies had found an ironic fulfilment. The Oberoi family had been 'sent' enough money, but it 'remained maidens no more'. The naïve innocence of the Bhaun and Simla days had been swamped by the war and whisky of Calcutta. The trajectory, triggered by the dramatic Associated Hotels of India (AHI) blast-off, would be halted in its blazing path only by the new imperative to build rather than annex.

Life had certainly become easier for Ishran Devi compared to the early days when she was 'bugged' in Band Quarter 4, the days when she had ironed out the creases in 'Rai Bahadurji's' clothes and life at Clarkes. Easier, but in other ways it was more difficult. The big league that her husband plunged into with such gusto quite overwhelmed her. While they shared the day's plans and problems as he shaved and dressed at the crack of dawn, she did not share his ambition. 'It's quite enough,' she pleaded. Like a latter-day family planning slogan she had said in Calcutta, 'Now we have two, that will do.' But the adrenalin was coursing through Mohan Singh's veins, and AHI activated the take-over tide. Nothing was going to stop him. Not even his beloved Ishran. She could not keep pace with his swift, sure strokes. She went under. Then surfaced again in her own way came ashore on her own private island of inner peace.

Ishran Devi immersed herself completely in the faith of the Sikh gurus, though she had not been born a Sikh. She organized *akhand path,* the three-day, non-stop recitation from the *Adi Granth,* that commemorates joyous domestic events, imparts auspiciousness to the start of new ventures, or defuses a financial crisis. At their Grand suite, she had a special prayer room and two *granthis* from the Bhowanipore gurdwara arrived every morning to conduct the ritualistic reading of the holy book. The night clerk, S.A. Franklyn, remembers getting *prasad,* the ceremonial offering, just before he went off duty; it was distributed to all the staff of the hotel. When they later moved to Delhi, she never failed to rise at five in the morning and be at the Sisganj Gurdwara by six.

It would be easy to analyse Ishran Devi's mid-life obsession with religion as an escape from the pressures of the high life thrust on someone who was still a small-town woman at heart. Mohan Singh may not have been a great socializer, but you cannot run a hotel as if it were an ascetic Himalayan cave. Religion pulled Ishran, she was not pushed into it in despair or in high dudgeon.

Mohan Singh did not love his Ishran any the less when, in later life, he pursued his other liaisons. Ishran's task was tougher, but she did not care for him any the less either. She was on the most gracious terms with her husband's women friends. She acknowledged the fact that they fulfilled his extrovert need for banter and laughter that she could not. Besides, Mohan Singh was both discriminating and discreet. That may have made it easier for Ishran. Or more difficult. It was also a more tolerant era, the word yet to become an acronym for the Equal Rights Amendment.

Despite her growing other-worldliness Ishran Devi would remain the bond that held the family together through the years of her husband's obsessive ambition. Rai Bahadur was not the only tycoon too busy tearing towards the top to have too little time to spend with his children. Not the first to believe that time is money, assuming that material indulgences would compensate for what he could not spare in terms of hours and minutes. This was a pre-postmodern age that had not heard of nurturing fathers or quality-time from supermom.

'Mom' in this case, was never the less 'super'. Always there to teach her daughters how to make the most of their lives. Swaraj recalls one episode from the acned ecstasy of adolescence when her mother did not thrust her value system upon her, simply told her that if she was not comfortable deep down about what she was doing, she should stop, however painful the short-term consequence. The sons were another matter altogether.

For all that has been said about Rai Bahadur being too busy, he always wanted to see what his wife and daughters brought back from shopping expeditions. He often told his wife that he would like her to wear a particular bracelet with the outfit she had decided upon for that evening out. When his daughters began learning classical music, he went himself to buy the harmonium from Calcutta's Lal Bazaar. Perhaps he no longer hand-picked each of Ishran's saris as he had from Loknath, the best shop on the Simla Mall, but he did take time off to choose personally every item for Rajrani's trousseau.

No one could have called him an uncaring man, even if sometimes, ignoring the basics, he strained at the trivial. The family laughs over the story of Biki's socks. He did not have much time to spare for any man-to-man—and male chauvinist—moments with his boys, but he once went to considerable lengths (scouring the shops in Calcutta) to get exactly the kind of woollen knee-high socks that he thought Biki should be wearing. Biki, at the time, was at St Paul's, Darjeeling, India's exclusive and most expensive public school patterned on English lines, complete with robed masters in the misty quadrangle.

Four decades after the imperial capital, Rai Bahadur shifted from Calcutta to Delhi. He did not choose, however, to live amidst Edwin Lutyens' architectural eminences. He preferred the vintage Maidens in the old city, with its colonnaded colonial facade, sprawling grounds and gracious ambience. He likened what Mr Maidens had built at the turn of the century as a 'travel stopping place for the right people'.

While the family moved to Maidens, Tikki set himself up in a lavish suite at the Imperial Hotel since it was closer to the seat of power—and farther from his mother's anxious eye. In any event, he spent six months of the year in Srinagar, in his beloved Puja House, the former Maharani's home which he had remodelled into an elegant bungalow, laying English tiles, wooden floor and Persian carpets, and replacing the front wall with a huge French window framing the spectacular view of the vale.

In 1959, Biki married Goodie, daughter of Punjabi landowners of Lyalpur. The fair, slim beauty, with her thick dark tresses, and made more exotic by her part-Persian blood, had caught the eye of Mohan Singh in Kashmir. He had mentioned her to his son who found himself entirely in agreement with his father's choice. The reception was at Maidens; the honeymoon in Jaipur. Then the couple went off to live in Calcutta where both their children were born. Natasha in January 1962, Vikram at the end of 1963. They, too, often holidayed in Kashmir with their friends, Piloo Mody, Ripu Bhagat, Colonel Harry Nedou and the Maharajah Holkar of Indore—going there to marvel at the changing seasons, for the shooting and, much more, the fishing. Goodie, now sitting in her distinctive all black and white Delhi home, says, 'Trout just didn't taste the same in the South of France as it did in Kashmir.' Biki later moved to the elegant house designed by William Perry, not far from his father's distinctly more modest one on the outskirts of the capital. Justifying the contrast, Rai Bahadur loves to joke, 'I was a poor man's son. Biki has a rich father.'

Swaraj and Gautam also remained at the Grand for several years with their boys, Ashok and Rajiv, and then shifted to their own home in New Delhi. Rajrani followed her Colonel husband to stations across the country, and her daughter, Rajni, and sons, Ajai and Vijai, went to boarding schools in Simla and Dehra Dun. But Prem and 'K.K.', together with their kids, Kavita, Ragini and Sanjeev, stayed at Maidens. To these children, who perceived him more as a businessman than as a grandfather, Rai Bahadur was 'Big Daddy' just as he was always 'Daddy' to his sons and daughters, Somehow *'Pitaji'* did not quite go with felt hats and spats.

Through all these affairs of the family, Rai Bahadur remained neck-deep in work. Other workaholics seemed cold sober by comparison. The clear mind and the quick grasp helped him keep an iron hold on the empire, no detail was too small any more than any dream was too big. He could not just sit back, occasionally check on the supplies, share a drink with a self-important functionary, and watch the money roll in. The state of the industry did not permit such a luxury. The British bureaucrats, who had been the mainstay of hotels in the past, had gone; the princes were going under with death duties; the new patronage was still to arrive on the social register. The business traveller waited apprehensively as the country plunged into its heady affair with the socialistic ideal. Destination India and the glossy poster were not even a gleam in an official's eye because a full-fledged department of tourism took its own time materializing.

Though Rai Bahadur continued to do business on the other side of the border, most of the profits of the Pakistan hotels went into the servicing of the loan taken from the local Punjab National Bank (PNB) for their renovation. The Cecil had been on the downslide ever since Simla lost its charmed Raj status. The Grand and the Imperial were the only ones that made money. Like a correctly demure one, Maidens followed two paces behind. But a lack of funds had never been a serious impediment in the way of new acquisitions. As long as he had the impressive real estate, the banks would loan.

Mohan Singh liked being the monarch of all he surveyed, and it was not long before he had under his belt the once splendid Swiss Hotel that he saw from his Maidens' window when he woke up every morning. It had once been the residence of Curzon, it was now owned by the Chunamals, an old Delhi family, and leased from them by Steiner, formerly of Associated Hotels. Rai Bahadur negotiated with both owner and Manager, and after a succession of moves, owned the whole lot: lock, stock and barrels in the cellar. Later, realizing that old Delhi could not support two luxury hotels, he converted the Swiss property into a swanky apartment complex.

Old Delhi was still beautiful, you could still see the moonlight that gave Chandni Chowk its evocative name. And sometimes, very rarely, the husband found the time to wander with the family through its serpentine alleys to savour his favourite *dahi bhalle,* or of a nippy winter afternoon, tuck into black carrot *kanji* and *paranthas* stuffed with radish, summoning through the mists a taste of the days back home in Bhaun. The only film he saw was *Mughal-e-Azam.*

Late at night, when he had cleared the last file on his table, and climbed into bed, he would lie thinking of his dream project, something more ambitious than he had ever dared before. The first hotel that he would build himself. Typically , it would be a landmark not only in his own career, but of the entire industry: India's first truly international hotel. But he would lose before he gained, and in between he would give the country another pioneering concept, its first palace hotel.

CHAPTER XXIV

A Palace Coup

Rai Bahadur was no stranger to the mighty Himalayas but he had never set eyes on the part of it fabled to be a paradise on earth. Kashmir became heir to its anguished, and now increasingly militant, legacy from the time that the titans of independence clashed over it. The Kashmiri Pandit, Jawaharlal Nehru, insisted on keeping his ancestral homeland for India; Mohammed Ali Jinnah, citing its predominantly Muslim population, was equally obdurate over wresting it for Pakistan. If the State's frustrated and misguided youth today fight for *azadi* with kidnappings and Kalashnikovs, that too is part of the bequest; the Maharajah of Jammu and Kashmir had his own plans, which did not jell with those of the two giants charting out the destiny of the subcontinent. His Highness Sir Hari Singh, KCIE, KCVO was determined that his ancient kingdom would remain an independent entity.

The debonair Lord Louis Mountbatten, referee to the historic match of wits and nerves in 1947, had veered to the viewpoint of Nehru, and a desperate Pakistan had sent armed raiders into the vale to precipitate a crisis. Ironically, this is what pushed the beleaguered ruler into the helping, and welcoming, arms of India. He hastily signed the Instrument of Accession, goaded by Sheikh Abdullah, the Lion of Kashmir and President of its dominant political party, the National Conference. Still intimidated, Maharajah Hari Singh abdicated in favour of his son, left his kingdom, left behind his palace. But took away everything in it, down to the washbasins. He left with a winding convoy of trucks carrying precious carpets, marble fireplaces, crystal, silver, paintings, furnishings, the elaborately carved furniture. Next, eight years of 'open house' completed the havoc at Gulab Bhavan.

In 1955, Rai Bahadur arrived on his first visit to Kashmir to participate in a travel agents' convention. At Delhi's old Safdarjung Airport, he met Tikki's friend, Ripu Bhagat, headed in the same direction. It was the height of the season and every hotel in Srinagar was booked. Rai Bahadur, who had shared more primitive lodgings with Ripu when they were building prefab housing in Siliguri, spent the night in his room at Nedou's. Early morning Ripu went off to meet the Kashmiri strongman and Chief Minister, Bakshi Ghulam Mohammed, and on his return he found a note in his older friend's scrawl, 'Thank you for the use of your room. I have moved to a houseboat. Please join us for dinner at 7 p.m.'

By then, Tikki had also arrived and the three men, mellowed by Kashmir's celebrated hospitality, sat in the elaborately furnished houseboat of the carpet and handicraft merchant who- perversely called himself, 'Subhana the Worst'. Moonlight dappled the waters of the Dal Lake, the chinars towered on its shore, and beyond this magnificent line of maples rose a splendiferous pile. A solitary bulb shone from its silhouette. Rai Bahadur could not take his eyes off it. As they dispersed for the night, he said, 'If I can get that, I'll make it into the most beautiful hotel in the world.'

The next morning Tikki activated his powerful Kashmiri network. D.P. Dhar, himself a princeling and later Indira Gandhi's confidant and minister, was his closest friend. D.P. knew that the Maharajah's son and regent, the *Sadr-e-riyasat*, Dr Karan Singh, who too would later join the Union Cabinet, could be persuaded to turn this huge liability to profit. He had a word with him. Then Rai Bahadur and Tikki called on Dr Singh. Over a silver platter of *koftas* simmered in milk, the deal was made. As discreetly as befitted royalty. It was only at the end that Rai Bahadur asked, 'Your Highness how much would you like?' Karan Singh replied, 'Rs 5,000 a month and a contract for twenty years.' Rai Bahadur said, 'With pleasure.'

Easier said than done. The palace had lain in grand decay for almost a decade. The grass was five feet high, the walls crumbling, the sweeping staircases giving way, and Tikki almost fell through a ter- mite-riddled floor. Besides, it was an absolutely empty shell. There was not a single stick of furniture left in it.

Rai Bahadur hired a few chairs and a large table, and moved into the precarious structure with Ishran Devi. Tikki pitched camp in a manner he was more accustomed to, checking into a hotel. Savitri Khanna joined them. An army of masons, carpenters, plumbers and cleaners was hired. Rai Bahadur redesigned the interior himself. The utilitarian furniture was ordered from Delhi, but local craftsmen worked long and caringly on the ornately carved Kashmiri sideboards and screens in walnut and rosewood. There was a billiard room, a gun room, dozens of bedrooms and private drawing-rooms to say nothing of grander audience halls; but there were just ten bathrooms, and they consisted only of three walls, and perchance, only perchance, a door.

Ishran Devi hacked her way through the neck-high grass with a cane and orchestrated the gardeners. By a stroke of luck they found the old *malis* who were able to restore to their original beauty the lawns and terraced hillsides tumbling to the edge of the lake.

But Rai Bahadur knew that though the Palace Hotel was now ready, it was not complete. Nothing less than its original furnishing could complement its architectural grandeur. This, however, lay in a godown far away in Bombay; moreover, he knew that the Maharajah, sulking there in self-exile, abhorred the thought of his palace being trampled all over by a bunch of tourists. Tikki, D.P.Dhar and Karan Singh all warned him that it was an impossible mission. They had reckoned without the two qualities which, more than any of the other determinants of his destiny, had taken the boy from Bhaun to the top: his way with people and his perseverance in getting what he had fixed his sights on.

The first thing Rai Bahadur did on his arrival in Bombay was to indulge in some minor espionage. He managed to get the keeper of the warehouse to allow him entry for a reconnaissance trip. He gasped at the Aladdin's cave of treasures; separated the antique, discarded in his mind the 'junk'. The priceless carpets were what he had set his heart upon. Then he sought an audience with the erstwhile ruler. After a couple of rebuffs, he was ushered into Maharajah Hari Singh's august presence. The initial hostility melted as the Maharajah warmed to this gentleman with such correct and winning ways.

Rai Bahadur edged the small talk towards the business at hand. The former ruler, with barely concealed sadness, asked him if he wanted to see the items before buying. The hotelier disarmed him by saying that this was not at all necessary; how could there ever be any question about His Highness's taste? Sir Hari Singh, now infinitely more cooperative, asked a secretary to bring in the inventory, and Rai Bahadur simply ticked what he wanted.

Finally, came the most delicate part of the operation. The Maharajah asked, 'How much will you pay?' Hesitating only enough to suggest that the idea had just struck him, and in a tone of restrained magnanimity, he said, 'I'll tell you what, Your Highness. The carpets may be old and used, but I will pay you as much as I would for new ones today. Rs 10 a yard.' The Maharajah visualized the miles of carpets, and agreed immediately. Today, just one is worth what Oberoi paid for the priceless lot: Rs 200,000.

The Kashmir Palace thus did not turn out to be only Aladdin's treasure cave; it also echoed its sequel of new lamps for precious old.

In 1980, with his sons grown up enough to help him in business, Dr Karan Singh asked Rai Bahadur if they would renegotiate the agreement, even though there were still several years left for the original one to lapse. He wanted Oberoi Hotels to handle only the management. Mohan Singh agreed, not very willingly, but he did not believe in taking friends to court. A fresh contract was drawn up by which the East India Hotels Ltd (EIHL) sold back to Dr Karan Singh all that they had put in: three million rupees worth of it, to be paid for over the next decade. For their managerial services they would get twelve per cent of gross profits and three per cent on sales.

In recent years, there has not been much to take a percentage of. The troubled valley lost all its tourists, and the Palace Hotel has been closed since 1990. But Oberoi continues to pay half the salaries of the staff that has remained. The Hindus who fled to the migrant camps in Jammu are being helped. Many of those desperate enough to leave their bracing homeland entirely, and brave the torrid summers of Delhi, have been given jobs in the Oberoi hotels in the capital.

CHAPTER XXV

Prince As Playboy

The rich and the famous would always pass through the portals of the hotels associated with Rai Bahadur Mohan Singh Oberoi. As Clerk or Manager or Owner, he always had an instinct for the finest, whether it came from the cellars or walked through the front door in a click of Spanish heels and a hint of French perfume. But in the glamour department, the father was no match for the sons.

Growing up in a hotel, where you had your own private suite and anything you wished for just a ring away, could hardly engender qualities of self-help. Besides there was an indulgent father determined that his own strict upbringing should not be imposed on his sons. Wasn't he making enough money to support as extravagant a lifestyle as they chose?

Far from being defensive about it, Rai Bahadur derived vicarious pleasure from it. Too busy to enjoy any of it himself, he viewed the young men's high living as a proxy endorsement of his own success. Moreover, even if his sons' well-heeled friends did not always contribute to the coffers of the hotel, they brought in style, an asset that may not be tax-deductible but is infinitely more valuable.

In the Simla season of 1955, Tikki Oberoi set eyes upon a girl in a yellow-print dress sitting in the garden of the Cecil and reading Radhakrishnan, a wild rose in her thick, black, waist-length hair. She was fresh, fragile and half French. Observing her from his window he turned to Lawrence Pratt, his British secretary—and said, 'This girl is going to be my wife.'

He wooed her with the determination his father normally reserved for winning hotels. He spared her the embarrassment of being selected Miss Simla Queen by making her leave the room at the crucial moment; his rickshaw arrived in the nick of time to save her from being caught in a drizzle on the Mall. Naturally, like the rest of his retinue, the four coolies of Tikki's rickshaw wore special livery, complete with cockscombed turban. Tikki asked her to tea in the Small Lounge, where, in another corner, Shashi Kapoor and Jennifer Kendall sat by the fireside whispering sweet nothings, probably in Shakespearean blank verse. He placed her across a tea table, looked into her hazel eyes, and asked her to marry him. All within a week of having seen her for the first time. The playboy of the Western world had not even kissed her.

The family was thrilled with the girl who was as elegant in her manners as she was exquisite in her looks. They hoped she would bring some focus and order to Tikki's life. Ishran Devi personally put together the trousseau, spending months deliberating over the brocades for her beautiful daughter-in-law-to-be, choosing the diamonds and the emeralds that would offset her porcelain features. Tilak Raj Oberoi wed Leela Naidu on 16 July 1956. He was thirty-three, she was seventeen. The simple Sikh ceremony with its seven *pheras* round the *Guru Granth Saheb,* was held at Maidens followed by lunch under a *shamiana* for several hundred invitees. In the evening, the guest list and the Imperial lawns spilled over. Every one of Delhi's somebodies was there: Rai Bahadur's government and business connections; Tikki's royal and army friends; the entire diplomatic corps; the scientific elite close to Leela's father, Dr Ramaiah Naidu, the nuclear physicist who was Science Director, UNESCO, for South-East Asia. Also Dr Radhakrishnan, still to become President of India, and Krishna Menon, still to resign as Defence Minister in ignominy. Rai Bahadur, with the sparkle that came into his eyes with just one drink, was the perfect host, revelling in the fact of 'at last having got a proper *bahu*'.

The marriage was incompatible right from the honeymoon in Puja House, Tikki's stylish cottage in Kashmir, where the new groom was welcomed like a maharajah with a line-up of retainers showering rose petals. Leela could not take his obsession with his friends, his shooting, his polo, his Johnnie Walker Black Label. He accused her of having intellectual pretensions and an interfering mother; he hated the idea of her wanting to be an actress. The birth of delightful twin girls the following July did nothing to stabilize the marriage that grew more tempestuous by the day. Leela walked out of the hotel suite two years later, leaving behind the one-year-old Priya and Maya, little dolls in their frilly French dresses, and pink booties, in their designer nursery.

Tikki had the clout. Tikki had the more expensive lawyers. Tikki had physical possession of the children. Tikki got custody. Rai Bahadur, however, put his foot down on this one occasion with his self-willed son; he insisted on Leela having access to the twins during the years that the case dragged on at the courts. And after.

Tikki had honeymooned in Srinagar with Leela. Kashmir was where, in 1964, he swept the honey-blond Jutta off her feet, five years after his first marriage ended in divorce. The statuesque Teuton, daughter of aircraft designer Ludwig Mittel Huber, who was then helping Hindustan Aeronautics Ltd to build fighter aircraft, had gone along to Srinagar with a friend who was camp-following Feroz Khan on location shooting. The Tikki-Jutta courtship was wild. The German had none of Leela's distaste for the high life. It was at a party at his *aprés-ski* hut in Gulmarg that Tikki announced the marriage—the first that the bride-to-be heard of the proposal. Typical of Tikki. Their son, Arjun, was born a year later.

Tikki had followed his royal role models closely, and soon rivalled them, point for glittering point. He learnt to be one of the finest shots in India, shooting game in the royal preserves of Cooch Behar and Indore, and fishing for brown trout in the crystal streams of Kashmir. He loved beautiful jewels and beautiful women. He loved his horses—and hated champagne.

Most of all, Tikki was the polo-playing 'prince', going on to acquire his own team, the Chocolate Babies, in their distinctive brown silk shirts. A leaf, perhaps, from Uncle Shiv Nath's brown and beige racing silks. He cut a dashing figure in his chukkers astride Pasha, a pony he had bought from a circus. He claimed that, with its Big Top disciplining, he hardly had to train it: it just went naturally after the ball.

Tikki was the 'regular old chap' of the international polo crowd. Had he been alive, he would certainly have been around to raise a toast to the bride of Britain's Prince Andrew; little red-haired Sarah, later known to friends and the world as Fergie, had pranced on the edges of the field as her father, Colonel Fergusson, and the young, dark and handsome 'nabob' pitted their skills against each other in a thunder of hooves.

Tikki had the distinction of beating the Jaipur team on its home ground. Winning the Jaipur Cup in 1955, with not a little help from Raoraja Hanut Singh, one of the best players in the country. Together with his sons, Vijay and Kishan, he was on Tikki's team. Jutta claims that, confronted by certain rout the next morning, 'Jai' asked to play with the opposition, but wanted to retain at least the dignity of wearing his own colours. No way, said Tikki, savouring sweet victory, and a Chocolate-Babies shirt was delivered from Delhi for him overnight. It was not 'my kingdom for a horse', but the years of friendship that prompted 'Jai' to offer Rambagh Palace first to Oberoi. But the fabulous business opportunity slipped away, not once, but twice.

It is not easy to stop bumping into the wealthy and the titled of many colours when your playgrounds are such places as Cannes and Monte Carlo. It is even more difficult if the owners of these terribly, terribly posh places are part of your inner circle, as was John Mills, no relation to the actor but mine host at *Les Ambassadors* in London. Howard Hughes was no recluse when it came to his pal Tikki. Rubirosa, one-time diplomat, full-time playboy and quintessential Latin lover, was his polo playing friend.

Wild might be too tame an adjective for the parties. Jutta, the swinging German who flung herself with gusto into Tikki's night life, recalled an evening when everyone was as high as a kite, including Rubirosa. At some point during the cavorting, Tikki's safe was opened for no reason that anyone can remember, and a very expensive string of emerald beads fell to the floor. The sobriety of the next afternoon revealed a layer of very worthless green powder.

Tikki never carried money on him, he simply signed, and Trilok, his valet, would arrive the next day to settle the bill. Witness the headline in one of London's shriller tabloids, 'Tipped off by Tikki !'. The report went on to tell the tale of the flamboyant hotelier-prince who had grandly presented his diamond cufflinks to a nightclub Manager to be redeemed against cash the next morning. However, when Trilok, himself in gold-trimmed, closed-collar Nehru jacket, presented himself the gentleman said he preferred to keep the cufflinks. The case reached the courts and a compromise of a hundred pounds.

Tikki did not sit at his desk for more than an hour, but he had a brilliant mind. Even before he joined his father at the Grand, he had successful businesses. When he moved to Delhi, he began Northern

India Caterers, which became the holding company of The Swiss Hotel, and later took on the management of a Chandigarh hotel. At the Grand, he was at the front of the house; his public relations were impeccable; he knew exactly how to win friends and get people to use their influence. Most of all, his forte was finance, and there is no denying that when the foundations of empire were being laid at the Grand, it was Tikki who helped ensure that his father's ambition would be adequately bankrolled.

In the last fifteen years of his life Tikki grew deeply interested in the business and kept in daily touch with all that was happening. He was a Jt. Managing Director of the East India Hotels Company, along with his brother Biki, and was a director of all associate companies. He chaired several committees relating to finance and development. Tikki had the ability to intuitively find and resolve key concerns of the group; Rai Bahadur affirms that his son's grasp of the hotel business and intelligence had a positive long term effect on the future of the Oberoi group.

Tikki was internationally known and this helped to make the Oberoi name internationally known. His open-heartedness and generosity ensured he was much loved by the family and employees and this was more than apparent at the time of his death at the age of sixty in 1984. His passing was a great loss to the Rai Bahadur, the family and the group, and we shall look at this more closely in a later chapter.

CHAPTER XXVI

Heir-Apparent Biki

Prithvi Raj Singh Oberoi—whom the well-heeled world knew as Biki—sowed his wild oats at the watering-holes of the world's wealthy, even as he studied in London and went on to master *haute cuisine* in Switzerland. In 1955, he decided to return home. He took his place by his father's side with a passion that rivalled that of Oberoi *pére*. At twenty- five, he was certainly more of a man of the world than Mohan Singh had been at that age, his experience of the finest hotels and restaurants making up for the lack of nitty-gritty that is mastered through years of working one's way up from the cellar. Not that Biki had not got his elbows greasy; *École Hoteliere* was as tough a task-master as they come.

Rai Bahadur was going to build a hundred hotels, and it helped to have Biki at hand. Rai Bahadur may have been far more indulgent to Tikki, but he knew earlier than anyone else that it was in Biki that he would place his faith—and legacy. As early as 1943, in fact. The boy was only fourteen, but it was in him that he confided the fact that he had wrested the holding of G.V. Pike and thereby bested Shiv Nath Singh in the race to get control of Associated Hotels (AHI). He knew his wily rival would have got the information out of Tikki; secrecy was of the essence till he had arranged for the money to pay for the shares.

From the vantage point of hindsight, Biki says he did not find growing up in the impersonal confines of a hotel anything to complain of. Watching and listening he got his first lessons in the business. To say nothing of the exposure to the rich and the powerful. Besides, it felt great to revel in the widening eyes of his school chums as he rang for anything he wanted from the private suite that was his at twelve. Today Biki will tell you, 'Give me a young man from a good background with a penchant for the good life, and I'll make him the perfect hotelier in three years.'

The years abroad convinced Biki that the Oberoi group would have to make its mark internationally, and to do so it would have to compete with the world on its own terms. Fortunately, that was his father's idea. Exactly. Biki was put in charge of the Pakistan hotels, not quite his notion of international, but a good place to learn how to open renovated wings and government doors with equal finesse. Here Biki came close to Zulfiqar Ali Bhutto, then only a Minister for Commerce in the Ayub Government. Piloo Mody, who was later to design the Oberoi in Delhi was 'Zulfie's' school friend from way back when in Bombay. Bhutto often invited the two of them to Swat to shoot the hill partridge, *chakor*.

With the architect, William Perry, Biki renovated the Pakistan hotels. And, right from those beginnings, he displayed his hallmark, the near-obsessive attention to detail. Neither time, effort nor money were of consequence in the pursuit of the right finish, the perfect grain, the flawless texture. The 1965 Indo-Pakistan war put paid to his efforts, the hotels being declared enemy property. But by then Biki had not merely cut his teeth, he had sunk them into the business.

The next stop was the world. Biki and his brother-in-law, Gautam Khanna, made a formidable team, following the whispers on the grapevine, assessing properties on every continent, driving hard bargains, drawing up contracts. Rai Bahadur almost never attended negotiations, except perhaps at the final formality. But, clearly, there was no way he would stay out of the picture. He knew every detail at every stage and went through the contracts with a fine tooth comb, subjected them to a mental third degree till he had dislodged every unfavourable sub-clause. Till the 1980s he would remain completely in command.

It was Biki's sense of style combined with his refusal to compromise that achieved the kind of standard in furnishings and food that people had said would never be possible in India. Achieving it in his hotels abroad was not half as difficult; there the problematic 'f' was finance. 'It pleases me a great deal,' he now says, 'to be asked how we manage to get everything done right in a country where so little functions smoothly.'

CHAPTER XXVII

Diversion

Let us for a while abandon the neatness of chronology and return to the farm where we first met the ninety-one-year-old patriarch. The mynah-bird marking out the sequence of his life on the extra window pane has withdrawn to its nest. There is no light for the pane to let in and thus serve its purpose. The shadows have assembled in silent armies behind the thickets, and now press against the glass of the door.

Khayali, one more of his good and faithful retainers, pads in, staggering under the weight of the silver tea service, the thinly sliced smoked-salmon sandwiches, the chocolate cake, the eggs stuffed with caviare. Rai Bahadur carefully lifts his large, fine-china cup of milky tea to his lips, and urges the feast on his chronicler. 'My digestion is not what it used to be. ' Munir has told us earlier of his weakness for *pakoras*, how they would stop near what was still the Punjab border when they drove to Simla from Delhi, of how the sahib would unscrew his hip flask, and of how he would get the piping hot fritters from his favourite shop by the wayside. *Pakoras* and *payas*, rich gelatinous trotters, now even more completely taboo.

We are alone with the shadows, Rai Bahadur uncorks the mind and quietly begins to talk of other memories. Of chance encounters that left their imprint, some transient, some indelible. Today Rai Bahadur takes a detour to talk of Gyan Singh Rarewala, a one time Chief Minister of the Punjab and Hill-States Union, and his daughter, Nirlep. The Rarewalas were Sikh aristocracy, closely connected with the house of Patiala, and with his Bhaun-old links with princely Punjab, Mohan Singh Oberoi knew them well. The acquaintance grew further in Chandigarh where he managed Mount View Hotel.

When Mohan Singh decided to build his own house, also on

picturesque Sukhna Lake, he got the same architect his friends had used. The architect's design was enhanced by Nirlep, who offered her considerable talents in landscaping the grounds. Impressed, Rai Bahadur began to talk to her a great deal about the laying out of gardens, which added a new dimension to a hotel's aesthetics. Nirlep had been studying the subject for five years, and had built up a collection of text and lay-outs from all over the world. When, much later, he began planning the New Delhi hotel, he knew just whose expertise on the landscaping he would count upon. Nirlep was delighted to oblige. No professional help was sought. Nor has he felt the need to make any changes ever since.

When, many years after, Mohan Singh built his farmhouse, he called upon her experience in the subject once again. Once again Nirlep flung herself whole-heartedly into the task. Like the hotel's the farm's grounds trigger spontaneous admiration. Today, the trees have grown to great height, but Mohan Singh summons the memory of Nirlep standing for four hours in the mud and rain, supervising the planting of the first, hesitant saplings.

Rai Bahadur encouraged this strong young woman to join politics, a diversion that he had also permitted himself. She took to it with a gusto greater than his. For a short time their terms in the Lok Sabha coincided, then Rai Bahadur moved on to the Rajya Sabha. Nirlep later went into religion in a big way, doing a lot for the Khalsa Panth. She died young, in early 1991. He cherishes her memory. She was a good friend.

CHAPTER XXVIII

A Style Called Imperial

Hotel Imperial, Janpath. It was the best address from which you could operate when visiting New Delhi to liaise with the licensing authorities, push the permit rajahs or merely move among the mandarins. And it was Rai Bahadur's. For all practical purposes. The Imperial had been given on a long lease to Associated Hotels of India (AHI) at Rs 35,000 a year, and Mohan Singh Oberoi inherited it, when he annexed the chain in 1943.

It had been constructed in the late 1920s by Sardar Bahadur Narain Singh, who, having built the New Delhi secretariat, had used his extensive contractor networks to create an imposing edifice, with columned porches, avenues lined with crowned palms, a grand staircase sweeping to its upper reaches, and a lobby that sprawled with the same uninhibited abandon as its lawns. Way back in the 1930s, Narain Singh had hoped that, repayment unable to be honoured, Clarkes would become the property of his son, Jagjit, in whose name it had been mortgaged. Fate stood the presumption on its head. Mohan Singh Oberoi not only retained Clarkes but also gained control of Imperial, the hotel that Narain Singh had bequeathed to his other son, Ranjit.

By the time Mohan Singh took it over, along with the hotels of the (AHI) chain in 1944, a patina of neglect had spread like a layer of grease on an unscrubbed scullery. He got to work, upgraded the facilities, redecorated the rooms, installed air-conditioning, glamorized and, more important, modernized, the bathrooms. The new Imperial's pride was the Moghul Suite, creation of its Italian Manager, fitted with chandeliers, period furniture, silk furnishings, the works. And while Makrana had been enough for Shah Jahan, for Italo Sibilia, nothing less than the varicose-veined marble from his native quarries of Carrara-would do. Rai Bahadur also added another imperious touch to the Imperial, another first in hoteliering: the tall, stately, Sikh doorman, in the full regalia of a Viceregal bodyguard.

It was also Italo Sibilia who introduced a sense of menu into the Oberoi hotels, leavened them out of the stodgy mince cutlets and caramel custard persona of their colonial years. He introduced the charcoal grill and the *flambé* at the Imperial's Tavern. Here, behind the innovative see-through glass, the chef in his apron, knotted scarf, and tall, white, starched *toque*, basted meats with a flourish, predecessor to the impresario *roomali roti* twirler in later frontier-cuisine restaurants. It had to be the legendary Italian who gave Delhi its first taste of pasta, and he must surely turn in his grave at the thought of today's Punjabi pizza with *chaat masala*.

Mulling over a Minestrone, he orchestrated the Indians in his kitchens, the 'mug' cooks from Chittagong who had mastered every layer of puff pastry as they worked their way through the kitchens of the Raj, and the Goans who had learnt their art aboard the ocean liners. Naturally, Rai Bahadur would not settle only for such second-hand expertise.

He coopted his new daughter-in-law, Leela, to get a French chef for the Imperial when she went to Paris for medical treatment after the birth of the twins; (Roberto Rossellini, who had earlier been quite bowled over by her gifts as an actress, had recommended the doctor who had treated his own wife, Ingrid Bergman). Leela got in touch with the chef of the Maurice Hotel, a gentleman appropriately if implausibly named Monsieur Gateau, interviewed several candidates, and chose Roger Moncourte. The clincher was his condition, 'Madame, I don't care about *le salaire*, but I must have good cooking wine.'

Moncourte arrived in Delhi, and went to town with his creations. He did great things with the game birds that Tikki, Biki and their friends shot. Incidentally, it was these same creatures that had got Ishran Devi extremely upset many years ago. The boys had brought in their mixed bag for her to cook, and seeing the massacre on her kitchen floor, she had turned vegetarian forever. While the French chef had no such inhibitions, his favourites were saddle of lamb stuffed with *paté*, rounded off with *Saboyan*. Or *Veal Orloff*, fillet stuffed with a *purée* of mushroom and onion and served in Bechamel sauce. Or *Asparagus Polonaise*, the tender spears tossed in melted butter. He was very good with *Lobster L'Armoricaine*, the original that takes its name from the village in Brittany, not the one corrupted to 'American'.

Moncourte was also fabled for an exquisite sole stuffed with a *duxelle* of mushroom and glazed with white wine. And his Pigeon on Toast. And the classics, *Coq au Vin, Baba au Rhum, Eggs Benedict*. Before this chef tossed together his combinations Delhi had known no salads other than the stodgy Russian. No wonder the French ambassador, doyen of the Corps Diplomatique, was such a regular. *Mon Dieu*! They were all delectations one couldn't Escoffier at!

Despite all the exotica, Roger Moncourte established a principle long before Paul Bocuse whipped up *le cuisine nouvelle*, 'Don't be a snob. Always go to the local market and buy what is in season.' He also had a yardstick to judge a restaurant. However luxurious its trappings, however lavish its menu, it was a *non-non* if the French fries were soggy, the mayonnaise had flour, and the tomatoes had 'fainted'.

Little wonder, then, that the Imperial was where the city's elite gathered in the Fifties and Sixties, a hotel in style and spirit a lot like the Raffles of Singapore. The government chose it for its official dinners. Across its carpets strode diplomats, visiting VIPs from the World Bank or UN agencies, foreign correspondents, editors who came to take the regulation Delhi pulse, agents of big business houses wheeling around to make a deal. There were also guests from Delhi's old families or one-time refugees who, using the Punjabi's native self-reliance, had made money and acquired the sophistication it can buy. Scattered through this clientele were a swagger of gay blades of varied lineage.

On mornings, evenings, afternoons, they measured out their life in coffee-coloured Oxford bags, while in the lobby women came and went, talking, if not of Michelangelo, then certainly of *dahi bhalle* and Mrs Bhalla. Rai Bahadur was yet to get the capital on the go-go with its first discotheque at Maidens, but, in the Imperial ballroom, you could still have a ball. Organized by the ever-innovative Sibilia. Like his boss, he, too, was a man with no interest other than hotels, and the boss would smile later, at ninety-one, and say, 'What hobbies could I have had except looking at pretty ladies?'

But Rai Bahadur has other memories of the Imperial. Tinged first by the sadness of leaving the family suite at Maidens, tinged much later again with the sadness of having to leave the Imperial.

The men in dinner jackets waltzed as they might have in Vienna as they boasted of the last time they had tangoed in Paris. In chiffons with broad brocade borders, the women flung decorum to the winds as they jitterbugged, rhumbaed or went into hysterics over that rumbustious number, 'It's a laughing samba, ha-ha-ha-ha- ha!'

The Imperial lawn was the venue of the capital's grandest weddings. The crass age of 'Pinky weds Bunty' was yet a *bhangra*-to-a-tin-band away, and those who had the wherewithal to afford a five-star marriage also still had the class not to create a nuisance for hotel guests, trample over the flower beds and pull all the toilet paper off its rolls. Years later, for just such reasons, Oberoi would put an embargo on these large receptions, gold mines though they were.

CHAPTER XXIX

Less Of The Lessee

The case was a long and bitter one. Fought from 1958 to 1968 from the lower courts to the highest in the land. The Imperial's lessor had filed a suit against the lessee, to recover premises alleging sub-letting and misuse of property. The battery of eminent lawyers appearing for Rai Bahadur Mohan Singh Oberoi, defendant, could not prevent the Supreme Court from dismissing the appeal and upholding the decision of the High Court favouring the plaintiff, Sardar Bahadur Ranjit Singh.

No one is quite sure as to why Ranjit Singh decided to take back his hotel from Rai Bahadur. Some say that it was over something as trivial as the discount allowed to him and the family when they used its facilities. The more plausible reason, however, was the vast amount of money that Rai Bahadur was raking in; just a month's taking from the shop licensees was what the Sardar Bahadur was being paid as rent for the entire year. Subsequently, Rai Bahadur did offer to raise the amount, going as high as fifteen lakh rupees compared to the original Rs 35,000, but by then Ranjit Singh was determined to carry out his vendetta till the bitter end.

Years later, Rai Bahadur would admit that he had indeed violated the terms of the agreement. He made alterations. He rented out entire corridors to shops as if he were giving out rooms to guests. This, too, was an Oberoi green-field venture—the shopping arcade was yet to become a feature of every large hotel.

One morning after Ranjit Singh had filed the case, Rai Bahadur called his daughter-in-law, Leela, down from her room and asked her if she could spot anything abnormal. Leela looked around carefully to find the ground broken up and the rubble camouflaged by potted plants. It was quite apparent that the unsanctioned structures, which he had now hastily pulled down, would catch the court officials' attention when they came to inspect the premises. So he hurried off to make more foolproof arrangements.

Rai Bahadur also concedes now that he made a mistake in not coming to a compromise with the landlord in the early stages of litigation. 'We were too cocksure, the lawyers led us to believe that we'd win. I didn't take the kind of personal interest that I always do.' Other acquaintances point out that the legal advice was not right while the case was still in the lower courts, that the licence deeds, which were all properly prepared and signed by the shopkeepers, should have been filed at the start instead of trying to effect a saving on stamp duty. The Supreme Court refused to allow them to make up for the default later.

The Supreme Court judgement handed down in 1968 was a landmark one, setting a precedent which has not been overturned either by another ruling or any of the later rules that govern property agreements. It laid down the law on the relationship between lessee and lessor, and under what circumstances it stands terminated.

The Court ordered Rai Bahadur to hand over the property in the shape in which it had been given to him, allowing him six months to vacate. He had spent a lot of money in upgrading what had been a great but old-fashioned hotel, and he asked the Sardar Bahadur whether he would take it back as it was. But Ranjit Singh, gloating over his hard-earned victory, was in no mood to compromise. He continued to dig in his heels; he was going to give Mohan Singh a run for his money. 'You heard what the court said. Restore it to its original form.' His lawyers conveyed the obdurate reply.

Now we see a ruthless Rai Bahadur Mohan Singh Oberoi. It is the wounded lion wreaking revenge. 'They want it exactly as they gave it to us, they'll get it,' he roared. He tore out everything he had so caringly installed. The paintings and the potted plants went first. He brought down the curtains, the carpets, even the clocks. Then he ordered the marble cladding off the bathroom walls, as also all the fixtures he had installed. He brought in old crockery and linen, even scoured the junk shops to get the obsolete toilet cisterns with chains. Finally, he ripped out the air-conditioning ducts.

It was summer in Delhi and the mercury was hitting 108 degrees Fahrenheit. The family had gone on its annual vacation to Kashmir. K.K. Mehra, his youngest son-in-law, offered to stay behind and help. Rai Bahadur refused. Alone he stood among the debris, from six in the morning till midnight, ticking off the items that were removed and those that were put back.

The process of handing over provided drama no less flamboyant than the order to do so. On site, the court clerk reads out the items, 'Four chairs, can you see them?' Sardar Bahadur's lawyer looking at the ones before him objects, 'Yes, but they aren't the original carved ones.' Rai Bahadur's lawyer says blandly, 'Item listed four chairs. It doesn't specify carved or plain.' Objection overruled. Next.

Seeing the devastation wrought on his hotel, Sardar Bahadur Ranjit Singh sued again, this time for the damage to his property. Rai Bahadur in the dock, all innocence, said, 'Your Lordship, the court asked me to hand over the property in the same shape as I received it. I had to comply. Else I would have been accused of committing contempt of court.' Case dismissed.

For all this, Rai Bahadur had lost. But, typically, he did not waste any energy mourning. He simply got on with the next project on hand. The most ambitious to date. The Delhi hotel he would build himself, and which no one could take away.

From the rubble rose the new Phoenix. The gracious old-world Imperial era was over, the period of streamlined new-world modernity clicked into place.

CHAPTER XXX

Breaking The Hex

The Oberoi Intercontinental, Rai Bahadur's dream hotel, the first he had built himself, to the latest international standards, opened in 1965. It was inaugurated not with wining and dining, but with the whining of the air-raid siren. The arrival of the age of the new Indian hotels coincided with that of the Indo–Pakistan war. Another war had won Mohan Singh Oberoi a title and a fortune. This time there was no such luck. Instead it further delayed the recovery of the fortune he had sunk into this hotel. The twists and coincidences that have shadowed every milestone of his life were in attendance here as well. Pakistan had marked the beginning of the Delhi hotel as palpably as it did its completion. And the completion is an entire story in itself.

Is it possible that the building of India's first modern hotel got bogged down for a reason most atavistic? That the alarums and excursions that did not let up for several agonizing, humiliating years perhaps had something to do with the hex of the ancient graves nearby.

Rai Bahadur had dreamt the big dream. His tour of the world's great hotels had strengthened the resolve. His faith in the country's future told him that the international business traveller and the front-of-the-aircraft tourist were only a matter of time, and he should be ready and waiting to catch the flood rather than be swept away by it.

For this new, discerning guest, there could be no existing edifices that merely needed modernizing, no relic managers, however efficient. This time, everything had to be built from scratch.

Conrad Hilton had said that there were three things he looked for when commencing a hotel: 'Site, site and site.' In the early Fifties, Rai Bahadur flew in an English architect and paid him Rs 10,000 simply to study Delhi's master plan, and choose the most ideal location. The architect found it, twenty acres tumbling over the hump of a hillock near the diplomatic enclave. Oberoi, used to the bustling centralness of Maidens, Imperial and the Grand, thought it too far out. The architect was convinced that the city would catch up with it. As it happened, their arguments were premature. The government asked them to surrender the land, and handed it to the princes instead.

The Jamsaheb of Nawanagar had managed to convince Prime Minister Jawaharlal Nehru that Oberoi already had an unhealthy monopoly on the hotel industry in the capital, and that the government should not waste incentives on him. The erstwhile rulers surely had the right background to build as luxurious a hotel, he argued, adding that the old conclave of princes would form a consortium and he would oversee the raising of capital. But the government should give them this land at a hefty concession. Sardar Patel had already exercised his iron will to get them to surrender their fiefdoms to the cause of a united independent India; this was the least the country could do in return, thought Nehru. Oberoi, always the pragmatist, deemed it unwise to argue. He would look elsewhere.

As it turned out, the princes did not want to entrust their money to the Jamsaheb, and since the government wanted a spanking new hotel in time for the UNESCO conference in 1956, it took over the land and decided to build one itself: The Ashoka Hotel.

In the meanwhile, Tikki, Biki and the architect had scoured the city and found a more beautiful site facing the fairways and trees of the Delhi Golf Club, in the environs of the tomb of the revered Nizamuddin. The Oberoi group wanted a monument to the living, but the market price for that was daunting. At prevalent rates they could afford only five acres in place of the twenty they had forfeited. Even this money Rai Bahadur would have to raise.

It was time to look across the border, and use the profits of the Pakistan hotels accumulating with the Punjab National Bank (PNB) in Lahore. Rai Bahadur had already repaid the loan for their renovation and he now asked the bank to pay him his balance of the Rs. 1.2 million in India. This sum took care of part of the land. East India Hotels Ltd (EIHL) went public in 1956, to finance the ambitious project. Construction began. Day and night, bulldozers levelled, foundations were hammered in, concrete-mixers churned, steel-girders were heaved into place.

Ishran Devi laid the foundation-stone in the traditional Sikh man-

ner. (She would continue to be accorded this honour for all sub-
sequent hotels.) She placed five *ashrafiyan,* gold coins, in the pit. Five
was the faith's auspicious figure, representing the *punj pyare,* the first
five converts to Sikhism, as well as the five *takhts* or thrones at
Anantpur, Patiala, Nanded, the Patnasaheb and the Akal Takht at
Amritsar. The last of the ten saints, Guru Gobind Singh, had also
ordained that five religious leaders should head the community for
all time to come and jointly decide on any doubts that might arise.

The hotel structure rose to six of its eight floors and then, one day,
everything just stopped. The money had run out. And there seemed
no way in which it could get flowing again. No one thought the country
was ready for the elaborate vision of Rai Bahadur Mohan Singh
Oberoi. The Industrial Finance Corporation (IFC) sanctioned a
one-crore-rupee loan, but disbursement took too long to materialize.
Desperate, Oberoi devised an ambitious and pioneering scheme in
1962, and East India Hotels Ltd became one of the first non-financial
Indian companies to receive fixed deposits from the public. The
Calcutta brokers, Amritlal and K.K. Bajaj helped rope in twenty
million rupees, at twelve per cent interest, investor confidence resting
on the success of the Grand. The company also held imposing real
estate in Simla and Delhi, besides the Pakistan property.

While her husband moved everything on earth, Ishran Devi moved
the heavens. *Kirtan, bhajan, akhand path,* but most of all the powerful
faith of a woman who was God's own creature, were used to invoke
the help of the Sikh Gurus—and propitiate spirits that might inadver-
tently have been disturbed.

The empty shell stood mockingly for six years, humbling the Oberoi
juggernaut. A concrete skeleton in the middle of a nation's capital was
as much of an embarrassment for the government. The State Minister
for Works, Housing and Civil Supplies, Mehr Chand Khanna, was
about to requisition the eyesore, and do what he thought best with it.
Fate, however, had reckoned without the patience and perseverance
of Rai Bahadur. He was not going to let a bureaucratic bulldozer
trample on his dream. It was time to bring out his own steamroller.

He knew that his good friend, Moti Khaitan, Chairman of Bata's,
who was one of the initial subscribers of East India Hotels Ltd, also
happened to be as good a friend of the Minister. What was more, he
was spending a holiday with him at the Khanna home in Mussourie.
Rai Bahadur drove up to the hill-station. Darkness had enveloped the

hills by the time he reached, and it was pouring with rain. There wasn't a hotel room available for money. Love had stopped being legal tender long ago.

He went over to see Moti. Moti wanted to help Mohan Singh but could not find a civilized way of exploiting his host, Mehr Chand. Yet he could not turn the dogged man out on a night like this. He asked him to stay, and decided to sleep over the problem. There being no other place, Rai Bahadur bedded down on the carpet.

At six the next morning, the Minister came in to ask his house guest if he wanted to go along for a walk. He saw India's greatest hotelier lying curled up in the cold on the floor. He was embarrassed. And impressed. If Oberoi could go to such lengths to save his hotel, he should be allowed to keep it. Mehr Chand Khanna spiked the confiscation order.

The problem of money remained. But just when it seemed that Oberoi would ultimately have to abandon his vision, the *deus ex machina* again arrived to save the day. In the nick of time, as it had before in Calcutta.

Rai Bahadur's chance meeting with obliging bankers seems preordained. This time he struck up an acquaintance in Calcutta with B.K. Dutta, Chairman of the United Bank of India (UBI). Of course he would advance him some money, provided he was allowed to set up a branch within the premises of the Delhi hotel. But the funds were still not enough.

Just then he heard that Pan Am's subsidiary, Intercontinental Hotel Corporation (IHC) had tried to get a foothold in India, but had been refused since the government did not think it needed any foreign expertise in this field. It was the socialistic heyday, the age of the Ugly American. But there would be no serious objection to a collaboration.

At this time, there was no question but that every option would have to be tried. So Rai Bahadur began exploring the American option with his usual perseverance, doggedness and diligence. It also helped, in no small measure, that he could count on a number of people in positions of importance, people he had come in contact with over the years and who had been won over by his fabled charm and, more importantly, who had faith in his ability to see things through once he had started them. This time, too, Oberoi's friends came to the rescue, as a result of which the Indian ambassador in Washington, B.K. Nehru, came to realize and understand the importance of this venture and went out of his way to convince the Chairman of Inter-continental Hotels, John Gates. Rai Bahadur did not really need their expertise, but he did need an American associate to access the P.L. 480 * funds with the US government.

Rai Bahadur asked Gautam Khanna to accompany him to the United States. They shuttled between New York and Washington for the next five weeks. Khanna, who was to face some pretty tough negotiators during his role in the group's international expansion, selects this as the most difficult. The meetings with US government officials and IHC executives seemed never-ending.

Pan Am's subsidiary pushed for a management contract, which was its usual deal with owner-hoteliers around the world; Oberoi was used to being both owner and Manager, the Indian government would not allow foreign management. An unusual compromise was finally worked out. The Delhi franchise would bear the names of both Intercontinental Hotels and East India Hotels Ltd. It was a ten-year agreement with an option to renew, which was subsequently exercised.

The IHC brought in an investment of only four lakh rupees, but this collaboration with a US company filled the condition for a P.L. 480 loan—Rs 7,619,000 at an interest of 6.5 per cent per annum. It also enabled an advance of U$ 717,000 from the Exim Bank in Washington.

It was during this time that Rai Bahadur became good friends with the President of the World Bank, George Woods. Although his institution was not involved, he was a very influential man. Even today his photograph finds a place on a shelf in the private drawing room of the Oberoi farmhouse, alongside two of Pandit Jawaharlal Nehru, one in thought and the other in a more relaxed frame with his daughter and two grandsons.

Six full years after the concrete-mixers had sighed to a halt, the

In 1954 U.S. Congress enacted Public Law 480 to govern the supply of US foodgrains to India. Its significant feature was that it allowed India to pay for these imports in rupees instead of hard currency. Eighty per cent of the sales proceeds of P.L. 480 were used within India by way of grants and loans to finance development projects. An additional seven per cent was available for loans to joint Indo-American projects in the private sector. P.L. 480 was scrapped in December 1971.

Delhi site once more clattered with the cacophony of construction. The Oberoi juggernaut had begun to roll again. By the time the hotel was completed in 1965, it had cost what was then a staggering Rs 45 million.

After the temporary setback of the Indo–Pakistan war, which marked its opening, the hotel made enough profits to pay back every paisa in four years. The hex had been broken.

CHAPTER XXXI

Flesh On The Bones

The Oberoi Intercontinental was not only an impressive piece of modern masonry. It was a state of mind. Indian hoteliering had entered the world of twin-sharing, wake-up calls, health clubs, ice makers, flower-arrangement rooms—and maids.

It turned out to be as problematic putting the flesh on the bones as it had been constructing the skeleton. Here, it was not money that was wanting. It was expertise, for Oberoi had set about creating a world-class hotel for which there was no local experience and several import restrictions. Intercontinental's part of the venture was not day-to-day management; its job was only to sell the hotel as part of its chain. But it still sent its General Manager and it still sent the new hotel its operating norms The search began for suppliers willing to alter their weaving machines and moulds to fit the American company's specifications for curtains, linen, knives, forks, glasses, even maids' carts. Indian hoteliers had never demanded them before for the simple reason that there had never been maids in Indian hotels before. The bearers had done the work, carrying brooms in their baskets and dusters on their shoulders. The suppliers who picked up the gauntlet and the design sheets never regretted it, for soon the entire industry would come knocking at their doors.

The Americans may have dispatched prototypes and organization charts, but Rai Bahadur being Rai Bahadur proceeded to make his own adaptations, especially as he had developed and perfected several systems of his own in the forty-three years that he had been in the business. Besides, the memory of money running out was too fresh, the loans looming over his shoulder too forbidding. He reduced, on an average, forty per cent of what Intercontinental said was needed.

T.K. Sibal—then freshly returned from hotel schools in Cornell and Austria, now Vice-President, Finance—has carefully preserved the documents that accompanied the floating of the hotel. They include Intercontinental Hotels' seven-sheet list of 132 designations from General Manager to 'Cabana Boys' for the pool-side club and their projected salaries. Rai Bahadur ticked the ones that met his approval, slashed off entire sections that did not. Accounts receivable assistant, time-keepers, pastry cook, *sous chef* (second in command) *tournent* (standby chef), *entremetier* (vegetables cook), silver-man, dish-washer were all deemed essential, but a bold line runs through the whole lot of laundry gradations of shirt-finisher, presser, hand-press worker, delivery man. In its place he has filled in, in his small handwriting, one designation with a flat rate of Rs 150 per month. He has halved several of the suggested salaries, but jacked up that of the security officer from Rs 700 to Rs 1,100.

Rai Bahadur introduced a number of check-points. He insisted on cooks going to the market themselves to pick up meat, poultry and fish, instead of having it delivered, as the American partners expected. He also wanted them to cross-check other prices while they were about it. He trained staff from scratch, picking up young men who did not know a thing about forks and knives, but did not have preconceived notions of what hotel service should be either. He did not take a single person from another hotel.

As always, Rai Bahadur would be in several places seemingly all at once, explaining the sophisticated circuitry of the room service telephones, showing how the plate-warmers ought to be fabricated, or even deciding the optimum height at which the toilet rolls should be placed. There was no chance of a replay of the story of the author who, crazed by the wallpaper pattern in his Bangkok hotel room, shot himself in the head; there was no wallpaper at the Oberoi Intercontinental.

Rai Bahadur reinforced the principle that had seen him through the hotels he had earlier merely renovated. He cut costs, but he never cut corners. Rai Bahadur laid down another rubric, which would later be reiterated when luxury acquired unimaginable extensions: choosing the expensive may cost money, but it also brings in more money. Which is why it had to be 'twice as expensive' marble over ordinary tiles in the bathrooms. However, he never lost sight of the lode-star, the bottom-line.

The streamlining of the system, checking of gadgetry, training of staff, dry runs in the restaurant for an intimate dinner for two or an elaborate banquet for 200, even the practising of smiles continued for weeks on end. The sons-in-law, Gautam Khanna and K.K. Mehra, William Land, the General Manager from Intercontinental, his Oberoi deputy, P.P.S. Lamba, and, most of all, Rai Bahadur himself— no one let up the pressure day and night. Public expectations were running as high as its curiosity. Neither could be let down.

Biki returned from Calcutta to contribute his expertise to the magnum opus. As he describes it, 'One day I reached the hotel. The Sikh guard opened the door with a salute that would have shaken a parade ground. A bellboy materialized immediately and took my briefcase. The receptionist glowed with genuine warmth.' The show was ready to roll.

The Oberoi Intercontinental commenced operations in September 1965. War had already broken out. With austerity the need of the day, they decided to forgo a grand opening, and simply offer champagne to the first guests. These happened to be the Pan Am crew, and they would rather have had whisky. Then the air-raid siren went off. Rai Bahadur and P.P.S. Lamba, whom he had trained since 1946, walked up and down the empty lobby. 'Let's celebrate,' said the boss bravely, and the two of them strode to the bar to toast the end of Mission Nervous Breakdown.

After all the headache and the heartburn you would think Rai Bahadur would give himself a breather. Indeed, his family made him promise that he would not even dream of another hotel for the next ten years. But barely had he managed to get his head above water than he had gurgled deep into liabilities once again. Literally so. Hardly a year after the opening of the Delhi Intercontinental, he bid for land in Bombay. The site was still under the sea.

CHAPTER XXXII

Keeping House With Style

With the Oberoi Intercontinental, something far more revolutionary had been introduced into Indian hoteliering than wake-up calls and health clubs. Housemaids. The tremors of outrage reverberated all the way up to Parliament, but Rai Bahadur remained unshaken. Every international hotel had them, and his would too.

Delhi's moral majority went into hysteria mode. Oberoi was exploiting young women, they cried; virtue could not be exchanged over the counter like a room key, they cried. They whipped up visions of women being served on a salver along with the welcome drink; of corridor orgies that would make an evening with Caligula appear like a Buckingham Palace tea party; of hotel guests admonishing some helpless, cowering, young thing with the proverb, 'As you make my bed, so shall you lie on it.'

Senior Managers, buckling under the controversy, begged him to reconsider his decision. Rai Bahadur countered: if international hotels had not become dens of iniquity on account of the women in black stockings and frilled white aprons, there was no reason why his should. He had set out to build his reputation, not ruin it. Why, equally, should anyone presume that Indian women would part with theirs so easily? Besides, would anyone find Abdul the room bearer shuffling around dusting a room at the Hilton?

He stuck to his guns, confident that neither the hotel's nor the housemaids' honour would be compromised. That the arrangement would raise the standards of both. That if the management was clear about the job description of this new cadre of employee, everybody else automatically would be, from guests to other staff. He also knew that his selection procedure would have to be very strict.

Here Rai Bahadur was on firm ground. He had already built up a highly trained level of housekeepers, supervised by the redoubtable

121

Savitri Khanna. The place and power he gave to his Comptroller of Household— Khanna was, by her son's marriage, a member of the family—was a measure of the importance he accorded to housekeeping, and by extension, personally to housekeepers. Hadn't Gertrude Clarke's contribution been equal to that of her husband? Hadn't his own wife's role in this department contributed to his early success? A housemaid was simply a housekeeper in the making. Savitri could be relied upon to ensure that they started with the right raw material.

The advertisements continued to be placed in the papers. The girls would have to be from decent families, should have completed school, should know English, and be personable. The salary was better than a modest education could fetch elsewhere without having to compromise virtue. They came hesitantly at first, and then in long queues. They came with fathers, uncles, brothers. References were checked up on; discreet inquiries made about claims.

It would be a lie to say that only the bona-fide applied. The American housekeeper from Intercontinental was taken in more easily by the smooth smartness, the fluent English, the upfront manner of those who were not there to scrub the sinks. But Savitri Khanna could spot the shady lady from a mile away. Sorry, she said.

It would be untrue to say that no one slipped through the sieve. To start with, there was some hanky-panky. But the senior housekeepers devised their own strategy. One of them might casually despair aloud over the difficulty of making ends meet. Sure enough, she would hear a hint of how easy it was to rectify that. A foreign guest gives a hundred rupees, but with an Indian she might have to settle for fifty, one of the girls would say. Her services would be terminated. There was also security on every floor that usually reported suspicious movements. And other housemaids, knowing that everyone would be tarred with the same brush, often reported on wayward colleagues. Once word got round on the tight control on loose behaviour, it was easy to clean up the act.

Staff members were taught to treat housemaids with respect, and senior housekeepers were the ones who most jealously protected the dignity of their wards. They instructed the girls never to behave loudly when travelling back home on public transport, and it was always ensured that they were seen safely off on the bus at night by someone from the hotel, or even dropped home by hotel taxi. In a hundred little ways the initial reservations were broken down.

Housemaids were indoctrinated in the importance of their jobs. Mrs Darshan Singh, now Executive Housekeeper in Delhi, recalls how, in those days, it cost a lakh to build each hotel room, so the girl in charge of 14 would be inspired by the pep-talk that told her she was responsible for 1.4 million rupees.

They drew the greatest dignity from the fact that the Chairman regarded them not as insignificant cogs, but as the key to the hotel's success. From the very start, Rai Bahadur knew that the room was the focal point of profit-making, which is why housekeeping and room service are given such a pre-eminent position in the Oberoi scheme of things, which is why, at staff meetings, the housekeeper very often calls the shots.

If the new hotel was to be a state of mind, the way of thinking of its staff first had to be rearranged. Housemaids were drilled relentlessly, to change, change, change. Not just the bedsheets every day, or twice a day if the guest had had a snooze in the afternoon, but also every hand towel even if hands had been wiped on it just once. Whether it was the edge of the draw sheet or the end of the toilet roll, it had to be folded just so. There was a set day in the month for turning round the mattresses, and there was no way in which one could be left for tomorrow. It was, in short, the established system, the unwavering standard, the total elimination of individual judgement. Rai Bahadur knew that discretion very easily deteriorates into whim. And then everything deteriorates. Period.

Housekeeping is much more than ensuring a clean set of bath towels. It extends to the maintenance of the building, the upkeep of restaurants, it even covers the garden. It interacts with virtually every department: laundry, room service, engineering, because all these 'enter our domain'. The senior housekeeper, a cross between Florence Nightingale and Sherlock Holmes, is an equal participant in daily managerial meetings at which all kinds of interdepartmental problems are hammered out.

The housemaid is the eyes and ears of the engineering and maintenance staff, passing on the information that something should be done about the bulb that has fused on the bedside lamp before the guest is given the opportunity to blow his fuse. Her job does not end there; she must return and check that it has been done. She is trained to report any guest comment, positive or negative, to her superior, not to decide for herself that it is insignificant; never to answer, 'That is the butler's job,' should she be pulled up for an empty water jug, but to say, 'I'll see to it, sir'; never to let an expression of horror or disapproval cross her face should she find a guest's children playing Picasso on the room walls. She simply has to relay the information to the housekeeper, who will pass it on to the Lobby Manager who, in turn, will decide whether to inform the General Manager or merely the painters.

Of course, there are occupational hazards, which come in all shapes, including the perfect one of the Pakistani cricketer walking about his room in the altogether. House rules, in the case of such an eventuality, state that the maid must not bat an eyelid, nor keep an eye on the ball, but return to pavilion at the earliest.

When Oberoi advertised for housemaids, he could never have guessed that this would bring in a spunky young woman from a royal family forced into such a situation by circumstance and her own headstrong ways.

Krishna Singh was slim, tall, and, even as a young girl, possessed a will as strong as her features. She was born in the fiefdom of Lalpur Basali, her father belonged to the Punjab Civil Service, and while he was posted outside Rajasthan, Krishna enjoyed the comparative freedom of a convent education. But then her father returned to the closed Rajput atmosphere of Narsingarh, and at fifteen, she was married into the royal family of Udaipur. She chafed under its conservatism, which included living in *purdah*, for ten years. The final straw was an argument with her husband over his refusal to allow their daughter to continue going to school. She walked out.

Well, sort of. The Maharana of Udaipur had already converted his palace into a hotel, and he asked her to help with the housekeeping. Behind the scenes, of course. She was still in *purdah*. It was not the happiest of arrangements and when she saw the advertisement for housemaids for the Oberoi Intercontinental, she was most disappointed that when an opportunity to break free arose, it was at so low a level. However, her godfather, the Raja of Deogarh-Madaria and father-in-law of former Prime Minister Vishwanath Pratap Singh, suggested that Krishna apply anyway, asking for a housekeeper's job instead. She got it. Oberoi had changed the face of hoteliering. Before this, a woman of her background would not even have stepped into a hotel. Her stint in the Udaipur palace hotel had different compulsions.

Mona Chawla, who would later take the skills she acquired here to her new post as Director of Housekeeping at the Taj, and Krishna Singh, were the first two Indians who began learning the ropes from Miss Evans, who had been sent by the International Hotels Ltd., and from Savitri Khanna, who by now had become something of an Oberoi institution herself. Since the Delhi hotel, for which they were recruited, was still a steel-and-concrete skeleton, they trained at the Imperial. It could not have pleased the General Manager, but Rai Bahadur was always a sympathetic listener to all their woes, whether they had been scolded for changing curtains too often or were being barred from the executive dining-room. This facility was suddenly withdrawn one day, and Mona and Krishna hated the *tandoori roti* which was the staple of the general canteen. After a few days, 'We went crying to the Chairman. "What's wrong with *tandoori roti*?" he asked. "I like eating it myself." "Yes," we said, "but not every day." The next morning we were back in the executive dining-room.'

Krishna Singh obviously had difficulty reconciling her background to her job, and there was constant friction between Miss Evans and her. The American refused to accept any of the suggestions that Mona and Krishna made largely because they did not toady up to her. One day, Krishna dashed off a letter of resignation, and, looking her squarely in the eye, handed it to Miss Evans.

Savitri Khanna was most upset by this, and, in an attempt to get her to retract, told her that the Chairman had given her the job and only he could let her go. She had not reckoned with the headstrong woman's next move: Krishna phoned the Chairman to inform him of her decision. He asked her to see him; she replied she was on duty. He said, come tomorrow. She said she would have left by then. When is your lunch break? he asked, and then the floor she was working on. Stay there, he said, *I'll* come. The mountain came to Mohammed, and patiently listened to the problem. He then went to the General Manager who summoned Miss Evans and asked for the letter Krishna had sent in. The American had torn it up, and brought it all pieced together and pasted on another sheet. This incensed the young housekeeper even more.

The matter was sorted out, Miss Evans was gently told to be more understanding; Krishna Singh was told to be less touchy. But the spirited young woman had by now made quite an impact on Rai

Bahadur Mohan Singh Oberoi. Her efficiency would impress him even more, and Krishna Singh would become the group's first Vice-President, Housekeeping, the first Indian woman with such a designation. She helped him greatly at the farm where he soon went to live.

CHAPTER XXXIII

'Have You Gone Mad?'

Delhi was a breeze compared to the Bombay operation.

If Calcutta was hailed as the second city of the British empire, upstaged only by London, Bombay laid claim to being the first city of India. Falling into Britain's domain via the dower of Catherine of Braganza, it was as 'chance-acquired' as Calcutta was 'chance-erected'; but, by the 1960s, it had outpaced the competition as market leader in mercantile Meccas.

It was now Bombay's streets that were paved with gold, and thousands poured on to them to make a buck, the quicker the better. Instant gratification and fame could also be sought out in 'Bollywood'. Thus, for business or other forms of bliss, Bombay had become the gateway to India in a manner more concrete than the triumphal arch raised by His Majesty's faithful servants to welcome King George V in 1927.

The Oberoi group was conspicuous by its absence. Was it, perchance, afraid to play on the home turf of the Taj Mahal Hotel, the Tatas' opulent and highly successful caravanserai which, along with the Gateway across the road, had become Bombay's most totemic landmark? A hotel chain without Bombay was like roast duck without *sauce à l'orange*. The missing link had rankled Rai Bahadur for a long time. If he was going to challenge the sovereignty of his only rival on the subcontinent, he would have to find a location even more beautiful than the picture-postcard idyll, sailboats bobbing in a harbour, that presented itself to those lingering over a *Cafe Viennoise* at the Taj's Sea Lounge. After years of his patented patience, he found it. There was only one minor complication, it was still covered by the blue-grey waters of the Arabian Sea. The ironies surface again. The waves would battle to reclaim their lost birth-right, for many years delaying the project and lashing its budget, but the hotel's ultimate salvation would come from the wayfarers who had given their name to this sea.

The first phase of the Backbay Reclamation Scheme of Bombay's master plan had proved inadequate to meet the ambitious city's needs. The Maharashtra government turned its covetous eye to Nariman Point, where Marine Drive ended in a clinch of lovers canoodling in cars at dusk. Conservationists warned that the reclamation would result only in a fatal embrace, the kiss would be only of death. The mayor clashed with ministers; environmentalists with civil engineers. An architect warned that the new skyline of Bombay would resemble the cardiogram of a faltering heart. Scandal mushroomed like slums. The plan was modified. The critics were mollified. Some of them, at least.

Bids had been invited long before the filling operations began. Rai Bahadur knew that even Hilton could not have bettered the site: a spectacular seascape stretching to the horizon, hugged by the winking lights of the marine expressway as it curved all the way up to the base of wooded and well-heeled Malabar Hill.

Rai Bahadur arrived with Biki, and checked himself into the Spanish Suite of the Taj. Aptly so, for he intended taking the bull by the horns in an afternoon of blood and bravado. He got a secretary to type out a letter making his bid, but left a blank in place of the amount on which the Government would calculate the ground rent; secrecy was of the essence. He filled in the figure, and silently handed the headed notepaper to Biki. The son held on to the edge of the table to regain his balance; it was a staggering amount, Rs 2,650 per square metre for the 8,364 sq. metre plot.

Biki told his father, 'Aren't you overdoing things?' Rai Bahadur replied, 'When you've set your heart on the best, you shouldn't leave even the slightest chance for someone to beat you to it.' Incidentally, when Sir Dorab Tata heard of the figure, his comment was equally low-key. 'Rai Bahadur, have you gone mad?' exclaimed the scion of the house of Tatas, owners of the Taj. Crazy or not, Oberoi won the race by more than a length; the nearest bid was a thousand rupees lower per square metre, but he could not have taken the risk.

Rai Bahadur remained as cool when he won his prize as when he had filled in the figure. Biki, still apprehensive about the deal, asked his father whether they would make it. 'Of course, we will,' said the hotelier. 'I want 500 rooms, a shopping centre, escalators, and lots of marble.' He added, 'To start with,' which did not help the son's anxieties one bit. As it worked out, it was Biki who complemented the project with an adjacent hotel that leap-frogged over even his father's extravagant vision.

That was much later. Beating everyone else to the bid did not mean you could start building. Or even filling. The government, already mauled by the controversy over reclamation, took its time over clearances, subjecting to a fine tooth comb such parameters as feasibility, requirement and capability. On the last count, Oberoi was on even less firm ground than his envisaged hotel. He may have built up a reputation for the past three decades, but his painfully visible inability to complete Delhi's Intercontinental had slurred all that. Besides, he was an alien in Bombay.

Now it was the turn of his patented perseverance to be turned on full throttle. Rai Bahadur refused to move out of the city till the green signal was given. His closest rival was Kanti Desai, son of Morarji Desai. One day, fortuitously, or by arrangement, Rai Bahadur found himself at the launching of the *Koyna* and the *Krishna,* two barges built by the rags-to-riches Raosaheb B.M. Gogte to transfer his iron ore to the giant ships docked midstream. Tara Berry, Principal Officer of the Mercantile Marine department, had been of great assistance in the building of the boats; his wife happened to be the Public Relations Officer (P.R.O) of the Oberoi group.

The launch had to be performed at the precise moment of the highest tide, at 9.27 a.m., but it was already nine o'clock with no sign of the man who was to do the honours, Defence Minister and Gogte's old school chum, Yeshwantrao Chavan. Finally, the mining millionaire mounted the rostrum and said, 'Ladies and Gentlemen, something unavoidable seems to have delayed the Honourable Minister, but since time and tide wait for no man, we will have to go ahead with the launch. The privilege will go to the fairest lady in the audience.' As the women in the gathering were being urged to make their claim, there was the wail of sirens, the roar of outriders, and the ministerial motorcade slammed to a halt. Yeshwantrao Chavan launched the barges as his wife, Venutai, broke the traditional coconuts on their hulls. After the ceremony, a portly gentleman walked up to Gogte and told him how much he had liked the bit about time and tide, and the fairest solution that he had found to the Minister's presumed no-show. 'May I know your name, sir?' asked Gogte. 'Mohan Singh Oberoi,' was the quiet reply.

The two self-made men took to each other and continued to meet in Bombay and Delhi. The older Rai Bahadur often helped the younger Raosaheb to see things more clearly, provided an object lesson in not being disheartened by failure, taught him that people are not intrinsically bad, and that you only had to try and understand their problem. Gogte knew the frustration Oberoi was suffering over the delays in clearing the Bombay project. He decided to have a word with his friend, the Maharashtra strongman.

Y.B. Chavan laughed him out of court. *'Kai sangta ho tumhi.'* (What are you saying!) he exclaimed, 'the man couldn't proceed from the sixth floor to the seventh floor of his Delhi hotel for eight years, how does he think he can build a skyscraper on our prestigious Nariman Point?' Gogte replied, 'Yeshwant, you are a politician, you do not know how business works. An entrepreneur may have initial setbacks, but that doesn't mean you condemn him as a permanent loser. All he needs is help at the right time. Just meet him.' The Minister did not think that was too much to do for a friend.

Rai Bahadur's proven persuasive skills went into turbo mode. The seasoned politician was as impressed by his grit and guts as the hardened Commandant in war-time Calcutta had been over his audacity and insistence. As is said in government parlance, 'Chavan agreed to do the needful'. Naturally, it was he who was invited to be chief guest and formally open the hotel in 1973.

But that too came later. Getting the government to clear his project was one thing. What about Rai Bahadur's financial advisers who were getting greyer by the hour wondering where the money was going to come from? They had pushed their luck in Delhi. There was no way this time that they could prevent the dream turning into a nightmare.

Even the Taj, at this juncture, was not doing well. J.R.D. Tata, the patriarch of the House of Tatas, does not recall any such move, but some years earlier, feelers had reportedly been sent to Rai Bahadur to take over the management of the Tatas' Bombay property. The idea was not as preposterous as it sounds today. The Oberoi-Taj race had not yet been announced, and the Tatas, establishing their name in heavy industry, viewed their solitary hotel as nothing more than an indulgence that they had landed up with because of their founder's inexplicable detour from his chosen path. However, JRD's closeness to aviation told him that, with the zooming in of fast and long-range jets, hoteliering would take off in a blaze of glory. Ajit Kerkar was lured back from England, and with his boss, spawned a hotel chain. The first addition was what Gillian Tindall dubbed the 'moorish skyscraper', The Taj Intercontinental, adjacent to J.N. Tata's portly dowager.

After the 1965 Indo-Pakistan war, Pakistan had confiscated all Indian property including Rai Bahadur's hotels in Lahore, Rawalpindi, Peshawar and Murree. The Imperial was lost to litigation. Corstophons had been sold to become a residence for the interns of Simla's medical college. Clarkes had never aimed beyond its modest reach, and the Cecil, with none of its old clientele left to revel in its luxury, had become a seasonal hotel, gradually reducing its operational span from six months to four, finally remaining open for just two months a year. Calcutta's political upheavals shook the business of the Grand. Delhi's Oberoi Intercontinental, however well it was doing, could not obviously underwrite the kind of costs estimated for the new hotel on the western shore.

To top it all, Rai Bahadur wanted his Bombay property to be even more ground-breaking than his showpiece in Delhi; indeed, he had promised Y.B. Chavan and the Chief Minister, V.P. Naik, that he would give the city the best hotel in his chain. In a city where buildings routinely scraped the skies, his could be nothing less than a high-rise tower, and, knowing him, no one even bothered to ask whether he wanted it to be the highest. Recalling perhaps the circumstances which had deprived him of the Imperial, he also wanted the hotel to have an entire shopping complex all its own, with no landlord lurking round the corner to pounce on violations of space.

East India Hotels Ltd (EIHL) floated a five-crore-rupee issue to buoy up Rai Bahadur's vision by the sea. He raised another four crore rupees through public deposits, again offering a twelve per cent interest. His friend in need, the United Bank of India(UBI), advanced two crore rupees, and the Industrial Finance Corporation chipped in. But all this did not quite add up to enough. If Gautam Khanna ranked the striking of the Intercontinental deal as his toughest negotiation, Bombay, in his book, has the distinction of being the most troublesome project to complete. The money was literally drowning. All kinds of expenses reared their heads.

Caissons, large watertight compartments, had to be built to lay the foundations under the water, the soil analysed, the land dried artificially. They had to wait patiently for the slow process of settling. Since he wanted all of thirty-four floors, the engineers told Rai Bahadur that the building would have to be rooted forty feet deep into the ground to ensure that it would not keel over. The incorrigible optimist viewed this not as extra expense, but as space for an additional basement.

One morning, a meeting was called to find ways of effecting economies. At the end of it, Rai Bahadur had instead persuaded the team to add two more floors to ensure that his was the tallest landmark on Nariman Point. As it happened, the Air India building next door turned out to be a higher flier, but Oberoi's hotel was still high enough to necessitate substantial additional expense on glass thick enough to withstand the notorious monsoon winds that sometimes roar through the city at 120 kmph, uprooting ancient peepul trees and whipping up forty foot-high waves on Marine Drive.

Work on the Bombay Oberoi ground to a halt as heart-breakingly as it had in Delhi. The basic problem was the high land price. The costing went haywire and delays aggravated the situation, escalating expenditure on steel and cement. But, once again, there was a last-minute reprieve. By now the controversy-embroiled P.L. 480 had been replaced by the Agency for International Development, (AID), and it was to it that the Oberois turned.

This time Biki, together with Gautam Khanna, betook themselves to New York and Washington. The old condition of American collaboration remained, but since Intercontinental Hotels Corporation (IHC) already had a tie-up with the Taj in Bombay, Oberoi teamed up with ITT Sheraton. Once again the war of nerves, once again an agreement that neither party was too dissatisfied with. Once again the grand scale and the tiniest detail, from the largest lobby ever seen in India down to the ebony black Watco oil finish of the wood and the angle of the Yamada Shomer recessed down-lights specified by Dale Keller & Associates, the anointed design consultants.

Indeed Dale Keller sent minutely detailed charts of decor, complete with samples of the mesh of the over-drapery or the gauge of the brass. They sent scale drawings of furniture, little stick-men sketched on them, to satisfy the requirements of ergonomy and economy, the exact space that should be left under a table to prevent wastage yet ensure that knees would not clash. They provided options. 'Table desk and other sitting work-tops heights are shown as 2ft 5 ins, but some authorities prefer 2ft 6 ins or 2ft 6 1/2 ins.' Or, 'As clearances are minimum they should be increased when conditions will allow.'

As in Delhi, American money was not all the manna from heaven that was needed. The Rs 4.30 crores from AID like the funds from P.L. 480 were linked to the buying of American equipment; sometimes not just brands, but even model numbers were insisted upon. It did not finance local supplies. This is where the brave army of Rai Bahadur's long-time associates went into action, people like his company secretary, Ramlal and his accountant, Banarsilal Khosla, who ferreted out funds from friends, financiers, money-lenders. A loan here, a *hundi* there, a promissory note from somewhere else. The grand dream did not arrive on a platter held aloft by a genie simply by calling up room service.

By 1972, the Oberoi Sheraton was ready, more or less. Though guests had been living there for a year, the formal opening was not till 7 April 1973. Y.B. Chavan cut the flower-bedecked ribbon with the Sheraton's traditional golden, sixteen-inch scissors, each of its inlaid semi-precious stones representing a country where the chain has established a presence. The scissors had earlier been wielded by such eminences as the Presidents of the USA and Argentina, the Prime Minister of Israel and the Lord Mayor of Copenhagen to inaugurate Sheraton Hotels round the world. The Finance Minister beamed at Rai Bahadur Mohan Singh Oberoi who had redeemed his promise of giving Maharashtra not just the finest jewel of the Oberoi empire, but also the highest in India.

At the black-tie dinner that evening, the siren that electrified the guests was not an air-raid one, but the Egyptian bombshell, Nagwa Faoud, performing her celebrated Oriental dance. There were other stars in pin-stripes and spangles; and a global glitterati glittered. Royalty, representatives of international business and the travel trade, entertainment celebrities from both sides of the Atlantic, a who's who of the world Press, and an awesome collection of Indian dignitaries.

Oberoi added his innovative touch. Before the guests were flown off to another round of scintillation in Delhi and a visit to the real Taj Mahal, Bhausaheb Mhase, Union Secretary of Bombay's unique and amazing food delivery network, the *dabbawallas,* handed Academy Award Winner, Joan Fontaine, a brass, gem-encrusted tiffin carrier. As honorary *dabbawalli,* the elegant actress then wheeled round the glass and marble lobby on the union leader's battered cycle, a-clatter with dozens of dented *dabbas*. In a manner of speaking, the humble Mhase and the legendary Mohan Singh were both in the same business.

Bhagwanti, mother of Mohan Singh Oberoi, and an abiding influence in his life

Rai Bahadur M.S. Oberoi with his wife—the late Ishran Devi

The Oberoi children—seated (L-R) Swaraj, Rajrani and Prem, standing (L-R) P.R.S. Oberoi and T.R. Oberoi

An Oberoi family photograph—Seated in foreground (grandchildren) (L-R) Vijai Kapur. Ashok Khanna, Rajni Kapur, Ajai Kapur. Seated (L-R) Swaraj Khanna. I.D. Oberoi. M.S. Oberoi, Rajrani Kapur, Prem Oberoi. Standing (L-R) son-in-law G.K. Khanna, T.R. Oberoi, P.R.S. Oberoi. son-in-law Col. J.C. Kapur

Tikki, the late T.R. Oberoi, Rai Bahadur's eldest son

John Faletti

Ernst Bret

Ms. Smith

Ernest Clarke

M.S. Oberoi with Henry Kissinger

M.S. Oberoi with Swaran Singh

M.S. Oberoi with King Birendra Shah
of Nepal

M.S. Oberoi and Pandit Jawaharlal Nehru

M.S. Oberoi with the Chairman of
the World Bank, Eugene Black

M.S. Oberoi with M.G. Ramachandran

The President of India, Giani Zail Singh, presents the 1983 International
Punjabi Society's 'Man of the World' award to Mohan Singh Oberoi

Arjun Oberoi and Vikram Oberoi, sons of Tikki and Biki

The patriarch at home on the Oberoi farm

SANAD

To

Mr. Mohan Singh Oberoi,
Managing Director, Grand Hotel,
Calcutta, Bengal.

I hereby confer upon you the title of Rai Bahadur as a personal distinction.

Viceroy of India.

New Delhi,
The 2nd June 1943.

The title of Rai Bahadur conferred on M.S. Oberoi in 1943

From
H.E. Mohamed Hosni Mubarak
President of the Arab Republic of Egypt
To
Rai Bahadur Mohan Singh Oberoi
Chairman Oberoi Hotels.

GREETINGS
In consideration of your good qualities and your
valuable service we bestow upon you the,

ORDER OF THE REPUBLIC
FIRST CLASS

We have ordered the issue of this Certificate to that effect.
Written and signed at the
Republican Palace Cairo
on
The 4th day of Rabi el Akheri
in the year 1405 of the Hegira Era
Corresponding to
The 27th day of December in the year 1984 of
the Christian Era

Signed Mohamed Hosni Mubarak.

M.S. Oberoi's citation on being awarded Order of the Republic (First Class)

Receiving the Udyog Path, 1989, 1990

Accepting an honorary doctorate from the I.M.C. U.K.

The Oberoi family gathered to felicitate M.S. Oberoi on his 'Man-of-the-World' title in 1983

Mohan Singh Oberoi's first hotel—The Oberoi Clarkes, Simla

At the Windsor, Melbourne, Australia

The Oberoi Grand, Calcutta—the taking-over of which set Mohan Singh on his course to fame

The Oberoi, New Delhi. The most exclusive hotel in the capital

M.S. Oberoi and P.R.S. Oberoi

CHAPTER XXXIV

High Rise, High Tension

'I have gambled all my life and still managed to sleep at night.' Mohan Singh Oberoi's one-time quip took a lot of battering during the first few years of the Bombay hotel; indeed, Rai Bahadur found it difficult to maintain his incompatibility with insomnia. The Oberoi Sheraton was estimated to cost seventy million rupees, a profligate enough sum compared to Delhi's forty-five million. By the time it was finally ready in 1973, eight years after construction began, the company had sunk Rs 180 million into the project with another ten million rupees soon spent on extension. At one point, interest on loans alone was adding up to Rs 120,000 a day.

The arithmetic had certainly got more complicated since the time of Clarkes when interest and repayment added up to Rs 9,000 a year or even the Grand when the lease was Rs 8,000 a month. It's just as well that no one knew at the time that the new Oberoi which Biki built in Bombay some thirteen years later, would cost Rs 650 million.

Every day's delay in the completion of the Oberoi Sheraton plunged the company deeper into red-facedness. And as they could not afford to wait till everything was in place, they opened each floor as it got ready.

The first group to arrive was Japanese, on 29 December 1972, and they were welcomed with garlands and a party in the Lancer's Bar. The Japanese guzzled their favourite beer, a drink that has its own compulsions. Soon enough, they needed to de-beer, but the lobby toilet was not quite complete. So there ensued the spectacle of one guest after another bowing his way out of the bar, and impatiently waiting for the solitary elevator in operation to go up to his room. The first suite to get booked was the Madurai, and the VIP who was to occupy it had to be delayed with small talk in the lobby, since the corridor carpet was still being rolled into place.

There was also the Sheraton playing supercilious international expert. As in the case of the Intercontinental, the franchise was a marketing one, but they still had their man, Glenn Brewer, as General Manager. Azhar Siddiqui, then Front Office Manager, was summoned by the American and asked, 'Young man, how do you plan to organize your beat?' When the young man explained, Brewer drawled, 'That way of functioning went out in 1948. I'm operating this hotel in 1972.' However, they all soon came to grips with the system that was made up of two parts Intercontinental, two parts Sheraton, and six parts Rai Bahadur.

The boss, of course, got his celebrated concentration into the act, putting aside all other concerns to see his baby through its early problems. Undeterred by his seventy-two years, Rai Bahadur camped at the hotel for six months. He stayed in different suites to ensure that they met with his exacting standards. They usually did not and he spent hours rearranging the furniture. He positioned himself in the lobby at different times of the day to clear the bottlenecks in guest flow and to overhear remarks so that he could provide service as his guests wanted it, not as he presumed they did.

This was the group's first high-rise hotel, and tempers went on short fuse as bed-tea and breakfast took a long time to get to the upper reaches. Rai Bahadur stood in his dressing-gown from five in the morning in the kitchen, often travelling up and down the service lifts with the orders to see how to shorten the delays. By the end of the week he had the answer: the entire room service bay would have to be moved to the other end of the kitchen, bringing it closer to the service elevators. Even though finances were scraping rock bottom, Oberoi took the plunge. The Indian segment of the market demanded bed-tea and breakfast in the room; the Indian segment had got accustomed to the Taj in Bombay; the Indian segment that had been wooed over had to be kept at any cost.

Room service got more zippy with another Rai Bahadur innovation: a 'pantry elevator' that would be stocked with the standard requirements of soda, ice, potato crisps, cashew nuts, and, most important, the wherewithal for tea and coffee. Room service orders would be relayed to the waiter manning the lift, and all he had to do was press the button for the relevant floor, pouring the boiling water into the teapot as he glided on his way.

In the first week, it seemed as if all Bombay wanted to descend on the lobby and gawk at the opulence, the Satish Gujral murals, the eleven brass-and-green-glass Dale Keller chandeliers, each with twenty lamps in four tiers. There were hundreds of people milling round the place, riding up and down the elevators, disturbing guests, and, on occasion, swiping a 'souvenir'. One day, Homi Wadia, then still the F&B Manager and not yet its Vice-President, decided enough was enough. Gathering a posse of security boys, he positioned himself at the door, and screened all those who were pouring in, especially at peak Marine Drive stroll time. He was doing quite well, when Rai Bahadur walked up to him, and demanded to know what this was all about. Far from being pleased over Wadia's initiative, he said, 'Open up the doors. I am very proud of my hotel, I want all of Bombay to see it and talk about it. In any case, the novelty will wear off in a month; then you will have all the exclusivity you want.'

Despite the millions scraped together and spent, business was lousy. For all hotels. There had been a sudden glut of luxury rooms in Bombay, and the industry was yet to get its act together to fill the new capacity. The Oberoi Sheraton itself had added 200 to its initial 500, Taj Intercontinental towered with an additional 350. Air India built the Centaur at the airport and the Calcutta-based India Tobacco Company Ltd (ITC) diversified from cigarettes to hotels under the Welcomgroup brand, starting the Sea Rock, in the plush suburb of Bandra. Indira Gandhi's petulant declaration of a state of Emergency in 1975 hardly encouraged the leisure traveller, much less the corporate one, to visit a country now clamped in all kinds of draconian restrictions.

At one point it seemed as though Oberoi's lumbering white elephant in Bombay would trample down the entire company; the crunch had become so severe that there was even pressure to sell it, and reduce the crippling liabilities. Rai Bahadur knew it, and it hurt. The darling of the AGM was letting down his shareholders. For the first time ever, he defaulted on the deposits. But he stuck it out. 'The crisis will pass,' he kept insisting, without anything to support his optimism. Anything, that is, other than faith in himself.

CHAPTER XXXV

Big Bucks In A Burqa

Once again Mohan Singh was right. And once again it was war that helped him make his peace with his financiers. This time the battle was far away, and the fortune came dressed in a *djelleba*.

Lebanon had erupted as the centuries-old power equations between Maronite Christian, Druze and Muslim, collapsed in the face of growing Arab nationalism. Beirut, the Paris of the Middle East, was bombed unrelentingly, and then balkanized. Shrapnel and rubble replaced plate glass and neon. French chic was swept away by communal hatred. Carbines took over from the cabaret. The pleasure-seekers from the Levant and beyond, who had once flocked there, fled. They first opted for London, but it was too alien. Besides they did not like being looked down upon by the very people who were making them pay through the nose. They flung themselves into the welcoming, and almost as alluring, arms of a city by the Arabian Sea.

The Arabs were no strangers to Bombay. Some of the Emirs had even built spacious art-deco apartment blocks on Marine Drive. But Bombay's relationship with the Arabs had, till 1976, been no great sheikhs. The Beirut War changed all that. Now, the city welcomed them and their money. They crowded its department stores, its bazaars, its pavements. They bought parrots by the dozen from Crawford Market; where they came from they did not see a bird for days, let alone one that talked. They staggered back with brilliant-hued bales of silk from Kalbadevi, and bargained over miniature Taj Mahals which they lapped up by the gross from Colaba footpaths. Two-bit sellers of agar wood and attars overnight became merchant-owners of huge air-conditioned establishments.

The Arabs chose Bombay because it was closer than Delhi or Calcutta, because it was laid-back, because its climate was equitable, because it was the biggest handler of 'No. 2 money' and because it was the No. 1 medical centre; they checked into 'five-star' hospitals, sometimes only for a tummy ache. When they came for a holiday, they brought their wives and brood. When they came for pleasure they came alone. A whole new profession of touts mushroomed to provide them anything they desired from donor kidneys to Nepali *chhoti bibis,* including a *kazi* for an instant *niqah* and an as instant *talaak.* Marriage and divorce were no problem when money was no object.

They loved walking by the sea, the breeze billowing *burnoose* and *burqa.* Most of all, they came to see rain. Unending sheets of it as only Bombay can provide. They created a new tourist season, at a time of year most hoteliers traditionally spent in perfecting their fly-swatting technique. Oil wealth swept up the foundering economy. All the hotels were buoyant again, bobbing serendipitously on great big waves of petrodollars.

Oberoi was in clover. The hotel had sensed the market, and played it to the full. It was the newest, biggest, flashiest. It made an all-out bid to woo the Arabs. Two hundred staffers were put through crash courses in the language, the services directory in the rooms became more user-friendly by switching over to the cursive Arabic script. Whole menus were changed, the roast loin of pork making way for *sheesh kebab.* The General Manager's wife who happened to know Arabic and Persian, was stationed in the lobby to handle guest relations—and relatives. The extra effort got the Oberoi Sheraton twice as many Arab guests as its nearest competitor which had been snooty about a clientele that was stinking rich.

Moreover, a couple of years earlier, when the Emirates of Oman and Qatar were looking for a residence and office for their Consul-General, the Oberoi group had welcomed them with special terms. It was a fortunate move since this made it the most obvious place for nationals from that part of the Gulf to drop anchor. The company's big white elephant became its greatest money-spinner, and never lost this pre-eminent position even after the Arab tide had ebbed. It was one of the most remarkable recoveries in Indian industry.

Having got his reprieve, Rai Bahadur wanted to declare an interim dividend in 1978 –as much to regain public confidence as to be able to float a new capital issue, this time to finance additional restaurants at the Oberoi Sheraton. He went to the US Embassy in Delhi to inform them of his plans; he could not move without their sanction since he was tied down to the AID loan. They refused, saying that no dividend could be paid till all uncalled share money had been collected.

Rai Bahadur Mohan Singh Oberoi came back to his office breathing fire. No one had seen him so angry before. 'What kind of Chairman am I if I cannot give my shareholders a return on their investment if I want to?' he fumed to himself. Then, regaining his customary cool, he summoned his accountants and told them, 'I am going to break free of that AID loan. Go through all our finances, collect from every source.'

The great mop-up operation began, the giant sponge went into suction wherever the Oberoi group had a stake. The Allahabad Bank gave a short-term loan of a crore of rupees; twice as much was collected from public deposits; funds were conserved by putting a squeeze on creditors, and never mind about robbing Peter, Paul had to be paid off. In ten days he was able to mobilize enough funds to drive up to the Embassy again. This time with a cheque for Rs 32.7 million, the balance due from the original Rs 43,500,000. With interest. He did not fling the cheque on the startled official's table. He walked out of the arrangement quietly and politely. He did not forget to say thank you. Few businessmen would have dared taken such drastic action since the loan was not due for repayment for another eight years. He caught the next available flight to Bombay, and removed the US AID's representative on the Board of Directors. Rai Bahadur was his own master again.

As it happened, Sheraton, too, was to play unfair. Shortly before the end of its ten-year agreement, it gave its franchise to the Welcomgroup's Sea Rock. Oberoi considered this a conflict of interest; Sheraton stuck to its guns; there was nothing in the contract with Oberoi, it said, to prevent it from getting involved with a second hotel in the same city. Oberoi refused the option on the additional ten years, and the two parted ways. Oberoi Sheraton, was renamed Oberoi Towers.

There was no drop in bookings; the name was now well established. It no longer needed to ride piggy-back on any international chain. In fact it was ready to go international itself, and did not want anyone to assume that it was Sheraton that was minding Bombay's highly successful Oberoi store.

CHAPTER XXXVI

Next Stop, The World

Hoteliering is like any other business. You have to keep going round in circles. Whether this motion is the vortex of the whirlpool that pulls you down or the ever-widening one of aerodynamics that helps the eagle soar, is up to you, but there is no way in which you can remain in one place. The static is the stagnant.

Rai Bahadur looked around for more worlds to conquer. The north, east and centre were his sovereign domain, the west was still rebellious but his foothold had been established. He could have proceeded downwards into peninsular India but then, historically, the throne of Delhi has never made much headway in the south. He would fill the gap later. For the present, he had more ambitious plans.

Having brought internationalism to Indian hoteliering, the logical next step was for Rai Bahadur to take Indian hoteliering into the international arena. Once again it would be a calculated thrust where other Indians had feared to tread.

It was not because he was no longer a young man that he did not go West. It was the East that was red with the dawn of international opportunity. Moving into a land that was home to the majestic peak that had bestowed its name on his hotel in Darjeeling, he would establish himself in the world's only Hindu kingdom, still so despite the *trishul*-rattling of India's own SS, the saffron secularists. From the windswept crags of Nepal, he would plunge into the sun-kissed sea of Indonesia where Hinduism had spread through several 'colonizing' Indian dynasties, there to survive in the *mudra* of a Balinese dancer or frozen in perpetuity in a temple frieze.

Between these two forays into Hindu strongholds would come an invasion into Muslim lands, starting with a civilization older than his own. At twenty-two, Mohan Singh's escape from a threatened Bhaun, along with his wife and first-born, was like the biblical flight into Egypt.

At seventy-two, like Mary, Joseph and the infant Jesus, he would pass under the unseeing yet all seeing gaze of the Sphinx, and from the dust of ancient empires, resurrect another relic of history.

The Arabs, whom he had welcomed in Bombay to the sounds of rejoicing and ringing tills, would *assalaam* him both into sacred Medina and Dammam, Mecca of the petrodollar boom. In between, he would arrive in Baghdad. He would also follow in the footsteps of Emperor Ashoka's celibate son and daughter who took the Buddha's pacific message to a now strife-torn isle, the ancient kingdom of Lanka. After this, the great survivor would go Down Under.

The first international venture was Nepal and, as among the mighty ranges in Kashmir, it was a travel agents' convention that triggered a second palace coup. One balmy evening in 1969, Gautam Khanna sat after the day's deliberations in the bar of the Kathmandu Soaltee. Prince Himalaya, uncle of King Mahendra, owned it, and the two got talking. In as many words as protocol permitted, Khanna told the Prince that hoteliering skills quite obviously had not been passed down through the generations. To put it mildly, the place was a right royal mess, in almost as bad a shape as Maharajah Hari Singh's abandoned Gulab Bhavan.

Twirling his mocktail, the Prince said in real seriousness, 'Why doesn't Oberoi take over the management?' Khanna, being a man as smooth as his Scotch, did not choke over it in excitement. He merely continued the discussion, and called Delhi later from the privacy of his room. Before it was time for him to depart, a gentleman's agreement had been arrived at. Within two days of Khanna's return to Delhi, Biki Oberoi took the Royal Nepal Airlines' flight to Kathmandu with a formal contract in his briefcase. The border had been crossed.

From being a mere importer of bathroom fittings and kitchen equipment, the Oberoi group now became an exporter of know-how, at a time when India was not considered an expert in any entrepreneurial area, least of all the world of hoteliering. The government was well pleased. For the chain, the international take-off would mean a forced departure from the policy that Rai Bahadur had formulated with his new hotels in Bombay and Delhi: own our own. This was the time of the shackling import restrictions of 1969 and even the liberalized Exim scrip of 1991 would not clear all the hurdles in the way of investment abroad. The company could not build, it had to restrict its stake to management. It could start an offshore offshoot, but government policies did not permit such a company to plough profits into a sister concern elsewhere outside India.

Admittedly, the Oberoi group's expertise being acknowledged in Nepal was not quite the same as international recognition. New Delhi's close and sometimes contentious links with Kathmandu made the country much less foreign, however sovereign. Having learnt to live with the UN label of least-developed land-locked country (LLC), Nepal knew that any know-how was still superior to its own. But, being the focus of international aid, it could have accessed any number of other hoteliering chains. It would not have been difficult, considering what a great adventure destination it was—overpowered by the highest mountain in the world, overflowing with pristine rivers, and overgrown with primeval forest. The Oberoi group's tie-up with the Soaltee would also bring the chain to the attention of all the international do-gooders who camped in Kathmandu bearing gifts of everything from prefab housing to polio immunizing.

In a short while, Rai Bahadur himself arrived and, typically, even though the take-over was not yet formalized, got down to clearing the grounds. Nirlep Kaur had opened his eyes to the vistas of landscaping. On this visit, she was no longer around, but Krishna Singh supervised the formidable housekeeping tasks with aplomb.

The Soaltee was a textbook case of how amateur management could ruin a great hotel. Its Nepali name was a catch-all word for hospitality, whether that of a close relative or a closer friend, but though the spirit was willing, the service was weak. The professionals moved in with a small task force headed by Biki. The daily 8 a.m. meeting laid down the day's game-plan. The categorical imperative was rubbish clearance, and, by the end of the first fortnight, thirty truckloads had been removed. Lorries wheezed up through the checkposts carrying tons of material from curtains to cauldrons. Kathmandu's isolated position hardly helped. As with the Grand and the Kashmir Palace, the massive cleaning up operation was accompanied by a recruitment drive. Where old expertise would enhance, it was re-signed on. Where only the new would do, it was taken on.

Finally, after two months of frenzied pull-out, put-in, hire, train, fine-tune, the Oberoi Soaltee emerged on a clear cold day in December 1969. Its resurrection was not as dramatic as the Grand's, its profits would never be spectacular, but it maintained its steady success from day one. The wheel of fortune was not only at its casino.

In Nepal the Oberoi group was impressing only the international do-gooders. Two years later, it got the chance to prove itself to hard-nosed international businessmen.

Many years earlier Rai Bahadur, depressed at the turn the Imperial case was taking, had been told by his friend, Moti Khaitan, of the mystic powers of Anand Mayee Ma. The hotelier might have acknowledged the existence of God, but he certainly was not the type to touch the feet of godmen. However, Anand Mayee Ma was a godwoman who had won over many cynics. A curious Rai Bahadur went with Moti to meet her on his next trip to Calcutta. The Mother radiated charm along with her aura. Her black tresses spilled over her white sari offset with its traditional red Bengali border. Anand Mayee spoke, 'You will lose one Imperial, but you will gain another.'

In 1969, he received a letter from the first General Manager of the Oberoi Intercontinental, William Land, now working for Singapore's Imperial Hotel. The Chinese owners had fallen out, and it could do with the professional touch. It was not really in the style to which the Oberoi group was accustomed, but it would help the chain establish a presence in burgeoning South-East Asia. Would the Sikh Singh care to come to Lion-city?

It was not an easy choice. Rai Bahadur weighed the minus of toning down the class he had so painstakingly made synonymous with Oberoi, against the plus of a gateway to international competitiveness. As always, Rai Bahadur could not resist the open door. With a little help from Willian Land, he won the management contract. When the owners could not settle their differences, the company folded up. Liquidators were no strangers to Mohan Singh; he had known them from Clarkes to Grand. He persuaded the bank to let his management continue; and he would find a new owner. He did. Mr Jhunjhnuwalla, an expatriate Indian industrialist. Anand Mayee Ma had been right. For the time being.

Rai Bahadur visited the Imperial several times, and not only because it shared the name of a hotel that had roused such conflicting emotions in him. During these stays, his Managers there got to see, close up, the traits which had carried him so far.

When the Imperial contract was being renegotiated, he sat in the Manager, Anil Madhok's, office for a full four hours subjecting the document to scrutiny. He did not once get up, did not shift his position, he did not so much as look up; he almost stopped breathing. It was as though he were in a trance. Finally, he came to the end of the document, raised his head and said, 'It's not at all to our advantage.' He then took out his fountain pen, and proceeded to make it so.

The hotel had two entrances, one from the front door, the other up through the shabby parking lot. One day, Rai Bahadur decided to close the latter. The Chinese staff were aghast; the decision went against the traditional wisdom that if money comes in through two doors, you do not post a notice telling it 'Right of Admission Reserved'. The equally money-centric Gujaratis have a similar proverb about not closing shop when Lakshmi arrives to anoint your head with a *chandla*. Rai Bahadur, however, felt his relationship with goddesses of fortune, almond-eyed or walnut, was strong enough to withstand so minor a displeasure. We must always present our best vista; a little loss of business is a small price to pay, he insisted.

On another occasion, he came to sign a contract for airline catering. The cocktail and dinner on the evening of his arrival stretched to 2am., the thirty-year-old General Manager of the Oberoi Imperial was dead-beat, but when he escorted his boss up to his room, the seventy-eight-year-old Rai Bahadur immediately looked around for the document that was to have been sent to him for perusal. The next morning at eight, the GM, barely out of bed, got a call from the Chairman asking if he had read through his copy of the contract. 'I plaintively asked, "When could I do it, sir?" He said, "Never mind, you can have a look at mine. I've corrected it." He must have stayed up till four or five in the morning going through the fifty-page contract with his trade-mark meticulousness.'

Once his stay stretched to three weeks. At the end of the high-pressure period, Anil Madhok felt he deserved a break after having been on his toes from early in the morning to early in the morning. Having checked in the Chairman at Changi Airport, he went off to unwind with friends and did not return till after midnight. At 1.30 am, his wife shook him out of bed to tell him that Rai Bahadur was on the line. The departure had been postponed to 8 a.m. because of a bomb threat.

Madhok could not trust himself at the wheel, so he told the Chairman that it would be quicker for him to take a taxi back to the hotel. 'I then took the longest and coldest shower of my life to wash out every trace of hang-over, and went down to wait for him. Despite the tiresome hours he'd spent sitting around in the security lounge, he said, "Good, now we have got a little more time to clear some more business, let's do so in the coffee shop." We did just that till it was time for him to catch the plane again.'

In 1986, Rai Bahadur had to weigh the old pros and cons of retaining the Imperial again. Mr Jhunjhnuwalla refused to spend the kind of money that was necessary for it to hold out against the competition, even in its own class. The earlier argument of a presence in a Singapore grown even more strategic to business interest, was correspondingly more valid. But Rai Bahadur took the hard option. No name was preferable to a bad name. He forfeited another Imperial. He had established much more of an empire by then, but it is still wondered within the organization whether egotistic considerations had not come in the way of future prospects.

If Rai Bahadur was clear on the priority of class, Biki was to set his standards even higher, refusing to take less-than-perfect properties in London and New York merely because they would have helped him get the longed-for toehold in the glittering foyers of the West.

CHAPTER XXXVII

Don't Blink First

In India, Rai Bahadur was a big fish in a small pond. Even if this came with the disadvantage of little fin-room, it took care of the fear of competition. Large international chains had entered India only with Oberoi tie-ups. Hilton's efforts to set up shop in Bombay had been aborted. There was no room at the Inn simply because there was no Holiday Inn in India.

The only rival was the Taj Mahal Hotel, the steel man, Jamsetji Tata's, pioneering thrust into hospitality. The Taj, however, had not gone beyond Bombay till it took over the management of Udaipur's Lake Palace Hotel in 1971, and even if its image was formidable, there were no real challenges for Rai Bahadur in India. Going abroad was not merely for pleasure, it was imperative for business.

Like the Intercontinental, the international experiment was again a whole new ball game. Rai Bahadur admits they made the mistakes of the greenhorn, plunging into ventures that later experience would teach them not to touch.

There were also times when Rai Bahadur had no choice. The Indian government insisted on him taking up a project in Zanzibar, and completing the hotel in time for its national day. It was great for Afro-Asian solidarity but hardly the same for his liquidity; yet it was virtually an offer he could not refuse. The Oberoi group had no say in the building of the structure; everything had to be flown in; too much was done in haste. Rai Bahadur made an honourable retreat as soon as he could. Indeed, Africa remained an impenetrable area for the chain. The blacks did not think the browns good enough, and efforts at joint ventures in Mozambique, Kenya and Nigeria were non-starters.

There were no Latin lovers either. When opportunities arose in Brazil, Argentina and Chile, the Oberoi group either could not muster its share of the investment or Indian procedures were too convoluted to make the snap decision needed to snap up the contract.

They learnt as they went along. At first, Gautam Khanna spear-headed the expansion, with Rai Bahadur entering for the *coup de grâce*. Tikki was never involved in the global strategy, but Biki, when he returned to India and joined the business, more than made up for both his brother's lack of interest and his own earlier lack of presence. It was a formidable task, picking up the messages on the bush telegraph, working out the game-plan, stalking the deal with patience and stratagem, then moving in for the kill. Oberoi's legal experts followed the spirit and the letter of the law, or whichever abetted the better deal. Dattu Telang was the live-wire activating international sales and marketing with friends in all the right places.

They mastered the art of not blinking first in the agonizing battle of nerves. They wised up to the owner trying to shorten the period of agreement so that he could dump the collaboration as soon as he had cottoned on to all the tricks; they learnt to insist on twenty to thirty year leases so that their share of profits could flow in over an extended period after that particular hotel's reputation had been built up. The duration of the agreement was invariably the bone of contention, and, sometimes, not all the silver marrow spoons in the kitchen could help.

They picked up the nuances of gross operating profits and group advertising plough-back, treading the tight rope of quantum of fee. It did not take them very long to demand, and get, the same percentages commanded by international chains.

They dug in their heels hardest in the matter of total independence in the running of the show. They could not afford to have an owner breathing down their necks, as had happened in the early years at Kathmandu, interfering in everything from employment to engineer-ing, from policy decisions to the price paid for the potatoes. Demand-ing to get things done their own way was more than a matter of throwing a tantrum; they were the management experts. It was their reputation at stake; if their takings depended on profits, then they were the ones who had to call the shots. All of them.

Rai Bahadur usually came in at the end. Or, rather, was brought in only at the end. Otherwise, in his enthusiasm, he would concede too much. The deals were usually with official parties, and he never believed in quarrelling with government, his own or anyone else's. 'The idea was to win the contract, not lose it,' was his defence. 'Don't slam the door,' he cautioned, 'it makes it more difficult to walk back in again.' Flexibility was a wise policy, he argued. 'Even if you do not make it to that contract, you will be the one called in the next time round.'

Biki endorses the wisdom. 'Your corporate etiquette, your manners at the negotiating table are very important. Hotel keeping is international, but it is a small world, and word gets round very fast. Being too clever by half is counter-productive. There really is no need for intrigue.' Operating from what must be among the most unconventional and scenic corporate headquarters around, his marble-floored and glass-fronted farmhouse on the sprawling Oberoi acres, Biki spells out how it is easier to do business with Westerners who will be more accommodating once they are convinced that you are straightforward and are not trying to pull a fast one on them, though, 'they, too, are learning the tricks of the Orient.'

His phone never stops ringing. Each buzz holds the potential for an extension of the empire. It is Budapest on the line wanting instructions on the restaurants of the spectacular new Gresham Palace Hotel. Another call comes from erstwhile East Germany. Would the group be interested in a *schloss* that its owner could get back from the government more easily if it were to be converted into a hotel? A banker friend phones to pass on the message of a property coming on the London market. (Waiting for Biki to finish this conversation, the chronicler is reminded of a comment from Trilok, Tikki's all-knowing valet-of-the-world, 'Where is there any place left in London for an Oberoi style of hotel? Park Lane or some place overlooking Hyde Park, at the most.')

But it all began because, way back in 1943, a man called Mohan Singh realized that he would get nowhere with an individual property or two, however imposing, and set about acquiring the homogeneous eight-linked Associated Hotels of India (AHI). In recent years, the chain reaction has been even more critical to success. The more hotels the group added, the greater their exposure, the better their chance of showpiecing themselves, of holding open the door to VIP guests to ensure that they, in turn, would open doors to them in their own country, *inshallah*. The high-profile presence in West Asia was built upon the name nurtured in the Arab world through Bombay and, then, Egypt.

It was in Cairo that the group cut their teeth on the subtleties of dealing with the Islamic world. The Egyptians, for their part, had never dealt with an Indian company before, and haggled on every clause, every term, every decimal ot every percentage. And for some reason, they never began their talks till seven or eight at night, by which time Khanna & Co were exhausted by the sheer boredom of having had to cool their heels all day.

But the luck of the Oberois' held. And still does. Mena House is today one of their most impressive properties. If you consider the Anwar Sadat-inspired Arab-Israeli talks held here or even the Franklin Roosevelt, Winston Churchill, Chiang Kai-shek meeting as too recent a period in history, you can always reach out from your balcony and almost touch the pyramids. Who else can offer you Cheops with morning tea?

CHAPTER XXXVIII

Grilled Cheops

Gautam Khanna stopped by in Egypt in 1971, from a trip to London. Cairo is not the normal transit halt, but he was on a hunting trip. He did not want an antelope or even a Cleopatra. All he wanted was to barge into the Nile. Egypt was a great destination, cashing in on a patrimony that began 5,000 years ago and taking in its sweep both Coptic and Islamic history. The charismatic Gamal Abdel Nasser had given it a present to boast of in addition to its past. But while it had the monuments, it did not have the expertise that would translate heritage into modern tourism. It was open season for the international chains, and Oberoi hoped he could take a pot shot as well.

Alas, the site on the banks of the legend that Khanna had set his eye upon had been grabbed already. The Egyptian government offered him the Lotfalah Palace instead. It was a beautiful piece of architecture, but he knew that its congested location would never meet with Rai Bahadur's approval. Khanna, thwarted as entrepreneur on the trip, decided he might as well play tourist. So he took a cab and a camera along the Pyramids Road to Giza, then still a narrow thoroughfare with a tramway bisecting it, and not, as it now is, an expansive—and expensive—avenue as imposing as a pharaoh's nose.

Khanna gazed at the wonder of the ancient world soaring to a cloudless, cornflower sky, its slabs held together only by ancient laws of physics. He pondered over the riddle of the Sphinx as the wind whipped the sand into a whirling dance of the dervish. Then, as he walked past the stalls, now with their votive offerings only to tourism, he saw another pile of stones that seemed to be almost as old as the pyramids but in an infinitely worse state of repair. He was surprised to hear that this was the historic Mena House, an institution that was to hoteliering what the Orient Express was to trains. It looked no better than a stable, and, his guide informed him, a Swiss hoteliering corporation had recently and sensibly turned down the offer to manage it.

Gautam Khanna's heart beat faster than Pharaoh Akhenaton's at the sight of Nefertiti. It might look as bereft as a plundered tomb, but forty acres at the base of the pyramids, with an attached golf course, was not something that routinely dropped into your mail box. Mena House had originally been a Khedive's hunting lodge. Gautam Khanna knew that this was the game he had to bag. He knew Rai Bahadur would flip for it. He did.

Perhaps it was not quite as dramatic a coup as that. The Oberoi group would have been happier at that time to seize one of the smarter hotels in town. But the chain was still not an international force. Despite the ideal of non-alignment binding Nehru and Nasser in euphoric embrace, for Egypt, India was just another Third World country, as low on corporate expertise as itself. Why ask the blind to lead the blind into a blind alley? But fate favours the underdog, especially the brave one.

Egypt may have been ready to welcome international collaboration, but the latter was not as ready to respond. Nasser's legacy was a bitter one, at least for the West which smarted over his sudden nationalizing of the Suez Canal, his USSR-financed Aswan high dam, and, most of all, his refusal to accept the Israel which the Balfour Declaration had thrust on West Asia. The powerful Jewish lobby in the USA was not going to look kindly on American chains presiding over the lobbies of Egyptian hotels.

Besides, in 1971, West Asia was political TNT. The Arab world marked time towards avenging its humiliation in the 1967 war with Israel, the Yom Kippur victory was two years away, and President Anwar Sadat's peace initiative even further off. Cairo did not seem to be the best place in the world for business opportunities. But Rai Bahadur knew first-hand that wars can save as often as they destroy.

Mohan Singh Oberoi accompanied Gautam Khanna on his return to Egypt. He had never seen the pyramids before, but this was not the first time that he was looking upon dilapidated grandeur. Mena House, too, was like the Grand Hotel in Calcutta and Gulab Bhavan in Kashmir. Like the first, Rai Bahadur would use it to make the great leap, this time into the big league of international hoteliering; like the second, but on a wider scale, he would make Mena House a landmark in restoration.

But, before this, he had to negotiate his way through the tortuous and sometimes simply tiresome perils of a contract. And even prior to this, he had to get the government just to agree to consider him in the reckoning. The luck of the Oberois' took over. He was introduced one evening to Amr el Alfi, Egypt's leading architect and interior decorator, and happened to tell him how much he would like to get Mena House. The man shrugged his shoulders and said, 'Very simple, the Minister for Tourism, Zaki Hashmi, is a good friend of mine. I'll get you the contract from the government but you'll have to give me yours.' 'Name your fee,' said Rai Bahadur. Amr did. Without bothering to convert it into rupees, the hotelier, echoing the word of the Commandant in Calcutta, said, 'Done.'

The public sector Upper Egypt Company had taken over the nationalized hotel from its Jewish owners, the Nungovich Company, and the crumbling pile, like any dowager whose better days were a long time ago, needed much more than just a face lift. Rai Bahadur and son-in-law camped in Cairo. The talks stumbled most on the substantial sum that would have to be spent to restore the hotel. Oberoi could not pitch in with any capital, but guaranteed a six per cent return on investment.

In the hours that they were kept waiting during the day for the night-time negotiations to start, Gautam and Rai Bahadur prowled around Mena House. And the old stones seduced them with their story. Creeping out of the dust-clogged lattice of the *mashrabia* wood-work, tripping off the chipped mother-of-pearl inlay, rustling through the scuffed velvet, the ghosts whispered. They told of how Khedive Ismail had built this place as a lodge in which to camp when he rode out on his Arab steed to out-pace the swift gazelle and fell it with an arrow.

Then the French engineer, de Lesseps, had cut a channel through a neck of continent to join the Red Sea with the Mediterranean, vastly shortening the route to the East and abandoning the Cape of Good Hope to despair. Empress Eugenie of France had come to Cairo to declare open the Suez Canal in 1869, an event for which the city went on one of the greatest binges of modern history. Its building splurge included the new Opera House, with Verdi commissioned to write a work for its opening; he filled it with the dulcet notes of *Aida*. The Khedive built a road so that the Empress could visit the pyramids in comfort, and the lodge was redecorated with the trappings of splendour for her halt there.

The grand fête put Cairo on the tourist map with a little help from the enterprising Thomas Cook. He was the first travel agent to start bringing tourists to Cairo, naturally also making arrangements for an attraction as alluring as the pyramids, namely, a Cleopatra-like glide down the Nile. Since cheques were not accepted, Cook devised a system of coupons to save his clients the bother of being weighed down by money, but *he* still had to carry bags of the stuff. Explaining his predicament, he wrote in a travel article,

> I expect on my return to show how it is possible to travel from London to Alex (andria) in seven days at a cost of less than 20 pounds, first class. The Egyptian Government will have nothing but hard cash, that is, gold. With the view of ensuring certainty of steamboat accommodation on the Nile, I forwarded as a deposit 50 pounds by cheque, I also took circular notes of the London and Westminster Bank, but neither cheque nor notes would be accepted—I must pay in gold, to obtain which I had to submit to a loss of 2 1/2%, and I began my transaction by emptying a bag of 1,300 sovereigns on the floor of the office of the Bay of Arsenal.

Thomas Cook made the arrangements and travelled with the royal couple himself when the Khedive and Khedivah took a trip up the Nile. The consort was towed with her entourage in a luxuriously fitted barge behind the Khedive's private *dahabeah*. At each landing stage the Khedive threw copper coins from large canvas sacks. As Cook was coming back to the barge after an evening in Luxor he saw the ladies, attended by a tall Sudanese guard, and hurriedly averted his eyes so as not to embarrass the viceregal harem. To his astonishment, the Khedivah herself hurried up to him and said, 'I have always desired to meet the great Mr Cook.' She was only lightly veiled and very beautiful. Thomas, undoubtedly, became her admirer for life.

Despite this, with tourists beginning to swarm all over the pyramids, the lodge ost its seclusion, and the Khedive looked for a buyer. The wealthy Frederick Head thought it was just the place for his delicate health, and came to live here in the early 1880s.

His good friend, Professor Saya, the Egyptologist, suggested he call it Mena House, after the pharaoh whose name led the list of seventy-six kings in chronological order on the famous Tablet of Abydos. Mena was the founder of Memphis—the original, not the Tennessee home of Elvis Presley. This King had united upper and lower Egypt, their two symbols of lotus and papyrus entwining among the hieroglyphics of his better-known successors.

The ghosts of Mena House talked to Rai Bahadur and Khanna about Frederick Head's death in England after five idyllic years in Giza with his wife, and the lavish home passing on to another couple, as English, more wealthy. Hugh Locke-King, like his predecessor, was of frail disposition, and needed to winter in Egypt. One of the reasons he bought the mansion was because he could not find a hotel with the standards of comfort that his wife, Ethel, was accustomed to. She was the daughter of the Governor of New South Wales and, later, New Zealand.

The ghosts might have had their memory jogged by Nina Nelson's charming monograph on the hotel:

> Once they moved into the spacious house it suddenly struck Ethel that it might be fun to turn it into a truly luxurious hotel.... With plenty of money at their disposal it was enlarged yet again, and the Locke-Kings set about turning it into the quintessence of comfort but with fittings, architecture and decoration remaining oriental in design. The furnishings were to be in complete contrast to the limitations of ancient Egyptian statues and bric-a-brac with which the Cairo hotels were heavily plastered.
>
> *Mashrabia* work reached its peak of perfection during the fourteenth and fifteenth centuries. From these latticed balconies women of the harem could see what was going on outside without themselves being seen. The balconies had smaller projecting niches where jars of drinking water were placed. The breeze evaporated the water and thus cooled it. Indeed the word *mashrabia* means the place of drink. The Locke-Kings succeeded in buying the most exquisite lattice woodwork from Rosetta and Damietta.

Other innovations by the Locke-Kings were lovely old blue tiles, mosaics and medieval brass-embossed and carved wood doors. . . . At a time when balconies were unheard of in hotels, the Locke-Kings decided that each bedroom should have an open balcony leading from French windows so that guests would be able virtually to sit out of doors although in the privacy of their own room. Mena House Hotel coupons were particularly popular during December (Thomas Cook and Son still use the word COUPON for their cable addresses dating from this period) and tourists mixed with friends of the Locke-Kings during the Christmas season.

Mohan Singh was just a boy when George Nungovich, who had started life as a porter on Cairo station and risen to become the most celebrated hotelier of Egypt, took over Mena House and turned it into an even more plush caravanserai than the one the Locke-Kings had bestowed upon the desert.

The shades of Mena House whispered to the new Managers of how the hotel became the darling of European aristocracy, wealth and scholarship and of those ready, willing and able to sacrifice life and English mustard to keep the flag flying from the periphery of empire. Egypt stood strategically, as gateway to Africa and India. A bankrupt Khedive had sold shares in the Suez in 1874, and perspicacious Britain had bought enough to gain effective control. For the next eighty years, using the argument of the waterway being the 'lifeline of Empire', it found plenty of reasons to meddle in Egyptian affairs. Kitchener, his path again traversing Oberoi's later footsteps, stopped by on his way to Khartoum. So did the archaeologist, Howard Carter, chipping his way to his tryst with the treasures of Tutankhamen.

More history shimmered out of the dusty *mashrabia* of Mena House. Montgomery plotting the battle of El Alamein, and in 1943, the Big Three, Winston Churchill, Franklin Roosevelt and Chiang Kai-shek confabulating in its lavish rooms while the pyramids looked on stonily, wondering what civilization had come to. The antic triangles could not have been amused either when the Duke of Windsor swung a ball off the golf course at its base, and the summit of Great Cheops' mausoleum became the highest tee in the world.

Rai Bahadur stood before Mena House as he had before the

Grand in 1938, 'And again, just very briefly, I marvelled at my own audacity.'

CHAPTER XXXIX

History Revived

━━━━━

Rai Bahadur persuaded the Minister, Zaki Hashmi, and ironed out the wrinkles in the contract with the efficiency of a collar press. The Big Dad of the Indian industry had arrived in the land of the mummies.

Atef Aboul Fadel, an Executive of the Grand Hotels of Egypt, that became the Upper Egypt Compay after Gamal Abdel Nasser's nationalizing spree, remembers his first sight of Mohan Singh Oberoi at the Cairo Sheraton where he and Gautam Khanna had set up base camp. The hotel's transformer had blown, there was no air-conditioning and Rai Bahadur sat stripped down to his underwear. Atef recalls his extreme scepticism over such a man's ability to restore Mena House to its legendary sophistication. The doubts were hardly diluted when they all went to the new Elephantine Hotel at Aswan, which was also part of the deal; the first thing the 'great Oberoi' did on arrival 'was to order a bowl of yoghurt, thin it with water, add some spices and drink it in one gulp.' One can hardly blame the Egyptian for not knowing the wonderfully restorative powers of *lassi*.

The three men got to know each other well, travelling between Cairo and Aswan. On one trip, Rai Bahadur and Khanna shortened the long journey with their Scotch. The devout Muslim and teetotaller, Atef, woke up with a terrible headache, and Gautam never stopped ribbing him, 'We did the drinking, and you got the hangover.'

By a smirk of irony, one of the brightest men in the Oberoi chain bears the same name as the man who now heads the empire founded by the builder of Bombay's Taj. The Oberoi group's Ratan Tata was, in 1971, just a young executive looking after the Singapore Imperial, and yet to prove his mettle. Rai Bahadur handpicked him for Egypt, and it was not because *ratan* and *mena* both mean gem. Tata would work the wonder, grow to head the entire operation in West Asia, and go on to become part of the élite corps of Biki's chosen ones. At six-foot-four he has always been head and shoulders above the rest. Now his stature has been professionally formalized as well; in October 1991, he was appointed President of the chain in India, a position created for him.

However, when he arrived on the scene of his first designated satrapy, young Ratan felt his excitement flaking off as distinctly as the plaster on the walls of Mena House, 'If memory serves, "Oh my God, what have I got into" was my first reaction. Half of the 200 rooms did not have baths attached. Every kitchen pot was caked with grease. Every floorboard creaked. The sofas might correctly be described as a skeletal service. But there was a staff of 700 people. All hanging around doing nothing.' They also looked as if they had been doing that since the time of Empress Eugenie's visit.

Ratan took a deep breath, not too deep a one for fear of asphyxiating on the dust of decades, and rolled up his sleeves. The great restoration began. The Oberoi group laid down its standard rule, 'No effort is too big, no detail too small'. The Chairman added quietly, 'There are too few places like this left in the world. Lose as little as you can of it.'

To its eternal credit, the chain did not proceed to Indianize the new property or even 'neutralize' it, but retained the original ambience that went back to the Ottoman empire. To understand this sensitivity, one has only to see what Marriott has made of the other historic Cairo property that was first offered to Gautam Khanna; its 1,200 rooms have completely overpowered the 'feel' of the old Lotfalah Palace.

The Oberoi group began with the easier part, a 'new' wing called Mena Garden which had been added but never opened. In fact the government had toyed with the idea of converting it into a hospital. The rooms were scrubbed, bathrooms modernized, wiring concealed and telephones installed. The amphitheatre of A,B,C,D & E blocks began to breathe again, rising from different levels of the hillock to a uniform upper circumference. The topography makes it an intriguing hotel. You can take the temperamental elevator up three floors, climb a flight of stairs and still find yourself at 'ground' level.

Then they came to the real challenge. Dramatic changes were needed in the layout of the main building, but no one quite knew how the walls were held up. For one there did not seem to be any joists. The revised blueprint demanded that the lobby be slid to the other end and a new entrance created. Yet, each time he started axing a passage through a wall, Amr el Alfi could never be certain that the whole structure would not cave in on him. The end of one problem was usually the beginning of another, and the joke doing the rounds was that the project would be ready only by the time Ratan Tata's son was old enough to take over as General Manager. The boy was then eight.

Amr el Alfi was as enthused as the Oberoi team. He would charge off into the *souks* of Cairo to hunt out old designs and the craftsmen who could replicate them. The unique and intricate fretwork of the *mashrabia* screens, very much like Rajasthani *jharokas,* were repaired or recreated. The antique cannon, muskets and blunderbusses from the Khedive's days were reinstated, now in the Mameluke Bar. There was considerable outlay on inlay as the gaps in the intricate mother-of-pearl were filled again. Antique ottomans were freshly upholstered in dull gold velvet. Once more the massive Islamic chandelier, made up of discs of blue and amber glass, gleamed softly from its commanding height.

Boarded up rooms revealed treasures, the finest of them being a pair of huge delicate vases. The Japanese ambassador declared them to be over 200 years old and probably matchless. They were installed, no case marring their exquisite beauty, on either side of the entrance to the coffee shop called Khan el Khalili, after the twelfth-century bazaar that is now Cairo's greatest tourist trap.

Not all revelations were as pleasant. Certainly not the discovery that the swimming pool had not been modernized since the time Ethel Locke-King installed it. It had no filtration plant, and an army of servants emptied it each night and filled it every morning. Or was supposed to.

Not all the renovation proceeded smoothly either. One day a marble slab slipped from its meshing and fell on an engineer named Alphons. He was crushed to death. Rai Bahadur supported his family, and his brother now works at the Oberoi restaurant in downtown Cairo, the Nile Tower.

The staff was quite unique. To say they had 'old-world-charm' would be only half true. If they had learnt anything about service in the hotel's better days, they had quite forgotten it. Even the Lobby Manager sat with his feet propped on the table. Getting government employees to buckle down to the demands of private sector work-style is not the easiest of tasks anywhere in the world. They had to learn that initiative, merit and hard work would take them far, that seniority was no longer the only criterion. Abdel Hamid Kansowa, also originally from the Upper Egypt Company, summed up the general picture, 'After twenty years in government service, a donkey can become a horse.' Oberoi paying four times the salary helped to inject some dynamism. But not entirely.

Together with the tapestry, the steam laundry equipment and the brandy snifters, Rai Bahadur also organized classes in English and French or sent staff to the American University at Cairo. It was worse at the Aswan hotel, where the native Nubians were even more reluctant to change their old ways, or even their traditional crossed-over kaftans; it took much persuading to get them to don modern uniforms. There, the Oberoi management brought in both tutors and dentists. The former to brush up the language, the latter to do so more literally. Fortunately, a large number of staff decided that the tempo was beyond their creaking bones, and agreed to retire. A corps of young, enthusiastic Egyptians—with better English, French and teeth took their place.

Ratan Tata put Abdel Hamid in charge of building up a trained cadre, but the pharaohs may have had an easier time finding skilled hands for their hospitality service in the afterlife. He was asked to recruit personnel at the Aswan hotel. The plan was to complete the job in a week; he had to stay six months.

Rai Bahadur insisted on employing personable young women, a practice he had pioneered in Delhi. It was easy enough among the sophisticated Cairenes, but at Aswan, this led to teething troubles of a different kind. Despite the town's exposure to the outside world, thanks to its modern temple, the high dam and the considerably older one of Abu Simbel, the conservative Nubians simply did not want their women to work. Anywhere. Even nurses came from outside the region.

Again, Rai Bahadur refused to relent. Finally, Abdel Hamid coopted hotel staff and tour operators to conduct a house-to- house survey. The objective was to identify the women who had graduated from college, but were sitting at home wasting their degrees. Gradually, they were drawn out.

Today Cairo's great respect for Rai Bahadur stems not only from the success he has made of his Egyptian hotels, but also because of the modern training programme he introduced into the entire hospitality industry there. Some of the finest Managers from India were dispatched to Cairo for the purpose, not returning till every last man was in place, and in perfect trim.

Finally, everything was ready. As in Calcutta, Kashmir, Delhi and Bombay, one day the butterfly emerged from the cocoon of scaffolding to wow the invited crowds. The garden was dotted with fairy lights. A dais was raised with palm logs. And, then, to the consternation of the Indian group, the garlanded fatted calf was led out. They feared it would be slaughtered right there. It was not. The chop fell out of sight, and the hallowed meat was distributed to the staff and the poor.

Oberoi gave Mena House back to Egypt, recreated a national symbol of forgotten craftsmanship. With it, he restored some of the face that had been lost along with the Sinai peninsula.

Calcutta's Grand Hotel had made its pile from the war, and then settled down to civvy street; at Mena House, however, battle was always round the corner, the thunder never distant. The Oberoi chain had taken over when Egypt had lost a war. Despite the opening in 1972, the hotel was still being brought up to Oberoi standards. Ratan Tata introduced the country's first discotheque, the Saddle, and Egypt's trendies bucked like broncos in it. A profligate sum of 13,000 £. E. (Egyptian pounds) had been spent, but it raked in some two or three million £.E. in three or four years, more than vindicating Tata's stand that it would compensate for the loss of revenue during the rest of the hotel's re-creation.

Half the hotel was still under renovation's burlap and takings were proportionately lower. It was at this time that Egyptian jets screamed into Israel even as the Jews celebrated Yom Kippur. The Arab world would get back some of its honour in this chapter of its never-ending enmity with the Promised Land, but the latest round of strife could not have come at a worse time for the hotel.

There was no question of cutting back on staff. If a hotel in the volatile Middle East were to do that every time the strafing started, jobs would never be safe. Ratan Tata, like his now legendary boss, was in several places at once, manning the station virtually for twenty-four hours, controlling costs, minimizing wastage, extracting loans out of the banks. He held the team together and gave it the critical thrust to see it through the first crisis.

Continuing its historic destiny, Mena House was the chosen venue for the Egypt-Israel talks, following Anwar Sadat's peace initiative. The guns would turn on the Egyptian President, on 6 October 1981 even as they raised their barrels in salute at an army parade. The country would be viewed with ambivalence by the Arab world for stretching out its hand in friendship to Zion, but the talks were the most momentous occasion since the mandate had presented Israel as a *fait accompli* on 14 May 1948.

The hotel bristled with security which outmatched the combined arrangements of previous summits and even the five-year-old son of Homi Wadia, who had moved there from Bombay, needed a pass-badge. The Palestinian flag being raised was explained away as a *faux pas,* but insiders insist that this was what President Sadat had wanted, that a table had also been provided for the victims of the new diaspora. Despite the security a suitcase with a bomb was smuggled in, but thankfully detected in time.

Causing as much of a kerfuffle was the discovery that the head of the Israeli delegation was missing just before the commencement of the first session. 'You'll never guess the cause,' said Wadia. 'It was the antiquated lifts, dubbed the "please and thank you contraptions", since they seemed to oblige only if such courtesies were extended to them. Even OPEC's powerful Sheikh Yamani had been trapped in them earlier. The lifts seem to hate VIPs.' They have recently been replaced with newer and presumably less finicky elevators.

The hotel was fully closed to the public, open only to the delegates. Exclusively kosher food was served. It was the first time that Egyptians were dealing across the counter with Israelis, and a receptionist could be forgiven for dropping the passport of one like a hot brick. He had never handled such a document before.

President Jimmy Carter addressed the meeting at 1 p. m. Flustered perhaps by the momentousness of the occasion, he said, 'Good morning, gentlemen,' and then hastily corrected himself to, 'Good afternoon.' The Egyptian and American Presidents were each presented a key of pure gold by the management of Mena House, in gratitude for the privilege of playing host.

Mena House would have enough of a respite to expand its facilities, gild the luxury, and snuggle deeper into the affection of the Egyptians. So did Mohan Singh Oberoi. Having learnt the way of doing business with these sensitive people, he would, over the years, establish a base as wide as the pyramids and, competing with the world's biggest chains, provide arguably the best range of properties in the country. Little wonder then that Egypt presented Rai Bahadur its highly coveted Order of the Republic—First Class, award in 1985, two massive stars of gold for having promoted modern tourism in the ancient land of Misr.

CHAPTER XL

King Of The Room Boom

Mena House was the 'Open, Sesame' to the Arab world. Negotiations for the Baghdad property began in the 1970s when Iraq and Iran were already at war, and there were no flights into Saddam land. Gautam Khanna took a plane to Amman, and hired a car to drive through the night and the sand-scape. In the middle of both, the engine fell out. He sat shivering, getting Dutch courage and Southern Comfort from a hip flask till another car passed by. It was packed, but with a little persuasion of the kind that transcends the language barrier, it agreed to take his driver back to town to bring in a more reliable vehicle. More shivering, more warmth. Then daylight and reinforcements.

The Baghdad hotel that Khanna negotiated was the fabulous Al Rashid built by the government at a construction cost of half a million dollars per room as against a super deluxe's more normal $200,000, the price pushed up by its bomb shelters, helipad and closed-circuit television. However, like many government enterprises, the hotel ran to seed; one day, chancing upon its shabbiness, the President ordered its management to be handed over to a private company. Enter, the Oberoi group. They ran it for five years till Saddam Hussein decided that a foreign group running a hotel where state guests stayed did not quite jell with national pride. He took it back. However, the group's presence remained in Iraq, at the Oberoi Babylon, on the banks of the legendary Tigris, fount of the Sumerian civilization. Much later, it would be one of the nucleii for international coverage of the 1990-91 Kuwait occupation till every foreign correspondent, bar the Arnett-work of Cable News Network (CNN), was ordered out of the country. The hotel remained, however, like Casabianca on the burning deck, when most other investment had fled Iraq, soldiering on till Baghdad and business were temporarily reduced to rubble.

Towards the end of the 1970s, the desert continued to be stormed.

P. R. S. Oberoi and Ratan Tata did not ever seem to be in one place for longer than two weeks at a time, especially after a very influential gentleman from Jeddah went back after a stay at Mena House. He wasn't charmed only by the pyramids that rose to greet him every morning from his balcony. Returning home, he told his construction company partners of the incredible meld of Arab culture and modern hoteliering that had been achieved at the historic hotel. Sheikhs Ali Tamimi, Abdullah Fouad, Omran al Omran and Rashid al Rashid asked the Oberois if they were interested in a collaboration.

Biki and Ratan arrived in Dammam, and almost caught the next flight back. There was no way, said Biki, that he was going to have anything to do with the strange apparition he saw in the desert boom-town, a jigsaw of imported prefab pieces. But Sheikh Ali Tamimi adjusted his head-dress, stroked his beard and said, 'This is only the first. If you don't take it, you'll be out of the race for the others.' Biki was already too much of a pro not to weigh the con. He signed on the dotted line, but only after he had laid down a condition of his own: 'In future, no project without our role in the planning and design.'

Thus began the enviable combination of Oberoi expertise and Arab expenditure which would help the group's expansion far beyond the flight of the desert falcon. Ratan Tata moved to Dhahran, heading a company called Saudi Oberoi. Its first achievement was the Dammam Oberoi, in 1981, its 300 rooms, forty suites and luxurious bathrooms making it arguably the finest hotel in the Gulf's kingpin kingdom.

Seven years later, the desert telegraph started clacking again. Another Sheikh would like to do business. Now, both Biki and Ratan, being infidels, could not enter the place restricted only to the faithful. Abdul Fadel was sent over into the controlled area, and while walking around, chanced upon a much better hotel coming up. So he called up its Kuwaiti owner, Abdul Aziz Al Shaya. Of course he had heard of the Oberois, and of course he would like to talk.

A unique remote-controlled operation went into top gear. The two parties, along with the British designer, would meet over breakfast in the Medina Sheraton, outside the sacred boundary. Then the instructions would be conveyed to their Muslim architects and engineers on the holy side. Ratan Tata became so respected a figure that they almost made him an honorary believer. He is now allowed into

Medina's controlled area, but he must return right after the *Isha* prayer. There is no way that he can spend a night in his hotel. He may, however, break bread at his company's ultra modern bakery at Riyadh and Yanbu, north of Jeddah, or drop in at the Green Island restaurant and health club in the capital. Relax there? Out of the question. Like his bosses he does not know the meaning of the word.

The desert would not fox the Oberoi group any longer. The Egypt operation would extend to the Egoth Oberoi at the El Arish resort, the first half of the hotel's name reflecting their public sector collaborator, the Egyptian General Organisation for Tourism and Hotels. You can also fly to upper Egypt, and from the shadow of the 5,000-year-old temples of Luxor and Karnak take a four-day Nile cruise aboard the *Oberoi Shahryar* or *Oberoi Shehrazad* up to Aswan. You could spend a couple of days at the Oberoi hotel on Elephantine Island soaking up the healing properties of the spa that impressed the Aga Khan and Anwar Sadat, wandering amidst its acres of orchard and garden that supply all the hotel's fruits, flowers and vegetables. Or you could simply sit sipping a *dom* juice on your duplex cottage balcony, watching the sailed *feluccas* glide past as they have since civilization began.

Back in Cairo, you can have a leisurely supper as you float down the river of many returns aboard the *Golden Pharaoh* or the *Nile Pharaoh*. The won't provide Cleopatra, but the aperitifs are better than ass's milk, and the belly dancer is more sinuous than the asp. Or, wandering through the ultimate guide-book ambience of the twelfth centure *souk*, the Khan el Khalili, you can loll languorously at its open-air tables, sipping Turkish coffee and drawing on a hubble-bubble with a hint of apricot. Or step inside to lunch on rice steamed with trotters or kebabs of many flavours served with *tahini*, sesame paste spiked with the pulp of smoked aubergine: *baingan-bharta* Egyptian-style, just like mummy used to make.

Future plans in Egypt include outrageous decadence at the Red Sea resort of Hurghada, an all-suite hotel where even the bathrooms will have spectacular views. Hurghada, with its clear, clear, water offers one of the best scuba-diving areas in the world. And it is expected to attract the cream of the European winter tourist. No discounts, no groups. With so many in the Oberoi chain now bearing the prestigious endorsement of the Leading Hotels of the World, the Red Sea is expected to part to allow those with disposable incomes to pass through with ease.

Desert and island, Rai Bahadur was not averse to being marooned on both in style. In 1973, the Lanka Oberoi gave him his first chance outside India to build his own hotel. It was an empty site, and the architect he wanted was Japan's legendary Yamasaki. But he declined, saying he was too old, and would not be persuaded by Oberoi Senior's example of life beginning at seventy-three. So the Sri Lankan government and the hotelier settled for something that promised to be as spectacular, an atrium design by the American group of Skidmore, Owings and Merrill. At the time, the Hyatt in Atlanta was the only other hotel in the world to have tried out this unique concept.

But hotels are not immune to politics, and when Sirimavo Bandaranaike took over as Prime Minister, she decided that her government was not going to put any money in the hotel. The Oberoi group found its funds after two years, from far-away France, and, fulfilling its condition of employing French construction firms, the bejewelled Lanka Oberoi was unveiled in 1975, sixty-foot showpieces of Sri Lankan craftsmanship cascading down the nine floors of the red and gold atrium.

Then, to the South Pacific and the secluded Bali hideout of an American playboy whose parties had been too wild for the Indonesian government. He had been ordered out. Gautam Khanna heard about it on the grapevine while he was in New York. He mentioned it to Rai Bahadur, adding that he did not think that season-dependent resort hotels were such a hot idea, however great the tan. Biki went over. He sensed the potential of the dilapidated cottages that were being rented out to hippies at a dollar a day, but he was not too sure either. He cabled his father to come and decide.

Some enchanted evening, the stranger saw the uncrowded beach, and fell in love with the solitude. So did the likes of Henry Kissinger when the hotel opened in 1978, the prototype of paradise with its seventy-five thatched *lanai* cottages and villas, five with their own swimming pools, nestling amidst lush tropical gardens right on the beach. It is so secluded that you can luxuriate in a bathroom where the walls are a thicket of foliage and the ceiling is the sky. The noble savage, however, does not have to manage without modern plumbing.

The Bali Oberoi did not shoot up overnight. Rai Bahadur stayed on for three months after the deal was negotiated. Every morning at five-thirty he made a round of the property with the chief gardener, Nengah Konok. The horticulturist was surprised by his new boss's knowledge of ferns, trees and flowering shrubs; bowled over by the passion with which he talked about nature. Thirteen years later, he would still recall with gratitude the advice that made his garden the pride of Bali.

In 1985, an American guest fell in love with the huge antique Balinese bed in the Presidential Villa. 'Name your price,' he said pulling out his credit cards. He refused to heed the management's pleas that they simply could not sell it. Finally, he agreed to settle for an exact replica. Local wood-carvers worked on the masterpiece for three months, and the hotel shipped it to him. He wrote back to say he was delighted, and that it was worth every cent of the $6,000 that it had finally cost him.

With each negotiation, whether on tiny island or king-sized transcontinental sprawl, the Oberoi group learnt a new rope, but each was also unique, and each brought its own surprises. Sometimes, the outcome had nothing to do with the talks across the table. In the then Soviet Republic of Turkmenia, discussions had gone off without a hiccup, and only the dotted line remained to be signed on. But the next day, there were a lot of red faces. The local government had gone ahead with the deal unilaterally, not played by Moscow rules. The Kremlin considered such a show of independence subversive. *Nyet,* it ordered. The way things changed shortly after in the USSR, *nyet* simply meant 'not yet'.

CHAPTER XLI

Big Daddy To The Company

At fifty, we found Rai Bahadur Singh Oberoi consolidating an empire he had wrested from others. By seventy- five, the next watershed, he had built his own, in the process, checking India into its first international class hotel. He had soldiered through the heartbreak of the years when grand visions threatened to turn into monumental disasters, yet he had emerged bloodied but unbowed.

By seventy-five he had gone global, and was still growing, confident enough to say that he would build a hundred hotels before he had finished with the century that had begun just eight-and-a-half months before his birth. He was too much in the thick of things to be pedestalled away as 'grand old man', but at seventy-five, he was already the legend. If most of Indian hoteliering's firsts were his, from room service to sales and marketing, it was due to some very distinctive traits.

His son-in-law, K.K. Mehra, tells of his ability to get you to do things his way without your ever realizing it. A little like the sexist one-liner about a woman chasing a man and allowing him to catch up with her—a predicament in which our man of the world may have also found himself. There was the occasion when 'KK' had denied a major contract to a civil works company that had been associated with the Oberoi group for a long time, but had not been doing its kind of jobs for some years. Rai Bahadur did not ask him to reverse his decision, he 'simply suggested that I analyse it. He provided enough indirect inputs to show that, financially, this was the best company we could deal with. I thus became a willing, not a grudging, partner in continuing with the old.'

On the flip side, a politically influential maker of cooking oil brought pressure on 'KK' to get the group to switch to his brand. When this did not work, he took his muscle to Rai Bahadur. The

Chairman agreed with the reasons for his son-in-law's refusal, so, putting on his most helpless look, he said, 'I am terribly sorry, but Mr Mehra's the boss in these matters, I wouldn't dare contradict him.'

He has a touching way of showing his appreciation. A senior liaison man helped him get a deal through and presumed he would be compensated handsomely. He came grumbling to 'KK', 'I expected a generous cheque, and what do I get? A basketful of *saag*!' 'KK' told him that those were not any old mustard greens, they were specially grown on the farm, and Rai Bahadur must have stood out there personally supervising the picking of the choicest leaves; it would have been much easier for him to have sent an impersonal bottle of Scotch. Besides, not to worry, it was not in lieu of payment. A very shame-faced man telephoned 'KK' two days later to tell him he was right.

Ragini Chopra, the chain's Director, Sales & Marketing, describes an incident in the Delhi hotel's coffee shop where Rai Bahadur quietly sat observing a girl who made a face on tasting her orange juice, did not drink any more, paid for it, and began walking towards the door. He caught up with her, asked her why she had left her juice unfinished and, on hearing that it was less than fresh, he said to her, 'You must never accept anything that's second-best—in life or in a hotel.' He then escorted her back to the table, pulled out her chair, and asked the steward to get her another drink.

There are any number of variations on the story of the cook who had retired after thirty years service, explained his problems to the Chairman, and requested an *ex gratia* payment. Rai Bahadur sent the file to the Vice-President concerned, suggesting that they give him a monthly pension of ten years instead. After that period was over, the money should not be discontinued, but the matter referred to him for review. Or of the telephone operator, hired on a year's contract, who suddenly died. Her death had nothing to do with the company, but when her father wrote describing his straitened circumstances, Rai Bahadur immediately sanctioned a generous sum. Or the retiring clerk who explained that legally due benefits would just about cover the medical costs of his bedridden wife, and nothing else. 'Sanction Rs 500 p.m. for five years' is the scrawled notation on the file.

All this goes from his personal income or the charity set up by Ishran Devi in the name of Bhagwanti Oberoi. He is very proud of the fact that the lowliest employee with a genuine problem will not hesitate to think, 'Let me ask the Chairman.'

When a promising young executive requested a loan to tide over the expenses of getting married and setting up home Rai Bahadur laughingly told him that he should be concentrating on his career instead. However, not only did he sanction the loan, he also told him how to get round the Vice-President, Finance who he said was 'sure to find ways of delaying payments'.

At a meeting, Rai Bahadur reiterated his belief that the hotels would be nothing without the acumen and effort of his Managers. Seizing the opportunity with a panache that would have befitted his boss, one of them stood up to say, 'Sir, we live in the hotel, but it would be much better if we could own a flat for the future.' This was the time that Swiss Hotel had been converted into a residential complex, and Rai Bahadur, pausing only for a moment's reflection, replied, 'Anyone who thinks the same way should meet me at Maidens at 7 a.m tomorrow.'

On the numbing February morning the Chairman drove the forty kilometres from the farm, took the assembled Managers round the Swiss Hotel enclave, showed them the different types of flats, and made an offer few wanted to refuse; a fifty per cent discount, a down payment of Rs 50,000 and the rest deducted in instalments over any period convenient. 'There's only one condition,' he said. 'Whenever you get an increment, half will go towards repayment.'

His granddaughter, Rajni Rana, is thankful that 'Big Daddy' insisted that she too buy a house on the Swiss Hotel estate. 'I can't afford it,' she had argued. He said she could have it on very easy terms. She never regretted it, later exchanging the highly appreciated property for an orchard in Dehra Dun. Naturally, the first thing he did when he visited her there was to start rearranging the furniture, and take the measurements of the driveway, so that he could send her proper gravel instead of the makeshift stone chips she had used. He looked so happy taking charge that Rajni did not have the heart to tell him she liked the place the way it was.

In fact, he seems to be Big Daddy to his Senior Managers as well. In the 1970s he kept advising them to invest in land. Advice is hardly the word. He virtually bulldozed them into it, however unwilling they were. He would go scouting in the area around his farm, choose, negotiate and send the transfer forms across, the places where the signature was required all marked in his own hand. The land is now worth a fortune, and its owners feel very foolish indeed over their initial grumbling against being 'bullied' into an investment they thought they did not want.

Hundreds of such touching gestures strengthened the foundations of the relationship on which, in turn, the superstructure of the company is built. You may call it motivated concern if you wish. Certainly, his business is all he has ever lived for, the single-minded pursuit of a single objective, but it is difficult to tell where self-interest ended and genuine warmth began. The fact is that both have gone in tandem.

It was the same with gestures of another kind. Like at the time of Nehru's death, when, without any tom-tomming, he catered for the special train in which family and close associates took Nehru's ashes for dispersal across the country. Or when, similarly, he went to the nth degree in providing luxuries for the Heads of State who arrived for the Non-Aligned Movement (NAM) conference in Delhi.

The personal touch has touched in many ways. At one time, Anil Madhok was Resident Manager in Singapore, and thus fairly lowly in the hierarchy. Back in Delhi on holiday, he was invited to lunch along with his family at the farm. Rai Bahadur walked out into the summer heat to take them from the reception area to his private quarters. He took Anil's little girls around, showing them his cows, his deer and his pet birds in their giant aviary. He collected peacock feathers for them. At lunch he turned to Mrs Madhok and said, 'Anju, I know you are vegetarian, so there's creamed spinach from the farm for you, but I have ordered minced chicken for the children; they'll find it easier to eat.' To the mortification of her parents, the younger daughter, only two, stood on the dining chair and began jumping up and down. Rai Bahadur indulgently said, 'Don't worry, all children behave like that.'

When he returned after opening the hotel in Adelaide, he brought back a memento for all his Managers: silk scarves for the women, ties for the men. Madhok's was sent to him in Singapore, with a hand-written-note—the notes are always hand-written—'I have just added another hotel to your chain.'

You could lose count of the little acts of concern. Azhar Siddiqui, another of the younger Managers, will never forget how, when Rai Bahadur got to hear about his nine-year-old daughter rapidly losing her eyesight, he immediately asked him to fly her for treatment to Singapore, told him to stay on there for the three extra weeks it took for the implant lens to arrive from the USA, and then insisted on settling the medical bills. 'Every time I've gone to meet him, he asks about her.' Siddiqui left the company for a while, but all trips to Delhi included a visit to the farm. 'If you don't go to see him, you'll get a note, very polite, but with the hurt showing through. And today even though it is such an effort for him to get off the chair, he still insists on standing up when a lady enters the room.'

Madhok tells the story of the time during the Emergency when his father-in-law's business premises were raided; Sanjay Gandhi, the 'extra-constitutional authority' of those days, was settling a political score with the other partner. The two senior men were arrested, and summarily pushed into the lock-up. Mohan Singh Oberoi heard the news on television, and immediately phoned Madhok to ask if he could be of any help. The matter had been settled already, but Anil was moved by the fact that the Chairman should put aside his pressing concerns to rush to the aid of a relatively junior employee's family.

Clearly, Midas had not lost the human touch any more at seventy-five, than at fifty. Munir, his faithful major domo, will point out that there has never been the feeling that 'I'm a millionaire, I'll move only among millionaires'. His son-in-law, 'KK', adds that there is no difference, either, in the way he relates to, say, a coffee-shop waiter or the President of the World Bank. He may have left the clerical days at Simla very far behind, but in many ways they have never left his consciousness. He thought nothing of going in person to the Ambassador Hotel to persuade Chef Mehrotra to return to his domain, the kitchens of the Oberoi Intercontinental's Moghul Room.

His cultural pursuits have been limited to the entertainment he has laid on for his foreign guests, the *raga* with *roomali roti* sort of thing. His reading is restricted to the odd biography of hoteliers such as Conrad Hilton; the only fiction that he had time for was Arthur Hailey's *Hotel*. Yet, he is numbered among the circle of such discerning eminences as Jawaharlal Nehru and his sister, Vijayalakshmi Pandit, D. P. Dhar, L. K. Jha and most of all, Indira Gandhi. Because of their long business association, Dr Karan Singh is a close friend, who has 'more than made up for his father not offering me even a cup of tea when I went to see him about the carpets.' On his birthday, India's former Minister for Tourism unfailingly receives a cake from the Oberoi pastry shop, always with a handwritten note from Rai Bahadur; on the peg table of the drawing-room at the Oberoi farm, framed in antique silver and 'crowned' with royal insignia, reposes a signed photograph of the erudite one-time maharajah and his stunning wife.

Dr Karan Singh is unlikely to forget the sheer professionalism of Rai Bahadur. 'He had just about regained consciousness after the stroke when I went to see him in the nursing home. Yet, before I even got a chance to ask him how he felt, he said, "Dr Singh, I've arranged for a new chef to be sent to Srinagar." The man had just had a brush with death, but he couldn't stop thinking of his hotels.'

Rai Bahadur got to know Sheikh Abdullah after he was freed from an eleven-year incarceration; the 'Lion of Kashmir' appreciated the Oberoi group's role in boosting tourism, and Rai Bahadur always brought back a present for him when he went abroad. Once it was an elaborate watch with different time zones; the towering Sheikh spent half the evening figuring it out with all the bubbling excitement of a child.

Certainly none of these people needed to befriend him for the kind of favours an international hotelier can provide. They deferred to him because of his contribution to the Indian image. The cliché of the begging bowl suddenly looked absurd on a buffet table laid with such elegance both at home and abroad.

If Biki has been able to work so smoothly with his father, it is because Rai Bahadur had no less modern a mind. Biki mentions the two-crore-rupee computerized system he installed recently in Bombay. On the innovation, as in the case of every other, he never heard his father even suggest that he had built up his empire without such expensive gadgetry, and there wasn't any need for it now. He had the same open mind on the decentralization that Biki introduced in the Seventies. In fact, Rai Bahadur went one further, at ninety-one, restructuring the organization and creating a president's post which would further streamline the company's functioning in India.

If Rai Bahadur achieved in one generation, as his eldest daughter Rajrani said, what normally takes two, it is because he cheated time, squeezing in an extra lifetime with the hours he kept. He told Munir, 'If you work for nine hours a day you'll achieve nine hours' profits, but if you work double that, your success will also double.' One can not fault the arithmetic. Even at this age he would feel uncomfortable all day if he had not risen at 5 a.m. and begun attacking his files. In the old days the dynamo was always charged, and charging around, well before day- break, well after the world had gone to bed. A hotel never sleeps, but a hotelier does not have to follow suit.

At seventy-five he was as energetic as at fifty, defying the rules of biological regression. It was a question of 'disciplining the mind, establishing a routine and not deviating from it'. Even in his busiest days, he cleared every pending file before he retired for the night. He deals with one problem at a time, never sees visitors or even takes a phone call while in a meeting or when processing paperwork. If you do not create a haystack, you will not have trouble looking for the needle.

He never forgets a detail on a document any more than he forgets a detail about a friend's or staffer's family life. While doing a round of the Adelaide hotel, the General Manager was astonished to hear his seventy-six-year-old boss inquire about an earlier plumbing problem on the floor he was inspecting. The repair had been necessitated three years ago and the information sent as part of the routine report. In the writing of this story, during the interviews he might say, 'I'll send you a note on this, or we'll talk about it next time.' He never jotted down anything to remind him, but the note would be sent, the matter raised, the couriered questionnaires answered point by point, and in the same order at the following meeting without him ever having a piece of paper to jog his nine-decade-old memory.

And, of course, he knows every inch of his hotels. When his daughter, Prem, was setting up home, he told her, 'We are auctioning some of the furniture at Maidens. There's an excellent chest of drawers in Room 26, I suggest you bid for that.' This anecdote says as much about his accounting as about his total recall. His daughters were set up in business, Rajrani running the country's first boutique at Imperial, 'Rani Saris', Swaraj the 'Ritika' book-shops in the Oberoi chain, and Prem the 'Silhouette' beauty parlours, all very successful enterprises. But they all pay exactly the same licence fees as the other establishments in the arcade. No one can, claiming family status, dine in the restaurants and walk off; everything is kept track of, especially after the hotels went public.

But empires are not built only on softness and simplicity. The vision has to be as wide as the detail is narrow, and the will as strong as the working arm. if I wanted something, I never let anything come in my way' is a true confession readily made, and his steamroller tactics are as much a part of company legend. When Netra Rana left Mercury Travels to set up his own agency, 'Big Daddy' gave his grandson-in-law his blessings, but added, in so many words, that he had better not work against Oberoi interests.

Ruthlessness and determination are two sides of the same specie. In both cases, obstructions had better look sharp. As a Member of Parliament he opposed tooth and nail the proposal to allow Hilton to construct a hotel on the spectacular sea-lapped site of Samudra Mahal, the Scindia of Gwalior's palace in Bombay. His sentiments were entirely noble. He had worked out the figures: 'The twenty-five per cent gross operating profits that Hilton demanded would leave the Gwaliors with nothing, even at an eighty per cent room occupancy. The Americans should not give Indians a raw deal in their own country,' he said to the law-makers.

His calculations were, however, also calculating, and his impassioned plea had a little more than mere national interest at its core. But, then, no one makes any bones about political lobbies, and no one can cavil or demur when they come to identify themselves strongly with five-star granite ones.

Besides, the sheer size of Rai Bahadur's contribution, the unassuming nature of the man himself, made it very difficult for any charge of pettiness to stick.

CHAPTER XLII

State Of The Unions

The biblical offer, 'Come to me all ye who labour and are heavy laden, was not directed at members of hotel unions staggering under the weight of room service trays, but it could well have been. Labour problems acquire a special dimension, as sinister as it is sensitive, when the shop floor is a marble one, and bankruptcy can be merely a bell-hop's scowl away.

The long-time President of the Federation of Hotel Associations of India, Ram Pershad, tells the story of travellers who arrived at Delhi's international airport at the usual ungodly hour that is neither night nor morning by any civilized reckoning, took two hours to clear the Gulag of Immigration and Customs, green channel notwithstanding, hung up the 'Do not disturb' card on their door, and flopped with relief on to their soft five-star bed. Barely had they dozed off when, through the glazing of their windows, the agitated slogans filled the room. It was impossible to rest amidst the unrest outside. They picked up their bags, checked out, and took their custom to a country with a more sleeper-friendly industrial policy.

It is not an apocryphal story; in a service industry labour agitations equal apocalypse now. A telephone operator's brusqueness could damn a hotel even before the guest steps into it. Half the battle for custom is won—or lost—by the time the guest checks in. Besides, unlike in another industry, you cannot prevent labour from interfacing with your customers. It's their very job. Room occupancy, like power, cannot be stored; if it's lost for the day, it's lost beyond retrieval. Word of mouth publicity cuts both ways with equal intensity. Losing custom is really as easy as picking up a suitcase.

In that industrial Valhalla when paternalistic management was yet to become a class enemy, a lot of pioneers did what was right before it became a legal right. Mohan Singh Oberoi's labour policy stemmed

178

from his own incredible rapport, at every level. When operations were small, this was no big deal. The real test came when the work force spread out under the labour laws of different state governments and even foreign ones.

Rai Bahadur's philosophy was, 'I'd rather have a bad settlement than successful litigation, because in the latter both sides could end losing.' The younger breed of Managers chafed under the directive to keep the door open for negotiations, to provide unions a way of returning to the table. If they were on strong ground, the Managers preferred to drive home the advantage, rather than compromise on discipline or principle. But Rai Bahadur, perhaps because he had grown in the business through both sides of the divide, abhorred the path of confrontation. 'Defuse the crisis, don't let it degenerate into a strike,' he would insist. If, sussing out the situation, he assessed that a union demand for the reinstatement of a dismissed employee was just a means of saving face, he would advise the Managers to accede, settle for an apology, avert a showdown.

Calcutta, springboard of militant trade-unionism in India, naturally threw down the first gauntlet. Long before the Marxists came to power. In 1949, the staff was in a belligerent mood, and a meeting called by Rai Bahadur at Prince's was only a short-lived pacifier. A one-day strike was called. The following morning the boss himself stood at the gate, informing workers that those who were dissatisfied should collect their dues and leave. Several did, but many soon came trickling back. The good ones were welcomed; the bad eggs, by now identified, were not allowed in once more to ruin the omelette. A few weeks later, Oberoi, on his own, announced several benefits, summing up the situation with the proverb, *'Bin maangey miley moti; maangey miley na bheekh.'* (Without asking you gain the pearl; demanding you are denied even alms.)

Soon, however, such unilateral solutions were no longer possible. A Left-dominated United Front government was installed in the state in 1967 in a hail of raised fists and slogans. Worker-power gave the English language a new word, *gherao,* literally 'surround', but referring specifically to the siege laid to Managers in one establishment after another, and acquiring a perverse snob value on the cocktail circuits of Ballygunge and Alipore. The situation at the Grand had deteriorated to such a degree that a room service waiter would refuse to do coffee shop duty. One made the beds, another had to be assigned to dust the furniture; the man who swept the bathrooms would not wipe the shower curtains: 'curtains are the job of laundry.'

Mohan Singh played his 'old-relationships' to the hilt. Then he won over the President of the Oberoi Grand Employees Union with his transparent sincerity. Oberoi, after all, had retained its faith in the city, had not pulled up its moorings and fled along with the rest to less harrowing industrial belts. Mohammed Ismail, the Marxist trade union leader and Member of Parliament, became a good friend, and he was not the kind of person you could put into your pocket. Terms were renegotiated, but Rai Bahadur ensured that he got the extra service in return for the extra emolument. The labour leader would often joke with Satish Kumar who orchestrated the seemingly impossible turn-around, 'Your unions are bourgeois ones, they are too pampered to agitate.'

Some years later, workers downed ladles in Srinagar, triggered by the brashness of a Manager who had failed to grasp that Article 370 applied to hotels as well. Kashmiri staff had to be treated specially. Again, lost honour was restored, and the hotel began functioning without another hitch.

Bombay in the mid-Seventies was a lot like Calcutta in the late Sixties. Trade unions fought long, acrimonious, even murderous, battles to wrest control of the Thane-Belapur belt. The reverberations were felt as far away as Nariman Point. Three unions embroiled the Oberoi in a tug-of-war for supremacy. The Shiv Sena flexed its newly acquired muscle, threatened Managers, screamed slogans outside the door, and finally broke the glass panes, and entered the *sanctum sanctorum* of the lobby.

Rai Bahadur rushed to Bombay, and immediately sought an appointment with the Shiv Sena 'supremo', Balasaheb Thackeray. He explained to him that the Oberois had come from Delhi and the Punjab to work for the glory and wealth of Maharashtra, that Bombay was Thackeray's showpiece much more than it was his. How would it help either if intimidated business travellers and tourists began to shun the city? The persuasiveness of the argument was underpinned by the genuine humility of the hotelier. Thackeray and Rai Bahadur are still good friends, and the Bombay Oberoi hotels have not had any major industrial relations problem since.

But Rai Bahadur's celebrated 'personal rapport' has not entirely been without heartburn; his accessibility has often been seen as a dilution of the chain of command. Azhar Siddiqui, when he was General Manager in Bombay, was once extremely miffed by the top boss mollifying union leaders whom he was trying to discipline. He dashed off a note to him saying, 'It would help, sir, if staff didn't have direct access to the Chairman.'

The time taken to reply was as studied as the contents of the memo that arrived after two weeks from the Chairman's office. '*I* may tell you whom you may or may not meet. *You* are not entitled to do likewise.' Siddiqui had realized even earlier that he had been too impulsive. He spoke to Biki: 'I'm in trouble, Mr Oberoi.' Biki, who had not yet taken over complete charge, knew all about the matter. 'Oh, the firing squad,' he replied, and advised, 'you'd better apologize in person when the Chairman is next in Bombay.'

Whenever he visited, the usual practice was for the General Manager to escort Rai Bahadur to his suite, excuse himself and return to his office. Rai Bahadur would normally telephone in a short while, and ask him to come up for discussions. On the next visit, Siddiqui sat glued to the instrument. As in the Cliff Richard song, he kept 'waiting for the phone to ring though I know it's all in vain'. Then, unable to bear the suspense, he took the initiative, and called Rai Bahadur's room, 'Sir, I've got some papers for you. May I come up?' 'I'm busy,' said the Chairman and disconnected. This set-piece was repeated for three days, by which time Siddiqui had virtually chewed off all his fingernails.

On the fourth evening, he went up to the Jodhpur Suite, knocked and said, 'Sir, I'll only take a minute. These papers need your signature. They are urgent.' They were nothing of the sort. Chairman and General Manager sat across from each other, both men intently studying the carpet through the coffee table's glass top. Finally Siddiqui took a deep breath and said, 'Sir, I owe you an apology.' The Chairman did not look up for what seemed like forever. When he did, he had tears in his eyes. 'How could you question my authority?' he asked softly. Siddiqui explained his position. 'You are like a father to me, but how do you expect me to operate if the staff all think they can go over my head?' Rai Bahadur nodded, stood up, shook hands and the General Manager returned to his office to allow his fingernails to grow again.

After half an hour the phone rang, 'Azhar, what are you doing?' asked the familiar soft voice. 'Nothing, sir.' 'Come up for a drink.'

As it happened, Rai Bahadur gagged on a piece of the favourite chicken *tikka* he always ordered with his Scotch. He turned blue in the face, his eyes rolled up, but finally, after much thumping and coughing, the offending piece was dislodged. Mopping his face, the Chairman said, 'For God's sake, Siddiqui, you should have taken a knife and made a small cut in my throat to help me to breathe.' 'If I'd done that after what happened earlier, sir,' said a by-now totally flustered Azhar, 'no one would have believed that I was trying to save your life.'

At the annual year-end staff party, the Chairman stood up to make his usual speech, 'Friends,' he said, 'I know you have problems. Some of them I genuinely can't solve. Some of them I could, but your General Manager does not allow me to meet you.' The twinkle shone through his glasses. But Rai Bahadur made it a point to tell future supplicants that they should sort out the matter directly with their boss. Not that he would not later check with him to see what exactly he had done about the problem.

A similar situation had arisen earlier. Dieter Jansen, the Sheraton-appointed General Manager in Bombay, had sacked an employee, who, predictably, took his case to Rai Bahadur, and was, almost as predictably, reinstated. Jansen was furious at being overruled in what he considered his domain. Mohan Singh Oberoi defended his action by telling the American, 'By firing the man, you played the role of a Sessions Judge. Mr Biki Oberoi is the High Court, and I am the Supreme Court. How can I run a company where there's no court of appeal? By that same token, I don't sack anyone, because there's no one above me for the person to appeal to.' This is what has built the confidence of the staff, an avenue for redressal. And he had explained a vital aspect of policy with a very simple analogy.

Satish Kumar in Calcutta adds a caveat, 'When the Chairman says, "Look into the matter", it means the matter does need looking into. And I can be sure that his office will continue to remind me of it till it has been settled one way or the other.' He does not have to tell his staff to do so. They have been perfectly trained. Rai Bahadur says, 'If an employee has brought a case all the way up to the Chairman, it's obviously a critical matter for him. We can't ignore it.' The boss may be accessible, but he still has enough of an aura for people not to come to him with frivolous complaints.

Anil Madhok recalls the time when the Gulf had become the closest thing to El Dorado, with hotel staff joining the droves of nurses and nannies, masons and mechanics—to say nothing of mutton—that went by the Boeing-load to Muscat, Dubai, Abu Dhabi and all the tiny sheikhdoms that had struck black gold. Rai Bahadur asked him whether he had lost any of his people, to which Madhok replied, 'Just one and I'm glad we've seen the back of him. He was nothing but a troublemaker.' Rai Bahadur looked at it differently. 'You should have persuaded him to stay. When he returns on holiday, he'll tell the others how much money he's making, how many gadgets he has, how great life in the Gulf is, and they'll be tempted to leave as well. Then you'll start losing the good ones.' He added, 'The Birlas and the Modis are much bigger than me. They'd like to build hotels too. They have the money, but they don't have our kind of people. If you have this attitude, you'll give them all the staff they need.'

He understood the human imperative in many different ways. In what was still the Oberoi Intercontinental, bar sales had dropped, a fact that came at once to the notice of the Chairman through the daily revenue report submitted by each outlet. He examined every possible cause: competition, drinking trends, government regulations, purloining. None of these seemed quite the reason. Suddenly Rai Bahadur asked, 'Hasn't the barman changed?' Indeed he had. He suggested they try to get the old one back, gently pointing out the forgotten truth that a barman is not there merely to measure out the Burra peg. He is a showman, a sounding board, a sympathetic shoulder. The attracting point.

Rai Bahadur advised his Managers never to say an outright no to an employee however certain they were that they could not possibly accede to his request. 'Always allow twenty-four hours to pass. You might well change your mind. Even if you don't, the person will have the satisfaction of knowing that you've given the matter due consideration. That helps him or her take the negative answer in a better spirit.'

For industry's trail-blazers, who have worked their way up through the ranks or, at least, shoulder-to-shoulder with them, labour, trade union, industrial relations, are all terms with a special connotation. If the man at the top measures his assets not in terms of his real estate or turnover, but in terms of his people as Rai Bahadur does, he cannot go very wrong.

His legendary personal rapport was not so carefully nurtured merely because he wanted to be India's answer to Dale Carnegie; he shrewdly guessed that hoteliering was a two-way street. You treated your staff well, they treated your guests well. Working his way up from the coal cellar at Cecil, doing the rounds of the world's best hotels, conducting his one-man time-and-motion studies in every operational area, poring over guest comments, Rai Bahadur realized that, to start with, his people had to be right, chosen, trained, motivated correctly, for they could not be replaced by a robot. As he worked alongside his father and then sat in the Managing Director's chair himself, P. R. S. Oberoi, too, learnt that while the computer could remind room service that the chief buyer of the German garment house in Room 665 liked her tea light and her toast dark, it could not deliver the goods with a smile.

Which is why, first Rai Bahadur, and, now, Biki, take very seriously their place on the selection panel for the Oberoi School of Hotel Management. Which is why both have always spent fifty per cent of their energies on personnel problems. Which is why Biki tells his General Managers, 'If you're not sure of his or her suitability, don't take the person.' Or, as the old editing rule insists, 'When in doubt, leave out.' If Rai Bahadur tolerated a lot more in people than his son is willing to do, it is as much a circumstantial difference as a temperamental one. The business is far more competitive, the wage bill is higher, and labour laws are far less flexible than during the time that P.R.S. Oberoi was 'Biki-baba'.

CHAPTER XLIII

Grow Your Own: The School

Call it foresight. Call it astuteness. Or call it a very calculating move. Whichever way you assess the Oberoi School of Hotel Management, you have to give Rai Bahadur a straight A. Give it grudgingly, if you like, for it can get a bit monotonous to find the same guy as the alpha male of the hotel herd.

Mohan Singh Oberoi knew he would have to find new, modern people to suffuse with life the new, modern breed of hotels he set out to build in the 1960s. And, as with his avocados and his iceberg lettuce, he knew that there was nothing better than growing your own. *Voila l'ecole!* Not that he would have put it quite that way. Neither French nor flamboyance was his forte.

Krushandl, Bret, Steiner, Grover, Hahn, and most of all the brothers Sibilia, Chico and Italo—these were the local satraps in pin-striped trousers who governed the old hotels that Rai Bahadur annexed as he swept Shiv Nath and Spencer's off the board with the checkmate at Tara Devi. Like Alexander with Porus, he let them retain their powers. But these Continental Managers were a dying breed, a repatriating one, and there were no more from where they came.

If Mohan Singh Oberoi was like Alexander in wanting more worlds to conquer, he was also not unlike Bertie Wooster's formidable Aunt Agatha who never went round in circles, wringing her hands and saying 'What to do?'; she acted. Rai Bahadur did not and did. He began structuring in his mind the perfect Indian hotel school. He had seen how well Lausanne's classical *Ecole Hoteliere* had sharpened his son's skills. He had also found a newer role model, with its motto, 'Anything in the world you want to learn, you can learn at Cornell'.

The first Indian Oberoi General Manager, P. P. S. Lamba, speaks in reverential tones of 'Dean Meek' who inherited a piece of earth by being opportunistic. Prof. Howard B. Meek had begun the Home Economics School at Cornell, and its students ran a hotel for a day as a part of their practical training. It did not result in total chaos in the kitchens, instead, it came to be quite a coveted 'take-over'. One night, after they had done a banquet, an impressed Statler of the leading U. S. Chain of the same name turned to Prof. Meek, and, like some potentate, said, 'Name anything you want.'

Prof. Meek grabbed the chance, and told him that he wanted a modern, fully equipped building for the hotel school. And that is how, in the early Fifties, Statler Hall, with Statler Inn attached, came into existence. Later extended and equipped with state-of-the-art facilities, it is the élite international nursery of the industry. At deluxe rack rates.

Rai Bahadur had realized the need for a professionally trained managerial cadre long before he thought of organizing it himself. Just after the Second World War, in fact, and Lamba was among the first who responded to his advertisement for 'fresh university graduates from good families' who would be sent for training abroad in hotel management. Lamba's uncle was aghast at his decision. 'You've smeared the family name,' he had spluttered like a mustard seed in hot oil. 'No decent girl will marry some one who works in a *dhaba*.' His sentiments were not unlike the horrified reaction of one of Jamsetji Tata's sisters when he told the family of his decision to create the Taj Mahal Hotel: 'You are building an institute of science in Bangalore, a great iron and steel factory and a hydro-electric project—and now you tell us you are going to put up a *bhatiarkhana* (cook- house)!' Rai Bahadur got his 'young graduates', but with the free-spending soldiers having returned home, all funds had to be conserved for readjusting the business to the demands of civvy street. The candidates had to make do with training at Faletti's, Lahore, instead.

Ten years later, in 1954, Lamba got his chance, a seat at Cornell aided by a Fulbright grant. Rai Bahadur was not too enthusiastic about American expertise at the time, and offered to send him to Lausanne instead. But the young man said he had made up his mind, and was prepared to resign if it came to that. His boss not only relented, he also paid him his full salary during the three years he was away.

Having crystallized in Rai Bahadur's mind, the Oberoi School of

Management became a reality in 1966. Rai Bahadur put the Delhi Intercontinental's F & B Manager, Sven Jorgensen, in charge. The school germinated at Imperial, grew at Intercontinental and then flourished into a sprawling institution at Maidens. It soon became the conduit for all those who enter the group with their eye on the main chance. Thousands apply for the 300 seats every year, straight out of college. Besides, in Egypt, Bali, Nepal, Saudi Arabia, Sri Lanka, one of the attractions of being employed in the Oberoi hotels there is the opportunity to train at the Delhi School.

When it came into existence, there was nothing quite like it in India. The catering institutes were half-baked, denied the authentic—and demanding—environment of an actual hotel. There still isn't anything quite like it. Welcomgroup's institution in Manipal suffers the lack of an attached hotel, and while the Taj has an in-house training programme, it has no centralized, structured classroom situation.

Of course, it cuts both ways. Its school gives Oberoi a fine-tuned managerial corps, but it also provides a diploma that is a passport to instant mobility in the industry. They tell you in Egypt that the Nile Hilton and the Semiramis Sheraton will take an Oberoi-trained Manager without so much as an interview. They tell you in Bombay that if you scratch beneath the senior management cadre of any hotel chain in India, you will find Oberoi school alumni. They tell you in Delhi that the company is fighting more cases against former trainees who have left without giving the bond money, than against labour or any outside party. But it is the price the patriarch pays.

The buck starts here. Sunil Juneja, who has stepped into Sven Jorgensen's shoes, explains they are not necessarily looking for the ninety-six per cent wallahs; they want young men and women who are intelligent and flexible, with flair and a good background. Services trump business families on the logic that the product is more disciplined. This is important, for it is a profession where power and glamour beckon from every corner yet the humility of serving is the corner-stone. A series of individual interviews and group-discussions reveals how the candidates project themselves, interact, articulate their ideas, use body language. General awareness, communication skills, mathematical aptitudes, are tested. Each round produces a shortlist, till the essence is distilled. By the penultimate stage, it is fairly clear whether they have it in them or not.

The final interview is, however, not just a token exercise with a foregone conclusion. P. R. S. Oberoi heads the grilling panel which consists of Senior Executives and Board Members; Gautam Khanna and Field Marshal Sam Manekshaw are almost always present. It is from those chosen that future Senior Managers will evolve; it is on them that the future of the chain rests.

But the candidates still have a long way to go. To start with, any illusions about unalloyed glamour are quickly dispelled by the sheer physical labour that is part of the training. The potential General Manager must know what it is like for the waiter balancing a fully loaded tray, and the only way to find out is to spend a fortnight in room service actually carrying the stuff up and down. Dropped trays, and drop-outs, are both casualties. Trainees go through kitchens and stores, purchase, engineering, accounts, housekeeping, security, laundry, personnel, front office, sales and marketing; they learn the computerized systems, human behaviour, general management, travel and tourism, horticulture, even architectural appreciation and law. As in the great hoteliering courses of the world, there is no specialization. That comes later in your career, because the only way to grow in hoteliering is in all directions.

If anyone raises a whimper of protest over having to do the dirty dishes instead of savouring the delusion of lording it over as F & B Manager, the trainee is not too gently reminded that the Chairman went through all this himself. He may have had no choice, but his son and MD, certainly did, and that did not prevent him from going through the mill as well.

Today, if Biki can confidently go ahead and open a hotel as soon as he finds a location that meets his finicky demands, it is because he has the managerial potential on tap from the power-house at Maidens.

CHAPTER XLIV

Squire Midas

The loss of Hotel Imperial in 1968 had triggered many changes in the hospitality business. Hotels moved out of the grand, leisured British style of hostelry into glitzy, jet-set-go Americana typified by the Oberoi Intercontinental. The Oberoi family moved out of the only kind of home they had known, the suite. Giving the country its first international hotel had meant giving up the cosy one-to-one relationship that they had shared with their chain. Now that it had to widen its capital base and go public, East India Hotels Ltd (EIHL) could no longer be treated like a private fiefdom.

The family still held controlling interest, so no one would have stopped them from continuing to use the same address. But Rai Bahadur did not think it was right. Ishran Devi finally got a home of her own, moving, together with Tikki and Jutta, into a single-storeyed house in Friends Colony. Oberoi wanted to have his own space. Why not use the sprawl of farm-land he owned as a permanent residence?

With the kind of foresight that marked all his moves, Rai Bahadur had, way back in 1952, begun acquiring parcels of land between the sleepy villages of Bijwasan and Kapasehra, outside Delhi. The area was barren scrubland with hardly another residence in sight, not, as it now is, the fashionable retreat of the capital's big money. Rai Bahadur bought seventy acres at Rs 3,000 an acre; today its value has appreciated. Seventy-fold. His granddaughter, Kavita Mehra, recalls, as a child, 'driving for ever' from Maidens to the farm which was still nothing in the middle of nowhere. 'Big Daddy sat on a stool in the wilderness and said, "This will be the vineyard. This will be the mustard field. Here the dairy cattle will have their sheds." We thought he'd gone nuts, so impossible did it seem for such emptiness to yield the kind of vision he conjured up. But he'd divided it all in his mind, and it grew to be exactly as he'd described it.' And some more.

He planned the layout of field and orchard, the winding pathways all covered with soft grass underfoot, the tree-lined avenues stretching to infinity.

Rai Bahadur came alone to live among the settees, dining suite, wardrobes and beds made redundant by some new renovation decree in one or the other of his hotels. On the wall, a clock wrested from Imperial; in the grounds a deer park filled with the *habitués* of the miniature zoo that he had created in the grounds of that same colonnaded mansion. The group's Vice-President, Housekeeping, Krishna Singh, would drop in regularly, and help him extend the sheds into comfortable living quarters.

If Biki's farmhouse across the hedge does not look like a converted barn, it is because it is not one. Its sleek lines of marble and glass, its rose-petalled moat of running water, its oriental art, its mahogany toilet seats, reflect the luxury that he has made his insignia. The pale Great Danes come bounding up, as high as heifers. In their paddock, his rippling horses stomp and chomp.

Initially, Rai Bahadur ran his farm and hotels in tandem, and the man flinging his empire across the oceans still had time to tend his broccoli. In later years the farm would be all. He would still know exactly what was happening in each one of his hotels, keeping abreast, even in his nineties, through his three pulse points—occupancy rates, restaurant business statements and guest comments, all submitted daily—but the farm would be his new tightly-controlled domain.

The oregano would flavour the hotels' kitchens. The gladioli brighten their rooms and lobbies. The eggs fulfil their promise on the menu of being farm-fresh. The ninety-seven acres, thanks to Squire Oberoi, have now become big business. The methodology that made him a personnel legend was put into practice here as well. The eagle eye that once knew which supplier needed to get his scales changed, would later keep track of how many kilos of Chinese lettuce went to each of the hotels; a notation in a nonagenarian's spidery scrawl on the margin of the 'fruit book' would demand to know why there was a discrepancy in the rates for grapefruit charged to the Grand and to the Oberoi, Delhi?

At ninety-one, Rai Bahadur closely monitors the dairy cattle. Roopwati, Reshma, Ganga, Munni—thirty-nine Hereford, Jersey and

Haryana milch cows twitch their tails in the sheds just beyond the farmhouse. Locked canisters of rich, creamy milk go each day to family members, who have all been given individual keys. When Jutta is away in England, the milk is still delivered to the Friends Colony house for Tikki's retainer, Trilok, Ishran Devi's driver, Shiv Singh, who now comes in every day to recite the prayers, and all the other servants; also for Salim, the sleek Saluki, who lies on his dead master Tikki's favourite Persian rug with an hauteur befitting the oldest domesticated canine breed in the world. 'Sweet milk'-whole for desserts—is sent along with skimmed to the hotels. The ledgers bear neat entries. The spidery hand queries: 'Gauri was covered on 29.1.91 so why again on 9.3.91? Confirm if conceived or not.' The cows are all artificially inseminated.

The eye on the bottom-line is as sharp. The costs are still counted. The electricity bill on the farm had gone out of hand; the calculating mind had not rusted; he brought consumption down by thirty per cent.

The acres sprawl, dapple, turn green and gold. The air is heavy with the scent of roses and the smell of dung. Geese honk and rabbits tumble towards the wire-netting to pull the tender blades of grass that are proffered by a podgy hand. The dragonflies eddy like dry leaves whipped up by a storm. A partridge nests in a pear tree. Peacocks sweep the dust, a *koel* calls yearningly from the depths of the mango, and the ethereal eucalyptus shimmers. Under an umbrella held aloft by the smart and sprightly young Chander Kumar, another of the Pahari staff, Rai Bahadur completes his walk round the farm. The stride has slowed to a shuffle, but he still feels monarch of all he surveys.

CHAPTER XLV

Another Brand of Power

His business brought him in touch with a lot of politicians, but that was no reason why he should make politics his business. Yet, Rai Bahadur Mohan Singh Oberoi decided to dabble in it. It was not too long or too serious a flirtation. Rai Bahadur was not stirred by ideology. He got into politics simply because he thought someone had to present the case for hotels. And, arguably, what was good for hotels, was good for him.

Although an admirer of the Nehrus, he stood as an independent, contesting his first seat in Delhi's municipal body in 1952. Four years later, his friends, notably the Raja of Ramgarh and Jaipal Singh, MP, convinced him that he should be in national politics. He stood from remote Giridh in Bihar, the suave, urbane Punjabi hotelier on the unlikely platform of the tribal Jharkhand Party. This was the newly-formed political unit of the Chhotanagpur Adivasi Mahasabha, established by Jaipal Singh, way back in 1939, to fight for a separate ethnic state. Rai Bahadur lost, but by a scant 3,000 votes despite being a total newcomer to both the game and the region. The victor was the doughty Congressman, Prabhu Dayal Himatsingka, who owned much of the forest land in the area. In 1962, Jaipal Singh helped the hotelier get into the Rajya Sabha from Bihar.

Having established his political credentials, in 1968, he won a seat in the Lok Sabha from the same state, this time with a more- than-respectable margin of 45,000 votes. He contested on the ticket of the Raja of Ramgarh's old Janata Party, and won with not a little help from Mahamaya Prasad Sinha, the dissident leader who had formed Bihar's first United Front ministry the previous year. Rai Bahadur returned the favour by contributing handsomely to Sinha's campaign. The 1970 election results did not favour him, but he was back in the Rajya Sabha again in 1972, from Uttar Pradesh, this time courtesy the

Bharatiya Kranti Dal (BKD) of that wily political war-horse, Chaudhary Charan Singh.

It was during this tenure that he made his presence felt. He fought to get for hoteliering the status—and concessions—of an industry. He had the entire Opposition galvanizing itself following his outburst against the government's proposal to bring in Hilton and give the American hotelier a colossal thirty-three-and-one-third gross operating profit. He called it an anti-country deal. If this also happened to be an anti-Oberoi deal, the next time he raised a furore—and a much bigger one—it had nothing to do with hoteliering. By now, Mohan Singh was no longer a greenhorn backbencher; he was National Treasurer of the BKD. However, when Charan Singh began merger talks with six other parties to form the Bharatiya Lok Dal, creating the first serious challenge to the Congress juggernaut, seven prominent members of the BKD rebelled, among them, Oberoi and the Party General Secretary, Shyamlal Yadav.

Both sides traded anti-party charges. The dissidents rattled their sabres, warning that, being part of the national executive, they would dismiss the Chaudhary, and install Rai Bahadur in his place. But Charan Singh was a far more seasoned politician, and, to no one's surprise, succeeded in turning the tables on his truculent office-bearers, expelling Messrs. Oberoi and Yadav instead in 1974.

The following year, in 1975, Indira Gandhi declared her infamous Emergency. It did not make Mohan Singh Oberoi abandon his personal loyalty to her, but he decided that politics and hoteliering were equally jealous mistresses, and there was no doubt in his mind over who had the greater hold on him. He had, however, quite enjoyed the political interlude. Enjoyed prestige of a different kind from that attached to brand leadership. Besides, the novelty of the election trail had quite exhilarated him: the gut interaction at rallies, pitching tents for the night, dusty jeep rides across the countryside, and the return to an India very far removed from the one he now moved in. He mingled uninhibitedly with the peasant crowd, and it was not the first or the last time that his companions would notice that he was still, at heart, the boy from Bhaun.

In fact he was so unassuming that, in some remote hamlets, it was Tikki's imposing bearer, in his grand livery, who was sometimes mistaken for the candidate, often because, he, too, was called Mohan Singh. Ishran Devi had dubbed him 'Hanuman', partly because he bore her husband's name, which, as a traditional wife, she could not take; partly because he had the organizational abilities of the monkey-god, who had mustered the simian army in support of Lord Rama.

Rai Bahadur's valet, Muniruddin, presents a cameo from the Bihar campaign. They had been attending meetings in and around Hazaribagh together with the Raja of Ramgarh, and had not eaten a thing all day. However, no dinner arrangements were made since, according to the original schedule, they should have left by evening. Oberoi got into his car, and told the driver to head back to Calcutta.

On the way, he asked Munir and the driver to eat at a *dhaba*, and said he would have his 'nightcap'. While the two went off, the boss spied a small teashop with his favourite *pakoras*. Even though these were the last of the day and rather sad looking, he asked the stall-owner to heat them. Munir came panting up, and the shopkeeper did a double-take on seeing the impressive uniform. As Rai Bahadur walked back to the car, the Bihari could not contain his curiosity. Munir told him, 'You may not believe it, but this gentleman who so humbly asked you for your stale *pakoras* is none other than Oberoi Saheb.'

Word of five-star splendour had accompanied the candidate to the inner reaches of Bihar, and the shopkeeper ran up to Rai Bahadur, touched his feet and said, 'It is my *kismet* that your footsteps graced my shop. If you give me your blessings, some day my little *hotul* will become a big one like yours.'

If anyone in the family could have made a political career it was Tikki. And if his father's forays into the arena had not inhibited the son from doing likewise, perhaps Tikki would have found his vocation. Tikki loved the power, the risks, the cutting edge of playing king-maker. He was close to all the leaders of Kashmir, most of all the highly influential D.P. Dhar. State Cabinets were made and unmade in young Oberoi's lavish cottage in Srinagar. Politics was his favourite subject of conversation, especially in later years, and if hotels were his brother Biki's passion, Tikki was very happy to say that politics was his. Tikki's second wife, Jutta, used to get extremely worked up seeing, 'half a million people on our lawn,' but her mother-in- law, who lived with them in the Friends Colony house, the ever-practical Ishran Devi, would just laugh and say, 'Take it in your stride, *beti*. See, doesn't Tikki look like Ali Baba surrounded by the forty thieves?'

CHAPTER XLVI

Getting 'Jeh'

Rai Bahadur Mohan Singh Oberoi did not need Rabbi Ben Ezra a.k.a. Robert Browning, to tell him 'Grow old along with me' / The best is yet to be / The last of life/ For which the first was made.... ' To begin with, who was growing old? He was only growing empire. And, till the Seventies, there were no rumblings of rival dynasties rattling their sabres.

The old hotels that had jousted with him for the custom of Calcutta's beautiful people had all gone, gone to seed, every one. In Delhi, the new ones were still to cast themselves into chains. The Taj Mahal Hotel stood in splendid isolation till 1971, when, for the first time, the group ventured out of Bombay to Udaipur's Lake Palace Hotel. Its pioneer status, and its grandeur, placed Bombay's Taj in a class of one, but it was the Oberois who had the chain, even if Partition had dismantled four of its links, and litigation the fifth and finest of the old Associated Hotels of India (AHI) legacy, the Imperial.

For Mohan Singh Oberoi the chronological watershed of seventy-five marked the last hurrah of his old rival and the first stirrings of competition. Shiv Nath Singh materialized again from the shambles of his Spence's Hotel, to meet his classical adversary in a final battle of nerves. He had heard about Hotel Fonseca, a small boarding-house being run as 'evacuee' property on the capital's Man Singh Road. The New Delhi Municipal Corporation (NDMC) had sued the proprietor for retrieval of the property; Fonseca defended his rights through the lower courts, but a later judgement had ordered him out.

Shiv Nath was as adept as his friend in spotting the potential of real estate. Together with his son-in-law, he bought over the hotel but, to circumvent legal hurdles, retained the name of Fonseca Pvt Ltd and kept the original owner as 'a one rupee partner'. 'The government is my headache,' he told the hapless Goan. Shiv Nath had not been fighting cases all his life for nothing; he managed to get a favourable judgement on the grounds that a running business could not be shut down in so peremptory a fashion. Then he went to Rai Bahadur with an offer.

Mohan Singh and Shiv Nath had remained good friends, meeting over a drink and chicken *tikka* in Delhi and Calcutta even when they were clashing in court, sharing memories and creating new ones. Rai Bahadur was keen to hear about all his Calcutta connections and there was no better raconteur than Shiv Nath to bring him up to date on the gossip as they supped. This time, Shiv Nath offered him the Fonseca property for twenty lakh rupees. Before he could decide, the NDMC took its case to the Supreme Court. And Shiv Nath, being Shiv Nath, without so much as a 'May I?' decided to shift his offer to the opposite camp. He knew the Taj would pay anything to get a foothold in Delhi. It did.

This was 1976, and the heyday of Sanjay Gandhi. Siding with the NDMC he sent in a van full of policemen to stop construction. Ajit Kerkar, who had turned the Taj around and set it on its new conquering course, asked Sanjay why he should have any objection to the Taj coming to Delhi, and Sanjay admitted that the order had been a mistake. He gave clearance, allowing them to continue building on the disputed property. The Taj Mahal Hotel on Man Singh Road was completed in 1978, but the ownership of the land still vests with the NDMC.

Shiv Nath Singh was out of the picture, out of Rai Bahadur's life forever, but, in retreat, he had lobbed a far more serious competitor, the Taj group. His malevolent laughter rang through the exit door.

Were he given to philosophical soliloquy, Rai Bahadur might have pondered over 'ingratitude more strong than traitors' arms.' Although he had never been in the Congress party, he was an unwavering admirer of Indira Gandhi. He had never once opposed her during his years in Parliament; he had acceded to her requests to return from his travels abroad to vote in favour of crucial motions; made changes in his own political affiliations to suit her strategy; never spoken against the draconian measures of the Emergency.

But Rai Bahadur knew he could not hold back the tide, and reckoned there was room enough for two in Delhi. As it would happen, the Asian Games in 1982 would throw open the flood gates and one chain after another would make it to the capital to nibble at the Oberoi-Taj hotel cake.

Several would jump on to the gravy train of Indian hoteliering, Intercontinental and Sheraton, Hyatt and Holiday Inn. Welcomgroup would open its arms wide; once, in Agra, it would take the Oberois into its embrace, draw on their expertise, and then jilt them at the eleventh hour. But Shiv Nath Singh's Delhi nominee would remain the only real rival.

Neither, naturally, admits to co-opting the dirty tricks department to keep the other out of its own established territory, and, to be fair, neither accuses the other of doing so either. Hoteliers, of course, are better placed than others to get the wheels of bureaucracy to move faster or slow down so excruciatingly that the other party gives up in sheer boredom. The only disadvantage is that rival groups have equal opportunity for wining, dining and general softening up. Covertly, subtly, indirectly, the tussle continues, for a new kid on the block can play havoc with occupancy figures.

For years, the Oberois could not get land in Taj city, Bombay; the same happened to the Taj in Grand city, Calcutta. The Oberois are just about establishing a presence in tourism's honey-pot, Rajasthan, where the princely rule has been that of the Taj, in the former palaces of Jaipur and Udaipur. All that remained was the signature on the dotted line for the Oberois to take over the Khasa Kothi Hotel from the Rajasthan Tourism Development Corporation (RTDC) when the employees' union brought an injunction on the grounds that private management might jeopardize their government jobs.

Coincidentally, in Calcutta, a union worked against the construction of the Taj, zoo workers claiming that the proposed hotel across the road would jeopardize the flight path of the real birds of passage that alighted by the thousand on Alipore zoo's lake.

Ironically, in Rajasthan, the prized Rambagh Palace Hotel, slipped out of the Oberoi group's hands not once, but twice. Sawai Man Singh II, 'Jai', had quietly entered into a deal with his chukker chum, Tikki Oberoi, to convert Jaipur's Rambagh Palace into a hotel. Perhaps one should hear the story straight from the thorough-bred's mouth. In *A Princess Remembers*, Gayatri Devi, the former Maharani of Jaipur, tells it:

> During the Delhi polo season that winter, Bubbles (their son) and I went to a lunch party given by the Oberois,

India's biggest hoteliers, and overheard talk of plans to convert Rambagh into a hotel. Neither Bubbles nor I had heard anything about this cataclysmic project before, and after quickly consulting each other, we excused ourselves and rushed back to tackle Jai with the news. We poured out the story to him certain that it must be only some ridiculous rumour which he would soon dispel. Instead he simply smiled. I knew that smile. It meant the story was true, that he knew all about it. He had not wanted to tell us before everything was settled. He was afraid that we would be upset.

Upset! we were speechless. Jai patiently went on explaining to us that times had changed and that it was no longer possible to keep Rambagh in the way it had always been, and deserved to be, maintained. He also felt that now he was no longer Rajpramukh. . . it was unnecessary for us to live in our previous style. If Rambagh was to be kept up in a proper way, it would have to be given up for a public cause. Jaipur badly needed a good hotel . . . .Other Maharajas were critical of Jai when they heard of the project. It seemed like such a concrete symbol of our vanishing way of life. Jai was the first of the princes to turn his palace into a hotel, but after a few years, others followed his example.

Biki fills in the inconclusive conclusion. The arrangement was that the royal family would retain only the private furniture and fittings while the whole palace and the rest of its contents would be made over to the Oberoi chain. However, they got to hear that truckloads of stuff were being carted away. Rai Bahadur confronted Jai; the Maharajah merely smiled. There was no more deal. Jai went it alone in the setting up and management of the Rambagh Palace Hotel in 1957.

Some years after the Maharajah's death, his son, Bubbles, mentioned to his good friend, Biki, that the hotel was losing money, and asked what he should do. Rather than jumping up with an exultant, 'We would love to take it over,' Biki, ever the correct gentleman, said, 'Get a professional group.' Bubbles mistook circumspection for refusal, and negotiated with the Indian Hotels Company, which naturally grabbed the opportunity and its management in 1972.

Rai Bahadur, however, consistently maintains admiration for the Taj, and personally for J.R.D. Tata. He never fails to greet him on his birthday or on every occasion on which the doyen of Indian industry figures in the news. For his part, J.R.D. will tell you, 'Even if the Taj Group is now bigger, Rai Bahadur is, without doubt, the father figure of Indian hoteliering in India and abroad.' He admits that he has 'the highest regard for him—I've known him some forty or fifty years—and I've been impressed by the standard of style, food and staff training in the Oberoi hotels I've visited. His achievement is all the more remarkable considering that he wasn't born with a silver spoon, that he reached the top entirely on his own.' The elegantly gaunt 'Jeh' presses his long fingers together, and willingly concedes that though he himself 'took close personal interest in the Taj as soon as (he) entered the business, till the Seventies hoteliering was only a diversion for the Tatas. Mohan Singh, on the other hand, knew right from the start that this was his *métier* and never digressed from it. Yes, you could call Rai Bahadur the country's only exclusive hotelier.'

Their correspondence has the ring of friendly banter. When J.R.D. wrote to congratulate him on his ninetieth birthday, saying, 'Now in my eighty-seventh year, you have my dear Rai Bahadur, again kept ahead of me by reaching ninety before me,' Oberoi wrote back, 'the fact remains you are much ahead of me. I was only three years old when Sir Jamsetji Tata built the Taj in 1903. (It is the head which wears the crown.)' At their standing and stage in life, one can hardly call them rivals.

The two groups, however, continue to make move and counter-move, continue to be quite obsessed about each other. The latest overlap is in Simla, Oberoi's 'home ground' where the Taj has been trying for several years to take over the magnificent and historic Viceregal Lodge, now occupied by the unglamorous School of Advanced Study. The Indian National Trust for Art and Cultural Heritage (INTACH) the 'heritage-*wallahs*', have consistently opposed the proposal. To the argument that the government cannot afford the upkeep of such a place, they have replied, quite logically, in that case, all Raj Bhavans should be turned over to hoteliers.

Many decades ago, an editor of *The Statesman* had pronounced, 'We have no competitors, only contemporaries.' Minus the pomposity, this quite sums up the position of the two Indian giants *vis-*

á-vis each other. Rai Bahadur has always insisted on owning his hotels rather than taking them on lease, in India at least, and Biki's policy is to seize the competitive edge on quality and not bother about number; at present, the Taj group has forty-three hotels and the Oberoi chain has thirty hotels.

When the Taj came to Calcutta, Rai Bahadur welcomed it: 'Competition keeps everyone on its toes,' he said, 'and the beneficiary is the industry.' Does the bottom-line fall with the monopoly? The senior Oberoi spreads out his patented philosophy.

'I never worry, it clutters the brain. Room occupancy may not fall, and then the tension will have been unnecessary. If it does, worrying will only come in the way of a clear-headed solution.'

CHAPTER XLVII

Curry Cook, Go Home

The Oberoi Windsor is reputed to have the most magnificent dining room in all Australia. What better contribution to a continent discovered by a Captain Cook? But things were not always this way. When the chain came on the scene 'cook' was, in fact, bandied about more than 'chef'. Eyebrows shot up in shock over the prospect of Victorian balustrades draped in saris. And nostrils flared in outrage over white Australian heritage going under a greasy tidal wave of curry.

No, sirree, the news of some swarthy swagman putting the Windsor in his tucker bag was not greeted with hearty shouts of 'Good on you, myte!' And Matilda certainly wasn't going to come a- waltzing with him.

Actually, the Oberoi juggernaut had first anchored beside the Australian billabong in Adelaide. Rai Bahadur had arrived on the antipodal continent as part of a parliamentary delegation, and realized that he did not have to emigrate to the place, as so many of his Anglo-Indian staff had done, to make it the land of opportunity. Said opportunity was right there at the reception desk where he checked in.

The Australia, as the hotel was then called, was in a mess. The phones did not work, it was not just the garden that was seedy, and the staff had neither enthusiasm nor uniforms. You did not have to pry into its account books to know that it was losing money. As is rather apparent by now, entrepreneurs are a little like lawyers and reporters; they thrive on other people's crises. 'Ambulance-chasers' is the evocative Americanism for this non-medical syndrome.

A financing consortium was formed to raise the three million Australian dollars needed to buy the hotel. Tamimi & Fouad, whose half-built property Ratan Tata had initially turned up his nose at in

Dammam, put A\$ 75,000 in the kitty; Oberoi hotels (Australia) matched this amount with an officially cleared remittance from India; Australian banks gave a loan for the balance with, as usual, the property as collateral. As *Newsweek* put it, Rai Bahadur, 'checked into his fourth continent'.

Always placing business first, he asked Krishna Singh to go over Down Under for a year to sort out what had been rechristened the Oberoi Adelaide. She was by now Vice-President, Housekeeping. Udaipur's once-purdahed daughter worked with the interior decorator who had come over from Singapore for the assignment, trained the staff, and put the Oberoi manuals on housekeeping, room service and public areas into practice.

Rai Bahadur visited occasionally. Small-town Adelaide loved their exotic celebrity, not that there was anything ethnic about this Westernized oriental gentleman, complete with felt hat and suspenders. Media coverage of the Indian 'doctor' who had saved the life of the city's largest hotel resulted in people recognizing him in the street, and stopping to shake his hand, though the Press did not know quite what to make of the man in the impeccable grey suit.

One evening a man came up to him in the lobby and said, 'You are Oberoi, aren't you? I've had a bet with my buddies that I'll get you over to the bar for a round of drinks. Come along, myte. Don't be bloody stuffy.' The bar was a rumbustious one, somewhat out of keeping with the staidness of the hotel, but Rai Bahadur did not need much persuasion. One round led to another and the camaraderie spilled over. Krishna Singh was somewhat alarmed when Rai Bahadur did not emerge for quite some time. All she could see through the glass door were a lot of very beefy Aussies having a very Australian good time, and no sign of the diminutive boss. Finally, she sent in an Assistant Manager to 'rescue' him. Quite unnecessary, he told her later.

The Oberoi Adelaide introduced the Sunday brunch, made classier with champagne. Whenever he was in town, Rai Bahadur presided over it, enjoying himself immensely, playing master of ceremonies, and subtly using it as a great business opportunity. But Adelaide was small beer. Rai Bahadur needed something closer to the style he had got his guests elsewhere accustomed to. Which was why father and son booked a flight to Melbourne.

Rai Bahadur and Biki were on one of their periodic trips to

Adelaide when Oberoi *pére* spotted an advertisement in the morning paper. The State of Victoria invited tenders for the management of The Windsor. The item pumped up the adrenalin as thumpingly as when Shiv Nath Singh had mentioned the name of the hotel on the Lahore-Calcutta Mail. The Windsor was of the same magnificent mould, of the same historical significance as the Grand. Indeed, the Australian dowager had, to start with, been called the Grand Hotel. Nomenclature was not very original in those days. The Windsor, with its vast Victorian facade, also stretched down an entire block of the city's most powerful avenues. Across the road was Parliament House, the natural vista was that of the Treasury Gardens. It was the most luxurious accommodation in the country. No wonder it was deferred to as the 'Duchess of Spring Street'.

Melbourne was not Botany Bay. Its first settlers were not those shipped out to make room in England's Dickensian prisons. They were adventurers and entrepreneurs who had been attracted, like John Company's agents earlier in another country, by the latest line in pagoda trees. The one they came to shake in Australia literally rained gold. The world's largest island and smallest continent was found to have the precious metal coursing through its veins. Melbourne had been established in 1835, and, like Adelaide, refused to accept convicts right from the start. Its streets were soon filled with fortune hunters, its population increasing by 2,000 every week in the 1850s. Having struck a gold mine, and then striking it rich in ancillary ways, its citizens proceeded to embellish their city with buildings that reflected their status, the architecture, like the name of their state, drawing inspiration from Queen Victoria back home.

The Windsor was one of these mansions, begun in 1883 by the Onassis of his times, George Nipper, and designed by the celebrated British architect, Charles Webb, as a monument to the colonial spirit, as solid as it was soaring. But it passed out of the hands of the shipping tycoon even before it was ready, not that this loosened its moorings in history.

James Munro, helped along by his partner, the parliamentarian James Balfour, completed it in 1888. With changing times, Munro became the leader of the Temperance Party in Parliament, and the hotel became the swankiest of Melbourne's newly voguish 'coffee places'. At a ceremony, Munro, with a great flourish, pulled its liquor licence from his breast pocket, and like a *flambéd crepe suzette,* set it alight, announcing, 'Well, gentlemen, this is what we think of the licence.' The Grand got its present name—and a new liquor permit—when a company headed by Lieutenant-General Sir John Monash bought it in the 1920s, spending over A$ 200,000 on renovation.

The aura of its celebrity guests—including personages no less than George V, and his son, Prince Edward—continued to rub off on the hotel. It would be appropriately schmaltzy to believe that the Grand changed its name to The Windsor because Australia was captivated by the idea of a man spurning the throne for The Woman He Loved, but there is the minor inconvenience of dates. In 1920, when the hotel decided to change its registration, King George was still very much around. Edward was still to ascend the throne, let alone abdicate and be given this duchy as some sort of consolation. But The Windsor did typify, even if it pre-empted, the kind of romantic style associated with the debonair Prince.

The starry-voiced Maurice Chevalier and the swashbuckling Douglas Fairbanks must have felt quite at home here when they visited, and even the Australian Prime Minister, George Menzies, spurning stuffy state accommodation, preferred to keep a permanent suite at The Windsor.

But the lesson of Ozymandias was as applicable in Australia as in Egypt. The arrogance of power gave way to the bathos of decay, and The Windsor's owners decided, in 1976, that they could not support such an expensive white elephant any longer, and that a large, lucrative office block in its place would do nicely, thank you. A hundred-year-old building in hoarier civilizations may fall without a murmur, but in a settlement that only went back to 1770 and in a city that had been around for just over 140 years, institutions such as The Windsor were precious relics and 'ancient' history. God bless the vigilant Press; a campaign was launched to save the hotel. The government was forced to intervene and take over.

However, it did not make much sense to do so, and then let it continue on its crumbling path to ruin. The Victoria government certainly did not have the money needed to restore The Windsor. It would have to lease it out to someone who did. Therefore the advertisement that set Rai Bahadur's eighty-year-old-heart a-flutter. Again, his was the highest bid among the forty-odd tenders. And that is when Matilda turned up her pert nose, and refused to go a-waltzing with him.

CHAPTER XLVIII

Rhapsody And Waltz

Rai Bahadur may have won the bid, but the reaction to this could hardly be described as tender. When it came to light that The Windsor had been leased for two years, with an option on another twenty, to an Indian, Australia's worst racism surfaced. The Press screamed even louder than it had over the decision to pull down the hotel. What was the point in the government saving the country's heritage, it cried, if it was going to sell it down the Murray Darling River?

The yellower among the papers even stooped as low as publishing a photograph of the bathroom in Biki's stylish Delhi farmhouse, with the caption, 'Marble and gold bathrooms, but do they know how to use them?' Fanning the flames of xenophobia was the thought of the Arab sheikhs, Tamimi & Fouad, in the background, rattling bags of petrogold.

Processionists took to the streets, bearing fiery placards saying, 'No Curry and Rice Houses in Melbourne'. The Oberoi staff was equally outraged over the virulence, and wanted to write letters to editors highlighting the chain's record in elegance, its pioneering of classiness. But Rai Bahadur asked them to ignore the criticism. 'When they see what we make of The Windsor, the carping will automatically stop.' The matter even rocked Parliament, but Victoria's premier, John Cain, was able to stand his ground.

The government knew that it would not find too many entrepreneurs intrepid enough to accept the long list of conditions that came along with the lease. Included on the Historic Buildings Register, The Windsor's old-world grandeur was also the greatest impediment to renovation. No changes were permitted that would alter its Victorian character, and not many would be willing to pump so much money into a project with do-gooders constantly breathing down their necks.

However, when Rai Bahadur sealed his tender, and agreed to toe the official line, it was not merely to make an egotistic point about what the Oberoi group could do. 'I knew a time would come when the discerning traveller would begin to reject the shoe-boxes with wedding-cake icing, and be willing to pay more than a little extra for hotels of history and character. So, for the present, it was important to give them back their past, whatever the effort, whatever the cost.' The obsession with magnificence had a very practical base.

For all the brouhaha, the shambles that The Windsor was in did not speak very much for its heritage. There was a 'junk shop' in the lobby, and a kiosk selling cigarettes and sweets as though at a railway station. If the light domes had not been boarded up, rain would have come in through the cracks; the carpets in many places were literally hanging together by a thread.

Rai Bahadur did not hold its present state of *déshabillé* against the hotel. This was the fourth time that he had seen a grande dame pitiably clutching on to a tattered gentility. He had given back the other three their pristine dignity. Now, on this young island continent, he started on a restoration project even more ambitious than the one he had undertaken in the timeless shadow of the pyramids.

It was Australian heritage that he had set out to restore, and he decided from the start that this meant nothing Indian, not one bronze Nataraja in a niche, not one curry on the menu, however universally popular both had become. For all the supreme indifference he had asked his staff to adopt, the criticism must have influenced this decision. Somewhere in the subconscious layers of his mind, a bruised pride was determined to prove its credentials with a vengeance.

Rai Bahadur and Biki began discussions with the government, the National Trust of Australia, historical groups, experts in Victoriana. The old mistress of Spring Street was lavished with more painstaking attention than a priceless Old Master. A team of architects and restoration consultants formed the task force, the former headed by Peter Lovell, the latter by Suzie Forge. They went over the sprawling property inch by inch. Lovell told Rai Bahadur that it was going to be very expensive, perhaps as much as two million pounds. The hotelier merely smiled and said, 'Go ahead.' The architect recalls that he kept smiling even when, in the four years that the project stretched into, costs spiralled to A$ 18 million.

It is easy to see why they did. A hunt was launched for every bit of memorabilia, every scrap of memory. A Melbourne resident volunteered the information that her grandmother celebrated her wedding anniversary at The Windsor and she remembered her saying that she 'flopped with relief into one of the large leather armchairs after the last guest had gone'. So leather armchairs it had to be. Antiquarian books were pored over, old records tracked down. The prize find was the diary of the original architect, Charles Webb, buried under a mound of crumbling documents in the library of the city's La Trobe University. To its notations, the restorers tacked on the personal recollections of all those who had had any connection with the hotel.

Hi-tech combined with the treasures from the attic: a computer determined the size and height of the chandeliers, matched the porcelain door handles, determined which wood grain would come closest to the original, coded the pattern of the old carpets so that weavers could replicate them to the last knot.

Lovell, on the explicit instructions of the man who never cut corners, worked with the care and exactitude of an archaeologist. In some areas, there were as many as twelve colour combinations between floor and ceiling. And in its hundred years, the building had been repainted several times. Scraping away layers, sometimes as many as ten, Lovell revealed the old tints and combinations. He traced the stencils used for the original etchings. When they took up the carpets they discovered exquisite tiling, alas a lot of it chipped. Webb's diary provided the name of the manufacturer—in Britain's pottery belt, Stoke-on-Trent. Messengers were dispatched with samples and instructions to get them to re-create the designs, whatever the price.

The staircase got back its magnificent sweep, complete with its frieze, timber balustrade and bronze lamps now burnished to flame. The intricate columns shown in Webb's diaries were missing. On Rai Bahadur's instructions, Lovell and Forge recreated them in their nineteenth-century technicolour dream-coat of buff, copper, blue and gilt. The Cricketer's Bar, naturally an institution in Australia, was virtually in Ashes; the wood panelling, the dark green wallpaper, were put back, and old cricketing prints coaxed out of collectors.

Rai Bahadur then turned his attention to the hotel's grandest feature, its dining-room. Lovell recreated its exquisitely ornamented ceiling and the eight enormous domed lights made of stained glass set in steel frames. The missing one was reconstructed using the intact ones as models. Bits of glass found in the attic were taken to a manufacturer in Melbourne who experimented for weeks to get a panel identical to the ones still in place. Photographs showed that there had been two black marble fireplaces in the grand dining-room. A country-wide search was launched for two identical pieces. They were found.

The architect discovered that the gold leaf used on the decorative rosettes was pure twenty-four carat, not surprising, considering that the original owner's fortune had been built on Melbourne's gold rush. He asked Rai Bahadur what he should use for the missing patches. 'The same as the original, of course,' was the unhesitating reply from the man who had started life as the son of an impoverished village widow. But, in all the enthusiasm to bring back nineteenth-century splendour, they did not forget to work in twenty-first century facilities.

Biki's critical eye surveyed every detail. When he was satisfied, in 1980, the national treasure was unveiled. The country's Press was invited for a preview. The gasp was now one of awe. Actually it was a stunned silence; reporters, photographers, TV crew wandering over the hotel were struck dumb by what the 'curry-cook' had achieved. The headline in the *Adelaide Observer* the next morning summed up the general opinion: 'The Windsor Jewel in the Oberoi Crown'; and Sydney's *National Times* honoured the herculean labour with an editorial. It wrote, 'The hotel Windsor has been done up. . . not just a cheap face-lift but transformed into what it once was . . . a national treasure.' *The Age* gushed, 'Windsor Dream Realized by a Tycoon with 300 cents', a reference to the salary that Mohan Singh had started on, way back in Simla.

At the banquet that evening, Australia's movers and shakers were equally moved by what a hotelier from India had done for them. Done it when he did not even own the place; that would come ten years later, when Oberoi hotels and their financing partners, Tamimi & Fouad would buy the Windsor freehold from the Victoria government for A$ 17.7 million, with willing help from local banks.

Matilda was quite breathless from the waltz.

It was as energetic a dance in Budapest. The Hungarians could have saved themselves a lot of heartburn and media protest had the Australians told them that their national heritage was in safe hands. In 1987, finicky Biki finally spotted a European property that measured up to his standards. The only problem was that it happened to be the headquarters of the secret police. But Sati Lamba, the Indian ambassador, was convinced that an Oberoi hotel would work wonders for Indo-Hungarian ties. He helped the breakthrough with Hungar Hotels for the turn-of-the-century, palatial Gresham Insurance Company building. East Europe had just begun to taste the pleasures of privatization, but the third party, a Swedish financing group did not bite. In the meanwhile, Budapest got a new municipal government which, like all new brooms, swept out pending deals. The determined Sati Lamba too had been replaced, but he passed on both his conviction and his perseverance to his successor, Mr Malik. After two-and-a-half years of the shuttling pendulum, the agreement for the Oberoi Gresham Palace was signed in 1991.

There had been as much brouhaha in the Press as there had been in Australia, over the 'sell-out' of history, however dilapidated its present condition. Once again the assurances, once again the opus of restoration, with an investment that is perhaps the highest of any Indian group in newly emergent, still-dicey, Eastern Europe.

When the Gresham Palace is completed, the Hungarians should be in as much of a rhapsody as a waltzing Matilda.

CHAPTER XLIX

Goodbye, Bhagwanti

Nearly four decades earlier, the redoubtable Bhagwanti Oberoi had passed away in 1945, in Calcutta. Mohan Singh, caught up in the tumultuous events of those cathartic years, still found time to mourn. He had never known loss and its first experience was that of what he held most precious. The mother who had been the overwhelming influence of his childhood and youth; the dominant woman who, refusing to wallow in the martyrdom of widowhood, had seized control of her own life, and shaped it with a strength that would later empower her son.

To her he owed everything. His indulgences and his discipline, his values, even his share capital. Bhagwanti, the bold, who kept a beady eye on his hotels in his absence, took on the Simla bureaucracy undeterred by her lack of English, always travelled unaccompanied from Bhaun to Calcutta, changing several trains and carrying her valuables in the secret pockets of the vest she wore under her *kameez*. Bhagwanti, the generous, who always had some money tied up in the end of her *dupatta* to give to someone whose needs could not wait. Bhagwanti, the mother, who lavished goodies on her son and grandchildren, sending parcels of her celebrated *matthi* and *laddoos* to Simla and even as far afield as Calcutta to which city she moved later in her life. Mohan Singh cremated her there. But not all the money he had made in the war, not all the luxury he now offered to his guests, could help him blunt the squalor that attended her corpse's final hours.

Calcutta's infamous Nimtollah burning ghat which had deprived his mother's death of its dignity, jarred on the solemnity of the last rites, intruded on the family's grief. Mohan Singh had hated the sordid, soulless surroundings of his beloved mother's exit from this world. The sluggish brown glide of stench of a polluted Hooghly. The irreverent cacophony of mundane details to be sorted out between petty officials and lowly orderlies who were rapacious or sullen and more likely both. The baying mongrels, the beggars no better off. The pervading ugliness. And, most of all, the queue of bodies lined up for their turn to burn into the great beyond.

He returned home determined that when the time came to mourn his passing, his family would not have to have their sorrow aggravated by such undignified delays. The idea grew in strength each time he came back from a funeral at Delhi's equally heartless Nigambodh crematorium.

Late at night, after he had closed the last of his files, he now began designing a private resting place on land adjacent to his farm. For months, this was the last thing he did before going to bed. He studied different memorials and mausoleums. He knew exactly what he was looking for. Finally he called his architects to draw up the blueprints of the design he gave them. Like everything about his life, the place of his leaving was planned to the last detail, down to the last shrub in the landscaped park.

When the building, a monument in red sandstone, was completed in 1982, it emanated a quiet grandeur. He named it after his dearly beloved mother. A ramp led up to a three-storey-high terrace on which the body would be consigned to the flames. The pillars of a central hall bore family portraits. The structure was set in manicured grounds adjacent to the farm. Gravelled pathways radiated from the centre, their edges banked with seasonal flowers. Lawns as soft as *pashmina* wool stretched to the periphery ringed by straight-backed ashoka trees. Departing from life, he decided, should be as aesthetic an experience as living it. Death, too, should have a room with a view.

CHAPTER L

1984

1984 was a year with its own kind of Orwellian significance. For the first time in Rai Bahadur's life, the dark cloud did not hold the underlying promise of silver. Tikki died. Tikki, the first-born son, Tikki, his 'rajah' who could do no wrong. Tikki, the playboy, straddling the Eastern and Western worlds. But also Tikki, the financial whiz kid, Tikki the political strategist. Tikki's savaged pancreas finally gave up on him.

Forty years of high living had to extract their price. Way back in 1967, soon after his second wife gave him his first son, Arjun, Tikki had doubled over with pain. The attacks continued off and on for the next three years till Dr Stoll operated on him in a Boston hospital, and removed his entire gall bladder. However, the following year, the same agony reappeared. This time, Tikki was in Acapulco. Dr Stoll was unable to help. So he was flown to the Harley Street surgeon, Dr Rodney Smith, who extracted several stones from his pancreas. In 1972, Tikki was crippled by diabetes, and his movements thereafter were dictated by his daily insulin injections that Trilok, his valet since 1956, learnt to give.

But Tikki did not abandon the high life. Ironically, in the early 1980s, he had begun to gain more control over his attacks, get better, take a greater interest in work. He visited his father regularly at the farm, even if it was often at midnight. The father had, long ago, pinned all his business hopes on Biki. Tikki never resented this; he had been involved closely with the hotels, but he had never wanted to take on responsibility for the empire. Despite the very Western way the family had of addressing each other, the father had lately begun to use the archaic *puttar* when talking to his older son.

Tikki was a superstitious man, so it was with some reluctance that on 13 January 1984, a Friday to boot, he had allowed his son to take the night flight back to London, and school. Trilok, who had gone to see him off, called from Palam airport to say that Arjun-*baba's* plane was delayed. Tikki went over to the house of a friend, Prem Patnaik, son of the Orissa leader, Biju, and stayed till eleven. He returned, sat down to a charcoal steak, and staggered to the bathroom.

His other retainer, Lakshman, found him dead on the black marble of his sunken bath, staring unseeingly at the mirrored ceiling. Dr Dhoopiya was sent for. He took one look at the pale and supine man and cried, 'Tikki, what have you done to all of us!'

The doctor phoned Rai Bahadur at the farm, only telling him that his son's condition was very bad. Mohan Singh rushed to the house in Friends Colony in his pyjamas, broke down, and wept like a child right through the night. As adamantly as Tikki had fought to live through a fifteen-year battle with agony and too good a life, his father had fought to accept the reality of his son's tattered health. Now the struggle was of no use to either. Ishran Devi lived upstairs, but she was the last to be told, the family afraid of the impact on her high blood pressure. As it happened, she took it the most philosophically. 'It is God's wish. Commence the reading of the *Sukhmani Saheb ka path*,' she said.

Mohan Singh had completed the tranquil and imposing private resting place just two years earlier, on the assumption that he would be the first to use it. Instead, it would receive Tikki, to him still the little boy who had brought him all his luck. The colossus was shaken. Ishran Devi stood by his side, despite her illness, still the quiet source of strength.

The body had been kept for two days till Biki, away in the USA with Gautam Khanna, could return. Now, taming his grief over the older sibling he playfully called 'boss', the younger son took charge of the arrangements, and comforted his sisters, Rajrani, Swaraj and Prem, sobbing over their fun-loving brother. His powerful and sophisticated friends wept openly in disbelief. True, Tikki had been ailing for the last twenty years, slave to his insulin injections, but to everyone he was still the man with the charmed life, the other name of *joie de vivre*: the flames could not possibly have the temerity to crackle round him in *tandavic* destruction.

In a corner stood the young Arjun, who had bid goodbye to his father, taken the plane to London, and landed only to be informed of his passing. He did not get out of Heathrow, simply took the next flight back. He stood remembering the father who may have been ill for the better part of his memory of him, but who had never let that come in the way of planning fun things for him. Of evenings over Monopoly, and Daddy always winning. Now, the time was past to pass 'Go' and collect 200 or 2,000 or two million. Arjun thought wryly of his polo-playing father's disappointment over a son who refused to get on top of a horse, over a boy whom he had trained to be one of the best shots in the country, veering towards conservation instead.

Leela, Tikki's first wife, was now in Bombay, married to the poet, Dom Moraes. She distilled the pleasanter moments from their incompatible marriage, remembered the suavity that had swept the sheltered girl just back from Paris off her feet.

Jutta, his second wife, was informed in London where she had been spending much of the year. Waiting to get a ticket to Delhi, she sat in the high-ceilinged chandeliered drawing-room of her fashionable Queensgate flat, and recalled the wild days of their Kashmir-to-Kanya Kumari romance, the crazy drive to the Nagin Lake, the months in St Moritz and in the shadow of Mont Blanc. She remembered Tikki's surprise announcement of his decision to marry her at a party in Gulmarg; how, gripped by sudden nervousness, she had sat in the Imperial suite in her blouse and sari petticoat crying uncontrollably just before the wedding ceremony; how Tikki had told her that if she was that worried, they could call it off; how she had pulled herself together, gone through the *pheras,* and then, in all her own bridal brocades, been whizzed off to the wedding reception of Bubbles Jaipur. Tikki's marriage to Jutta too had soured. But she made it in time for the funeral.

It was Rai Bahadur who was the most shaken by the death of Tikki, the one who took the longest to get over it. If he still has. Every morning for a whole month after, he climbed the three-storeyed ramp to the spot where his son had been cremated. He still keeps Tikki's celebrated wardrobe with its embroidered dressing-gowns, French silk shirts and over a hundred jackets. And, since the day his son died, he has banished all music from his house. For months after, whenever someone dropped in to extend sympathies, the father wept, and if, so as not to sear the old wound, the visitor chose not to bring up the subject, Rai Bahadur would turn to his confidante, Krishna Singh, and say, 'See, they have forgotten him already.'

For the first time in his life, Rai Bahadur knew unmitigated despondency ; the iron grip that he had maintained, even at the age of eighty-four on every detail of operations, slackened. Biki, who had managed the empire for the past ten years, was now totally in command.

But Tikki's death was not the only blow that the year was to bludgeon him with. There were two more. Ramlal Chowdhury, Principal Secretary of East India Hotels Ltd (EIHL), passed away in Calcutta, his financial wizard, the man who had ferreted out from every possible source the funds needed to save Oberoi's face and hotels. The news had to be broken to Rai Bahadur very gently. Once again, he broke down. Despite his deteriorating health, he insisted on going to Calcutta to console and condole with Ramlalji's family.

Then, on 31 October, as she walked to her office, Indira Gandhi was gunned down by her Sikh guards. She was the politician Rai Bahadur most admired. He had supported her on every move, turned a blind eye to her excesses, defended her against her critics, including Tikki, who had been scathing about her tax raids. Stood by her when fair-weather friends had disappeared to bask under newer suns, and only a solitary visitor's car stood under the otherwise overflowing porch during her two years in the political wilderness.

As soon as he heard the news, Rai Bahadur decided to go to Teen Murti House where the slain Prime Minister's body lay in state. He refused to wait till officials were notified and a special VIP pass organized. Krishna Singh felt that she had better go with him. The eighty-four-year-old international celebrity stood for hours in the pushing, jostling general queue, that was getting more and more restive by the minute. Finally it broke through the security cordons, and went on a hysterical rampage. Rai Bahadur and Krishna Singh were trapped in the stampede, manhandled, lathi-charged and finally tear-gassed.

It was with great difficulty that the octogenarian and his companion fought their way through the melée and stumbled back to the car. By this time Rai Bahadur was trembling, out of breath and soaked with perspiration. The country-wide riots, blood-bath and savagery that was to claim thousands of lives had already started in Delhi. It would have been extremely foolhardy to attempt to go all the way to the farm through the crazed mobs, even if his chauffeur had not been a Sikh, the targets of the vengeful butchery.

Harjeet Singh drove as fast as he could to the Oberoi Intercontinental. Which was just as well. Rai Bahadur shortly suffered a stroke, and being in town, medical help could be summoned with less difficulty than if he had been at the far-away farm. That was the first time Rai Bahadur realized that he could no longer ignore the fact that he was eighty-four. He would have to make some concessions to the body he had pushed so unrelentingly, and which had not once whimpered in protest.

CHAPTER LI

The Ascent Of Biki

Back in 1973, the world's glitterati may have glittered unabashedly at the opening of the Oberoi Sheraton in Bombay, but a cloud had passed over Rai Bahadur's face as he stood behind the vast stretch of plate glass looking out into the neon-streaked night. In a diagonal across the harbour, Malabar Hill was ablaze with extravagant stacks of light; down the curve of Marine Drive, the deep-balconied buildings of the Fifties oozed a solid wealth; along the buttered expressway, the jam of cars stuck in a prosperous tailback symbolized a city that had arrived. All bespoke a metropolis where big bucks were made and big bucks spent. No reason for a hotelier who had just uncorked a gigantic honey-pot to frown.

But Rai Bahadur was not looking at future custom. He was looking at the plot to the right of him. Rai Bahadur did not like one-upmanship—not anyone else's—and it was clear that the Air-India building there was going to go up one floor higher than his own. Rai Bahadur then looked at the vacant plot to the left of him, and, signalling his son over, he said, 'Biki, do you think you could build another hotel here? Not as large, maybe just about 200 rooms, but really classy?'

Biki gave his father the kind of look he had found necessary eight years earlier when his shocked eye fell upon the astronomical figure of the bid for a chunk of unreal estate. He thought of the intervening uncertainty, the herculean task it had been to wrest the land from the sea, the colossal amount of money still owed. 'Daddy, we've just opened this hotel,' said Biki. 'We don't even know if it will be a success. How can you possibly ask me to build another?' it will. Will you?' asked his father.

The son did not reply right away. But when he did, it was the father's turn to be stunned. By the time Biki finished creating

Bombay's The Oberoi in 1986, fifteen years after they acquired the lease on the land, he had given a whole new extension to the concept of luxury. Five-star was no longer an adequate classification for this new brand. A fresh one had to be created: super deluxe. The quantum leap was now his. And it came to be said that if, for the father, building hotels was a mission, for the son, it was a passion that often lost sight of the bottom-line. The Oberoi finally cost Rs 600 million, three times as much as the old. But Oberoi Sheraton Towers had proved to be a gold-mine, and there was no need to go with a begging bowl to the American agency AID.

When Rai Bahadur gave Delhi the Oberoi Intercontinental in 1965, it changed the social life of the capital. Overnight, eating out became the in thing. Earlier, if you did not favour *dhabas* or belong to a stuffy club, you really had no choice but to entertain at home. But, soon, 'Meet me at the I- con' became the new mantra. Inviting friends and associates there acquired the VAP factor—venue-added prestige.

Twenty-one years later, The Oberoi in Bombay redefined style, with its atrium, its tinkling piano, its pampering in the rooms, a quiet opulence in the granite and splendour in the glass. The next year, the Intercontinental in Delhi followed suit, being rechristened The Oberoi after being completely refurbished to measure up to this lavish new brand. Here, too, the lobby sets the tone, punctuated with a white marble fountain, scattered with four bronzes by the celebrated sculptor, Amar Nath Sehgal, and rounded off with a filigreed Tree of Life. Between faxes, users of the Executive Centre, might care to contemplate rare lithographs by Emily Eden, who was better known for her diaries. Elsewhere, you could also chance upon an original Daniell, either Thomas or his nephew, William. Up on the rooftop, the Taipan glows with the pastel shades of original, 19th-century Chinese water colours.

The upgraded brand complemented a social stratum that had evolved and matured as new money stopped feeling the need to shout and learnt to make the quiet statement. It was a class that was worthy heir to the old patrons of hotels such as the Grand, the Imperial and the Cecil. As well travelled, as discriminating, and, arguably, wealthier than many of the maharajahs in the final daze of faded glory. But this kind of custom was just a snack.

At its core, The Oberoi brand was positioned for the top-end international business traveller, giving him, and now increasingly her, a world-class hotel. These guests wanted the ultimate in comfort, and paid for it at the full rate. They entertained lavishly, ordered the finest wines, the choicest food. It was worth letting go of some other profits to keep their custom. The son and father agreed that the international business traveller, asks, above all, for tranquillity from his hotel. Mark, then, The Oberoi lobbies. The seating areas are pushed back. A certain aloofness about the granite discourages the local populace from killing time here, strutting around, being seen.

The Oberoi concourse does not aspire to being a railway platform. The tone has been raised by lowering the decibels. Again, it is not the kind of place where you will find children somersaulting on the carpets and using the sofas as a jungle gym. Note, also, that the staff is always at attention; it is only the guest's prerogative to be at ease.

Too cold, says the competition. Perfect, says the guest as he escapes from the culture shock, the madding crowd, the heat and dust, into the security of the sound-proofed, satin-lined cocoon.

Oberoi is prepared to lose domestic revenue to keep it this way. Few exceptions are made to the rule of 'no large wedding receptions', the great money-spinner, but also the great clutter- maker, even if 'Bunty' does not any longer arrive preceded by a tin-band to marry 'Pinky'. Indian weddings are not the quietest of affairs, and the guest would rather not lose himself in the caparisoned crowd as part of the in-house entertainment. Similarly, membership of the health club, swimming pool and the rooftop bar is restricted to the bona fide hotel guest. He is the reason for The Oberoi being in business, he should not have to wait his turn.

Since The Oberoi caters for the business traveller rather than the leisure tourist, the decor is singularly lacking in ethnic encrustation. History is nice to look at, ordained Rai Bahadur, it can be grossly uncomfortable to live in. The long-legged Westerner does not want to uncoil himself from a low-slung divan. Indian silk upholstery, yes, but on proper, comfortable armchairs. Lacquered swings are lovely to behold, but a terrible distraction while conducting a business discussion. Nineteenth- century hunting lithographs on the walls, yes. But no hookahs to trip over.

The essence is gracious living that transcends boundaries of time and place. Biki's years abroad, moving among the cream of society, have given him an unfailing instinct for class. His objective, not surprisingly, is not his hotels being the best in India, but being among the best in the world.

He once told Rajiv Kaul, the General Manager at Delhi, 'All you have to do is create the life of a gentleman.' So, it follows that, in his hall-marked The Oberoi brand, the carpets have to be hand-knotted, the crystal hand cut, the curtain rail solid brass, the silver pure Sheffield. Even the coffee shop must have a full-linen service; no papering over, thank you. The pillows have to be stuffed with down; exactly 1,650 gm of it each, not a feather less, not a feather more. And the stem of the rose on each restaurant table has to be twice as long as the slim brass holder in which it is placed.

By the same standards, the towels will continue to be discarded after sixty washes, instead of the international hotel standard of 100-plus, till a reverse-osmosis plant has been installed to tackle the sediments in Delhi's water; the Calcutta Grand already has one. Drinking water is given the infra-red treatment to make it as clear and sparkling as a mountain stream's. Seven of the chain's thirty-nine are now entitled to include themselves under the exclusive label, 'Leading Hotels of the World' and The Oberoi, New Delhi, was recently ranked by the discerning *Harpers & Queen* guide among its '100 Best Hotels in the World'.

It's a question of perspective, and Biki likes to tell his General Managers the story of the three men who sat by the roadside hammering at a rock. When asked what they were up to, the first one said, 'I'm breaking stones'; the second said, 'I'm carving a statue', the third said, 'I'm building a temple'. Rai Bahadur expressed the same sentiment somewhat differently, 'The idea was never merely to make money. The compulsion was to think big, and let it happen. The profits would automatically come in.'

Biki might hold that the future lies in deluxe hotels, but that does not mean the group intends handing the rest of the business to someone else, on a salver complete with long-stemmed rose in a silver bud-vase. Standing with his back to the fireplace in a house on swanky Chester Row that belongs to a friend in London, P.R.S. Oberoi, now Managing Director of the group talks of the different kinds of traveller and the disservice it would do to both the country and the industry if the company were to concern itself only with the hall-marked The Oberoi. 'Air fares abroad are now cheaper, and eighty per cent of Americans have not yet travelled 200 miles beyond their homes.

There's a huge market out there, ready to burst through Immigration. But it is a diverse market, and the catering for it must be correspondingly segmented. The different types of hotels must be branded separately. General Motors makes both the Cadillac and the Chevrolet, but both are very different cars, and the buyer knows what he's paying for and what he'll get.'

Enter Trident and Novotel, the other two in the Oberoi group's new three-tier system. 'Look at the map of India,' says Biki. 'How many cities can take the deluxe category? Eight at the utmost. The four metros, Bangalore and the golden triangle of Jaipur, Udaipur, Agra. Once you've covered these, you can pack up and go to sleep, because the big-time foreign traveller and the top-notch Indian businessmen, the only ones who can afford to spend $170 a night, are not going to any other city.' So you need a slightly lower category, the Trident, as the group already has in Madras; other smaller hotels in the chain will be renovated to fit this brand.

A third budget segment, slotted at a rate lower than that of the better-class motel, awaits unveiling: Novotel, in collaboration with the French chain of the same name. Rajrani's sons have been working in different Oberoi hotels for some time; Novotel brings in Swaraj and Gautam Khanna's son, Ashok, who is handling the project under his uncle's direction.

In terms of returns on investment, Novotel is expected to bring in the widest smile. However, in terms of sheer revenue raked in, nothing can touch The Oberoi. Each devaluation of the rupee enables the jacking up of rates. In 1990, Biki's persistence paid off, and the government allowed hotels to charge foreigners on a dollar rate. Earlier, both were the losers in the context of the falling value of the rupee. Indians, however, pay a marked down rupee rate to cover the twenty per cent luxury tax imposed on their bills. 'We don't want Indians to end up paying more in their own country,' says Biki.

If Rai Bahadur had said earlier that quality costs money but it also brings in more money, this is not substantially different from his present argument that as long as you do not pass off a dud, the international business traveller will not bat an eyelid about a $50 price hike. Class has to take itself seriously. Biki will point to the escalation in the whole top-end business. 'Consider what a seat on the Concorde costs; a decent lunch for two sets you back by a hundred and twenty pounds in London. More people now are making more money, and they are prepared to spend it. But they make their demands. Obviously, we are satisfying them.' Father and son agree that they would prefer a lower occupancy at a higher rate than vice versa. 'Of course, a high on both counts, would be even better.'

CHAPTER LII

Symphony in 'E'

Hotels are as capital intensive as they are people based. The gestation period is high, the returns comparatively low: a good hotel takes nothing less than seventy crore rupees to build, but you would be lucky to get an annual turnover of forty crore rupees. Another industry could easily make twice as much. On the other hand, the property value appreciates like no other, and, in a few years, its worth could quadruple.

But a hotelier cannot simply sit back and become a real estate agent. Rai Bahadur's empire would have been assigned to the mothballs of history, like so many great hotels, had he not realized the imperative of constant growth, constant change. Biki today compares his job to showbiz: 'It's glamorous, glittering—and you have to come up with something new all the time. Changing trends in taste and life-style demand renovation, sometimes you have to have change for the sake of it, simply to keep up the image of dynamism.' Newer, smarter, brighter, quicker—that is the only way to grow.

Biki inherited a world that, having become more standardized, yearns for the personal touch; this, precisely, provides the competitive edge. Anyone can duplicate the physical facilities, given the finances; anyone can put the guest's name on his or her matchbox together with a cling-wrapped plate of complimentary pralines in every room. It is the service that is the amorphous essential that supports the entire business, gives muscle and, more important, tone, to the bottom-line.

In Biki's book, service is not just speed, it is 'sunny-side up' in more than just the breakfast eggs. Service is the warmth of the 'Good morning', the care over a flower arrangement, the pride in a bed well made. It is the way the entire staff behaves, friendly without being familiar, polite without being patronizing. According to him, quick but off-hand service is bad service. Not that he is very tolerant of the reverse either. Encapsulating this is the Oberoi rubric that the customer is never a 'client' but always a 'guest'.

Which is why, recuperating in London in 1991, Biki was extremely annoyed over what others might dismiss as a trifle. Hearing of Rajiv Gandhi's assassination on the British Broadcasting Corporation (BBC), he called Delhi immediately to ensure that adequate security precautions had been taken at the hotel; he also wished to send a wreath. Asking for the Lobby Manager, he found that he had to repeat what he wanted several times. It was only when the person at the other end identified himself, that he realized he was speaking to a trainee Receptionist. 'The Lobby Manager is not supposed to ask the telephone operator to direct his calls to the Reception. The guest doesn't know that he's got the wrong man, and is perfectly justified in damning a hotel that has a Lobby Manager who can't understand what a wreath is.' One of Biki's first tasks on his return to Delhi was to find out why the system was not followed, and where, along the line, the selection and training of the Receptionist had gone wrong. The swish of an axe was clearly discernible over the hush of the plush.

Since hoteliering is so full of intangibles, the best way to go about it is to define with absolute clarity all the tangibles, eliminate all the probables. Which brings us to the famous Oberoi systems, as cast-iron as the old kitchen ranges. Since you cannot be everywhere, concluded Rai Bahadur very early in his career, you have to have a system from which there can be no deviation. And since the only unchanging thing is change, the refining of the system never stops, nor does the training. The boast cannot be: 'We do it right most of the time.' It has to be: 'We do it right every time.'

This is hoteliering's equivalent of quality control. Therefore, the General Manager is as pleased as he is concerned when a guest complains that the coffee shop waiter did not pull out the chair for his lady companion, the pleasure stemming from the expectation of such graciousness even in so informal a restaurant.

It may be a glamorous business, but it is not an easy one. For instance, it takes years of togetherness for a house to become a home, but in a hotel the same warmth is expected from total strangers and at the turn of a door key. Besides, people want the comforts of home, but will not make the allowances they would back there. They are paying for it, aren't they? And through the nose.

As remarked before, it is a reputation built—or shattered—on the seemingly trivial. In an American study, 'Supercilious Behaviour of the Front Desk Clerk' headed the list of ten things that most turn off a guest. Oberoi *père* & *fil* have tried to eliminate many more. A telephone not answered before the fourth ring, a mispronounced name, a welcome smile not warm enough, a welcome drink not cold enough, receptionists not a hundred per cent bright-eyed and bushy-tailed at two in the a.m., given the odd hours at which international flights come in, all these and more are frowned upon.

If the General Manager is the conductor of this thousand-piece orchestra, he is also something of a municipal commissioner. A hotel like The Oberoi is a minor township, incorporating housing, water, sanitation, conservancy, security, restaurants and bars, as well as home delivery for both *shammi kebabs* and laundered shirts. There are shopping malls aplenty, even parks, taxis and sightseeing packages. To say nothing of business services.

Older staff might mumble that, in the earlier days, you would have to have gone through the mill for thirty years before you could become General Manager, whereas now, fresh out of the Oberoi School of Hotel Management, you can become one at thirty. Indeed most of them do, this now being the new average age of 'Senior' Managers in the Oberoi chain.

But there is no denying that hoteliering has made a paradigm shift, however timeless the old essentials might be. It is not just that the Bearer Subedar has given way to the Butler Manager. Sanjeev Malhotra, the General Manager of Oberoi Towers, may have less scope to become a legend like Italo Sibilia at the old Imperial, but his task is infinitely more complicated. He may no longer be great at whipping up a menu, but he has to be much more alert that the men do not whip up something less delectable. The old, day-to-day, be-everywhere approach has given way, at least in the larger units of the chain, to overview, marketing, PR, profitability, returns on investment, and catering for the sophisticated needs of the business traveller, the beluga caviare of the Oberoi chain.

Still, since the macro is made up of the micro, Rajiv Kaul in Delhi, Deepak Talwar in Calcutta, Shankar Mani in Egypt and Kamal Kaul in Bali can never really stop worrying about the details. The closed-circuit monitor is always on to make sure that there is no bottleneck in the porch; the beeper at his waist is always on to ensure that the bar is not neck-deep in bottles.

If the objective is a symphony in E—elegant and exclusive however expensive—the orchestration needed is mind-boggling. Not just at the General Manager's level but in every section. If almost every department enters the 'domain' of Housekeeping, the Food & Beverage Manager has virtually half the hotel reporting to him or her. In the space of thirty minutes, the F & B Manager in Delhi approves the assortment of salads for an 800-cover banquet and the Taipan's brand of jasmine tea, assesses the computerized plate-based analysis on why some dishes keep coming back half-eaten, and sorts out a snafu in butler service.

He then goes into a huddle with Inder Dhawan, his Executive Chef. They agree that they should never mess around with the classic dishes; never make the vegetarian go through the entire leather-bound edition before he finds something he can order; not adjective their shrimps with 'ocean-fresh' —there is no ocean near Delhi. The super-deluxe restaurant must take into account the new health consciousness, yet provide enough of the cream and almonds for the guest who, with irrefutable logic, argues that if he wanted to eat simple *dal-roti,* he would have stayed home.

It has helped considerably that chefs are no longer the tantrum-throwing prima donnas of yore. After all, the Executive Chef and his F & B Manager had probably studied together at the Oberoi management school. Besides, with the switch to gas and electricity, tempers have come down correspondingly with the heat in the kitchen.

Not the least of the F & B Manager's tasks is to ensure that the stewards in the breakfast room learn to distinguish between British and American guests. The latter want their coffee even before they order their pancakes with maple syrup, whereas the Englishman would be disoriented all day if you poured out the Earl Grey without having served his eggs & b. Sunny-side would be categorically down.

For his part, the Lobby Manager has to be the General Manager's eyes and ears. Great thought goes into the positioning of his desk, accessible without being obtrusive, just up front enough to see what's going on without giving the impression that 'Big Brother is watching'. He is the man on the spot. The guest goes to him with complaint and query; even rings him up from his room at 2 a.m to ask what the eerie sound is that is keeping him awake. 'It's only the peacocks, sir, in the. thickets of the Delhi golf course.'

He comes into his own at night, when he is virtually in charge of the whole hotel. The General Manager is informed the next morning about who got locked in, who tried to set himself on fire in the room, who tried to smuggle a woman in. Everyone knows that the tarts are not only in the pastry shop, and everyone in the Front Office soon learns to distinguish a call-girl from the more outrageously dressed but bona fide clients of the discotheque.

If she has entered draped on the arm of a guest, and she does not look like Pretty Woman was before Spoilt Playboy emeried her edges, Lobby Manager pretends that she is here only to admire the etchings. Lobby Manager may or may not put his foot down and pick up the phone, if, after an indecent interval, said companion has not emerged from the elevator. One of them repeats a dialogue from the Seventies. 'Sir, it's 1.30 a.m., will your visitor be taking some more time?' 'No, no, she's just leaving.' 'Sir, it's 2 a.m. House rules don't permit visitors staying the night.' 'I know, I know, she's just leaving.' 'Sir, it's 2.30 a.m. Would you like me to change the billing instructions from single occupancy to double?' 'No, no.' She leaves before the company gets to know of the executive's devotion beyond the call of duty. At 3 a.m. it's the Lobby Manager's phone that rings. 'I say, young man, do you happen to have a detective thriller or something else I could read?'

CHAPTER LIII

Carry on, Jeeves

Mohan Singh Oberoi introduced room service way back in the early Thirties at Clarkes to remove the clutter of personal retinues tripping up the efficiency of kitchens. Thirty years later he got all Delhi agog by employing housemaids; Abdul the room bearer no longer shuffled in with *chhota hazari*, the crispness of the toast depending on his mood that morning. Everywhere, sparkling jackets and well-pressed trousers replaced the anachronistic feudal uniforms. Except for the doormen. Smart young men and women replaced the unlettered chap who had come as the *badli* when his maternal uncle thrice-removed went on leave to his *muluk* and both stayed on and on. In tradition-bound, union-dominated Calcutta, Biki did the unthinkable: he brought in a retirement age. Then he out-Jeeved Jeeves.

If the Oberoi trademark was to gift-wrap the routine in style, then there had to be something more to room service than the waiter arriving with a rose on the tray. If hoteliering was to provide the elegant life of a gentleman, then there had to be a gentleman's gentleman. Every guest at The Oberoi would have a personalized butler, ordained P.R.S. Oberoi. It was more than just upgrading the waiter. A bright, young law graduate, Arunesh Mayer, was dispatched to the media-hyped Ivor Spencer School of Butler Administration.

Mayer returned and set up his own training programme for the young men specially hired for this job. At The Oberoi in Bombay and Delhi, the butler adds the satin finish to the already decadent pampering. You do not have to wrap gifts, call the airlines to reconfirm your onward booking, think up what to serve at a party in your suite. You do not even have to to draw your bath. All you have to do is press the butler service button on the console by your bed.

After months of training, after months of conditioning never to say 'no', a particular butler came a cropper when a guest asked for a shave.

A powwow was called, and the correct response decided upon. In future, faced with such a request, the butler would say, 'It calls for a professional job, sir. For what time should I fix an appointment at our barber's shop downstairs?'

The clientele is international and, just as much as the maids did earlier, the butlers learnt not to turn a hair on being asked to bring some 'souspix' or a plate of 'Flenchflies'. Nor must he blush to the roots of his hair and take to his heels when a scantily clad lady guest says, 'Rub my back.' He must first ensure that her American accent has not altered the perfectly acceptable 'Run my bath' to this seemingly immodest proposal. If, however, the former is what the lady does have in mind, there is a preordained response. 'Excuse me, madam, but house rules don't permit my presence in the bathroom when a guest is in it.' Said in as level a tone as can be summoned in the circumstances.

And when the guest returns home and his wife demands to know who packed his suitcase with such womanly finesse, he can hiss conspiratorially, 'The butler did it!'

CHAPTER LIV

That's How The Money Rolls In

Rai Bahadur started life with nothing. His mother gave him the first leg up, and as his daughter, Rajrani, commented, the first project is crucial. Combined with the dreaming and the daring was the 'calculating' mind. His costing was impeccable, whether he was drawing up a menu, or sending up a tower to scrape the skies.

Today's multi-crore Oberoi empire began in 1934 with an outlay of just Rs 16,000, young Mohan Singh's share of the money to make Clarke's Hotel in Simla hospitable. He soon raised this investment to Rs 120,000 to buy it over. Thus, right from the start, he established a financial-rule that stood him in good stead through the decades, namely, own the property so that it can be used as collateral for further loans. He acquired this initial capital through Bhagwanti's wealthy connections, and as we saw earlier, paid them back with the money he could borrow from the Punjab National Bank on much easier terms.

Shrewdly managing Clarke's, he made enough money to access what would turn out to be the real case generator, Calcutta's Grand Hotel. The business of running this hotel was channelled through Hotels (1938) which he formed with his four partners, Kahnchand Kapur, Shiv Nath Singh, Hari Ram and D.W. Grove.

Catering for the army during the war accumulated unplanned profits, allowed him to buy out his associates in just 12 years, and bring the Grand's property under his banner through acquisition of the entire Rs 3,452,407 worth of share capital of its holding company, Chowringhee Properties, in 1949. Its liability of Rs 4.7 million in debentures was also assumed. The first series of these, valued at nearly Rs 3 million was redeemed by 1964, and the remainder by 1972.

The Grand's wartime windfall was wisely invested in another golden goose—nine, in fact, those of the Associated Hotels of India Ltd., which, in a master manoeuvre, he had annexed in 1944. Already an expert at acquiring run-down property and developing it with his unique managerial skills, he picked up the Palm Beach Hotel in Gopalpur-on-Sea for just Rs 300,000 in 1947, and five years later, the spectacularly positioned, Hotel Mount Everest in Darjeeling. He paid Rs 500,000 for it, plus a debenture liability of Rs 800,000 which, with his Midas touch, he was able to clear from the hotel's own resources by 1963.

However, the biggest financial coup came with the creation of what is now the flagship company, The East India Hotels Limited. It was formed in 1949 with an authorised capital of Rs 20 million, a long way from the Rs 16,000 with which he had started just 15 years ago. It was a milestone for other reasons too. The public issue floated in 1956, was the first ever by a hotel company in India, raising Rs 6.5 million for his ambitious Oberoi Intercontinental in Delhi.

This was also the first time that an official institution agreed to put money into a hotel venture, the Industrial Finance Corporation advancing Rs 11.6 million. The balance of the nearly Rs 49 million needed was made up by a United Bank loan and Rs 16.5 million from public deposits. The Rs 12.4 million pledged by the USA's Exim bank also broke new ground, pioneering foreign investment in the Indian hotel industry.

None of this phenomenal growth would have been possible without heart-stopping risks, and the one that sent all calculations awry was the project, that rose like a reluctant Venus from Bombay's Arabian Sea, the Oberoi Sheraton. For this, the group borrowed Rs 42.2 million from USAID, Rs 56.8 million from the United Bank of India and Rs 95.5 million from public deposits. An additional Rs 23.4 million was raised through a share issue, while the collaborators, ITT Sheraton contributed Rs 5.9 million. The later 190-room extension was again bankrolled by the public, through convertible debentures worth Rs 75 million.

*

Yet these dizzying financial heights would not have held if our protagonist hadn't kept as much of an eagle eye on inventory control as on the investments.

In the old days, he always based the contents of the day's menu on those of the ice box and kitchen cupboard. Fresh orders were never placed without an exact inventory of existing stock. Guests had to specify beforehand if they were vegetarian or otherwise to avoid waste. 'Messing per head', as it was called, was calculated to the last decimal. But, he cut only costs, never corners, knowing that old-fashioned micro alone could make futuristic macro possible; that if the first was cautious, the second could be grand, soaring, no-holds-barred.

This policy never became obsolete. Making a round of the scullery after breakfast hours at the Oberoi Intercontinental, he found that the butter remaining in the fluted pots went down the drain. He told the F & B Manager to have the unused parts collected and sent to the pastry shop. Better cakes, better custom.

P.P.S. Lamba and he once travelled up to Simla together by taxi. The driver hared round the hairpin bends without either slowing or blowing, and Mohan Singh kept gently cautioning him to do both. Finally, the driver shouted, '*Lalaji* stop saying "*Horan bajao, horan bajao*". I want to save my Exide.' Lamba sniggered at his stupidity in not realizing that using the horn would put no strain on the battery, but Rai Bahadur expressed his admiration of a man who was conscious of his losses, even if mistakenly.

The lode-star was always the bottom-line, and the avuncular Company Secretary, Satyabrata Roy, sitting in the registered office of East India Hotels Ltd. (EIHL) at Calcutta's 4, Mangoe Lane, repeats his boss's sentiments, 'A hotel is not Shah Jahan's Taj Mahal. When constructing it, you can't lose sight of the profits it can make.'

You can, however, afford to be extravagant, since the costing rule of thumb allows you to charge 0.1 per cent of the construction cost of each room: $100 a night if the latter worked out to $100,000. Which makes Biki's obsession with luxury practicable. But he cautions, 'The more you've spent on your hotel, the higher the margins, provided you get the occupancy.' The Oberois have not lost much sleep on this account.

It was Rai Bahadur who first pushed hotel rates into a quantum leap. His peers in the industry sniggered, and sat back smugly, waiting to hear the crash. Six months later, they were all quietly rearranging the rack rate behind their own reception counters. The Oberoi Intercontinental began with an average charge of ninety-five rupees, today it is Rs 3,400. After it metamorphosed into The Oberoi in 1986, profits tripled largely because the revised room rates offset the Rs twenty-seven crore spent on the renovation.

This money was raised through debentures, and a confident public responded, as it had eight times over the years, collectively pooling Rs 100 crore. After all, wasn't this the man who had dared jettison his powerful financier, USAID, because it refused to let him declare an interim dividend for his investors? When a severe financial crunch followed the delays in building the Intercontinental and there wasn't enough to pay back the matured fixed deposits, hadn't Rai Bahadur personally taken charge, supervising refunds in instalments with full interest? Conversely, if EIHL shares have not snorted into the arena of rampaging bulls, it is because Rai Bahadur insists on not playing the market, but allowing share prices to find their own level.

In the early years, his meeting with bankers at critical junctures may have been largely fortuitous, but keeping them owed nothing to chance and everything to clean financial practices. S.B. Roy spells it out, 'If bank loans were so readily given, it is because banking norms were meticulously observed. We put our cards clearly on the table; never exceeded our sanctioned overdraft limit, and ensured that interest and repayment schedules were adhered to.' Even when Rai Bahadur was floating on the euphoria of being nominated Man of the World, he still sent a telex from New York to Roy, reminding him of repayments due.

The Secretary dismisses out of hand the suggestion that bankers can be plied with pampering into compliance. 'Hospitality isn't going to make anyone fork out vast sums of money. We have maintained good personal relations, but this, too, was possible only because we never abused the professional one. Besides, you can't give bankers free hotel rooms. It violates their business ethics.'

Every loan was a challenge, the outcome resting on a delicate interplay of personal and professional rapport, to say nothing of scores of meetings. Rai Bahadur went to the banks; he went to the public; when pushed, he even went to international aid agencies. But he gave financial institutions a wide berth. He knew how easily they could turn the tables on a company.

If you cannot avoid them, at least do not antagonize them, he advised H.P. Nanda, caught in the Reserve Bank-blessed machinations of the (NRI) tycoon, Swraj Paul, to take over Escorts. Surrounded by his collection of hand-cut crystal, wearing a hounds-tooth tweed jacket, the dapper Nanda considers Rai Bahadur a 'friend of friends', recalling how he stuck by him when all his old associates distanced themselves, too afraid of being on the wrong side of the government.

Mohan Singh kept abreast of the lopsided tug-of-war from far-away Australia. When Nanda was told to bear the astronomical legal costs himself, and not charge it to Escorts, Rai Bahadur promptly offered him and his team a fifty per cent discount in all Oberoi hotels. Incidentally, the country's top-flight corporate lawyer, Fali Nariman, also slashed his fee to a third. Nanda won.

The empire has expanded spectacularly but the family grip has remained intact through Oberoi Hotels (Pvt.) Ltd., which holds controlling interest in East India Hotels Ltd. and other Oberoi companies in India and abroad. For the properties in India, sales turnover in 1971 was Rs 4.90 crore; in 1991, it had blasted off to an auspicious Rs 101 crores. During the same period, fixed assets in the country spread and appreciated from ten crore rupees to Rs 234 crore. Biki blueprinted the government stipulation that foreign guests pay in hard currency. Moreover, in 1990, Rai Bahadur's hotels brought in Rs 3.2 crore in foreign exchange through dividends and management fees.

Not bad going for someone who started life at fifty rupees a month.

CHAPTER LV

Beatific Giver

'In the early hours of November 2, 1988, she quietly slipped out of this world, leaving her husband, four children, thirteen grandchildren, ten great-grandchildren and thousands of people who worshipped her as a goddess to mourn her going.' This uncharacteristic schmaltz is Khushwant Singh's, a columnist who has demolished with a vengeance the dictum, 'concerning the dead, nothing but good', reserving his sharpest barbs for obituary comments. But he wrote about Ishran Devi:

> What is it that gives some women an appearance of eternal serenity? . . . None of this meteoric rise in her husband's fortunes brought the slightest change in Ishran Devi's values. Religion became her life's passion. I saw her on many occasions at religious ceremonies and could never take my eyes off her. Her eyes were closed as if lost in deep *samadhi*, and seeing her at formal receptions, talking to presidents of international consortiums, ministers and diplomats. . . I often wondered how Ishran Devi was able to combine her spiritualism with the earthiness of the rest of the Oberoi clan. . . .

His wife's passing, four years after the death of beloved Tikki, accelerated the slowing down of the man who earlier never stopped. But the discipline asserted itself, he knew he could not allow himself to sink into memories, for sentimentality at the age of eighty-eight was quick-sand. He willed himself together, established an iron-willed, walk-work routine. Yet, of an evening, he permitted himself the luxury of remembrance.

The images flashed upon the mind's eye. Ishran, who had charmed him with her engaging manners, her quiet strength even as an adolescent; for that was all she was when she became his bride in Bhaun. Ishran, for whom he had satin slippers in jewel colours made at his uncle's shoe factory. So what if they were a size too small; her heart was large enough to forgive him for this and future trespasses. Ishran, who had quietly brought him her modest store of gold to help him take his first step towards empire.

It was to her that he first communicated the news of every conquest, even though she despaired deeper with each new hotel, and gave up trying to dissuade him after the Associated Hotels (AHI) coup. He realized that he did not know half of what she had done to keep the family together when he had been too busy to play father. He had provided the toys, clothes, servants, the English marmalade on the toast, and she'd had to try and undo the effects of over-indulgence. She had succeeded with Rajrani, Swaraj and Prem, because in old-fashioned India, daughters did not get spoilt. She had failed completely in Tikki's case; less so with Biki because, by then, the father had realized the destructive powers of pampering.

In later years, she spent six months at her beloved Clarkes where she had worked so closely with her husband before the seven- league boots put such a distance between them. At the Simla hotel, too, she followed her routine. Two hours of *maun,* silent meditation, after an early bath. A frugal meal of two *phulkas* and a vegetable cooked by herself on a simple heater in her room. She never ate any bought food, she even made her favourite cottage cheese herself. The evenings were again devoted to a long prayer session, either a reading from the *Granth Saheb* or a discourse, perhaps by the learned Sant Gulab Singh at Knockdrin, the bungalow once occupied by British bureaucracy, then by the Maharajah of Faridkot, and now the family home of the artist, Billy Malhans.

Her driver, Shiv Singh, is among the band of faithful retainers who joined the company as young men fleeing the straitjacket of their villages in Bihar, Garhwal, Kumaon or even Nepal, and then were drawn into the family, there to stay till the end.

The *granthi*, who came in every day, had taught Shiv Singh how to write his name in Gurmukhi, and as he sat practising it on a slate in a corner of the veranda of the Friends Colony house, 'Burri *memsaab* asked me if I'd like to learn to read and write the language fully. Of course I said yes, since I knew only Hindi. Then she asked the *granthi* if he'd mind teaching me. *Gyaniji* said he'd do whatever she told him.

'The next day, he got me a primer, and my lessons began. I used to drive her to the park every day, and take my book along to practise while she walked for an hour. One day, *memsaab* made me sit before the *Granth Saheb* and to pray the *ardas,* the invocation. I was very nervous, and made a lot of mistakes. But at the end of it, she patted me on the back and *said "Shabash!"* I was only a humble driver, and not even a Sikh but a Hindu, yet she entrusted me with the honour of reciting from the *Granth Saheb* when she could not read it herself due to her weakened eyesight. There was no bar against a non-Sikh doing this, provided he didn't drink or smoke. I'd never done either.'

But she continued to remain in the material world. She passed on several of her housekeeping skills. Krishna Singh pays tribute to Ishran Devi's contribution to the thrifty systems which, as much as her husband's 70-mm vision, helped build the early Oberoi conglomerate. How to salvage towels with a tear but still with plenty of wear; how to convert tea-stained tray-cloths into smaller teapot holders; how to take care of carpets to make them last forever; how to make a lime pickle with almost as extended a longevity.

Like her husband, she knew exactly what was where. Some years after Cecil had been padlocked by Rai Bahadur till he could bring it up to the Oberoi standard again, she asked for an inventory of the brass planters in the closed hotel. The figure did not tally with the mental calculation she swiftly did, so Kavita Khanna, the Assistant Manager at Clarkes, was sent on a hunt through the stores till every one of the missing pots was located. There were eighty-seven of them, and she knew precisely how many were on each landing or stair.

Ishran Devi was as indefatigable as Mohan Singh. Even at eighty-two, wracked by bronchitis and hampered by near blindness, she went over from Clarkes to Cecil one morning after her prayers, taking along a few servants. She made them pull out the priceless rugs that were moulding with neglect, and stood with a small handkerchief at her mouth while they dusted, shampooed, dried and rolled them up correctly (along the pile), according to her instructions. Like her husband, she just got down to the business at hand without fuss, let or hindrance. They had both learnt a lot from each other.

Her humility, like that of Rai Bahadur, was genuine, whether it was cleaning up by herself anything she had spilled or her insistence on her driver, cook and bearer sitting together with her under a tree and sharing the packed meal on their way up or down from Simla. The old waiters at Simla recall how she would stitch some of their smaller clothes for them herself, to save them tailoring bills.

When an engineer asked for from Maidens to fix a problem at the house did not arrive for three days, Shiv Singh told her, 'You are the *malik*, you can easily speak to the General Manager.' Ishran replied quietly, 'The only *malik* is the one above; we are merely the *chowkidars*, the keepers of the gate.'

Swaraj's son, Ashok, noticed even as a young boy that his grandmother never seemed to have an idle moment; even her meditation seemed so dynamic beneath the serenity on her face. Prem's daughter, Kavita, observed that she was always giving—of herself, her efforts, even the gifts that someone may have brought. It was not being ungracious, she just automatically began to wonder who would like it more, who would need it more.

Certainly, Ishran Devi had the same genius as Mohan Singh for multiplying money. The Bhagwanti Oberoi Charitable Trust that she set up and supervised to the last detail, grew from its original corpus of Rs 10,000 in 1963 to several hundred thousand in 1990. If you want to be as exact as its Manager O.P. Arora, at the close of the accounting year 1990-91, it stood at Rs 3,934,915.98. He, too, notes that her saintliness did not interfere with the shrewd way in which she could judge people, at once seeing through charlatans who thought they could get away with a slice of the charitable cake. The Trust disbursed funds for education, ran a dispensary, provided clothes and blankets to those beggared by upheavals which were not of their making, and fed the poor at *langars* in gurdwaras.

Till the end, Ishran Devi continued to be the anchor of a wandering family. She always held an *akhand path* on Rai Bahadur's birthday as well as all other auspicious occasions, and insisted that he, however busy, attend. The grandchildren spread out across the world to study and work, but whenever they were in Delhi, they always lunched with her. Every day. Granddaughters are the beneficiaries of another exclusively family trust that gives them Rs 1,000 on each birthday; about the grandsons who were left out, she would say, 'They have me.' Besides, they had a place in the Oberoi empire, the sons of the sons. more than those of the daughters. It is only Arjun and Vikram, who, together with Biki, are the legatees of the House of Oberoi.

It borders on the outrageous to sit with an *éminence grise,* and question age-old verities such as his decision to pass on the business only to sons and their sons. 'I couldn't have imagined it to be otherwise. The more members holding shares, the greater the chances of the business house breaking up. Haven't you seen it happen in so many industrial families?' asks Mohan Singh Oberoi. 'Besides, my daughters are well taken care of; they earn a lot from the businesses I set them up in. I have also provided for them in my will.'

It seems equally audacious, or just unfair, to raise doubts at this stage in his life over what his wife thought about his women friends. He replies, 'When we got married and she came to live in Simla, those were the happiest years of my life. I never loved her any the less till the end,' he insists. 'I gave her place, dignity. She never stopped caring for me or consulting me on matters relating to the family and the Trusts she set up.'

Even though he was eighty-eight and a shadow of what he had been before the stroke in 1984, there wa not single evening that he did not go all the way from his farm to Friends Colony where Ishran Devi was seriously ill. When she was moved to Bombay's Jaslok Hospital, he camped in the city, spending every minute of the visiting hours with her, morning and evening. His daughters kept telling him not to strain himself so much lest he suffer another setback. But he continued the routine, and he adds, 'If I had not reached by my usual time, either in Delhi or Bombay, my wife worried, and would ask someone to call to check if I was all right.' As he sits alone and ninety-one at his farm, it is Ishran Devi who continues to smile beatifically from the photograph on the table by his side.

Ishran Devi grew to become one of the most loved and respected figures of Sikh society. Industrialist H.P. Nanda vouches for the fact that the highway leading to the farm had never seen a traffic jam like the one caused by half of Delhi thronging to bid the serene giver a final goodbye.

She did not leave unprepared. Exactly on 18 October 1988 she had told Shiv Singh, 'I don't think I will live longer than another fifteen days. As soon as I die, start the *Sukhmani Saheb ka path*. Have the *akhand path* for three days, and distribute *prasad* by the generous fistful. Don't ever close the prayer room of the house, but keep up the daily recitations.' When Rai Bahadur came that evening, she asked him to continue to take care of Shiv Singh so that he could perform this ritual. He still does; he will to the end of his days.

On 3 November, tc the sonorous chant of her beloved Sikh

scriptures, the *japji,* the *antim ardas,* the repetition of the names of the ten gurus, the gurus' sons, the first five converts, the famous martyrs, the five *takhts,* Ishran Devi was cremated at the perfectly sculpted, peace-enshrouded private Oberoi resting place. The man who had built it made the painful effort of heaving his stroke-weakened frame up the three-storey-high ramp. He piled the sandal-wood logs on his wife's body himself. He stroked her face with both hands before it was covered, then removed the cloth once more to repeat the gesture. As the pyre turned to ash, Rai Bahadur sat in a corner, weeping softly over the fact that fate had cheated him a third time.

CHAPTER LVI

Back To The Rescue

The Kuwait-triggered Gulf War was the last straw on the back of the up-market Indian hoteliering industry that had staggered all through 1990 under the impact of domestic instability. The business traveller stayed away because there was no government worth the name to make industrial policy decisions that would last out the month. The U.S. State Department was not the only one that informally advised its citizens to avoid India if communal carnage, caste conflagrations, arson, loot and general disruption were not their chosen points for sightseeing.

The political imbroglio spelt ruin for all hotels which depended almost exclusively on the foreign client. For the Oberoi chain, the plummeting room occupancy came on the heels of a fire at the Towers in Bombay, which also razed the rents of the shopping arcade and forced renovation. In addition, airline crews decided to take their custom closer to the airport. The Oberoi group made eighteen crore rupees less than its sales forecast for 1990-91. To top it all, Biki was in London for several months, recovering from major surgery.

Everything that could have gone wrong did. But Rai Bahadur remained unfazed. He issued instructions that Biki was not to be troubled. His own farmhouse became the power centre, with the nonagenarian Chairman, making clear-headed decisions to see the chain through its most critical phase since the building of the Delhi and Bombay hotels. He loved it. His metabolism improved as the adrenalin once again coursed through. He could not get a spring to his step, but the shuffle showed a marked acceleration.

Occupancy had sunk from eighty per cent to fifty per cent in Bombay; in Delhi, with more hotels squabbling over the diminished slice, it dropped as low as thirty per cent. Rai Bahadur tackled the slipping revenues not with any dramatic shutdowns, but with his old, time-tested, forte of the small solution. His ability to break down a problem to its simplest component and proceed from there had not gone into hibernation despite his abdication in favour of his son; it was being put to profit at his farm every other day. All he had to do now was to multiply its application in the hotels.

Instructions radiated from his farm to all centres. All renovation was to be deferred; telex and fax were to be used only for business that could not wait, and regular mail or courier services should carry the rest. Subscriber Trunk Dialling (S.T.D) facilities were to be drastically cut down. Staff should use public taxis instead of the private ones that were exorbitantly more expensive for short distances. Vice-Presidents were to set the example and not remain islands immune to the new austerity; their petrol allowance became a fixed one instead of actuals, and they, too, had to travel economy on foreign trips.

Heat-light-power is a hotel's highest expense, and pruning here went on a war footing, especially since hysterically raised tariffs on account of the Gulf crisis had vastly inflated the electricity and gas bills. Rajiv Kaul and his Delhi team were summoned. Typically, instead of saying, 'I want this done,' Rai Bahadur said, 'May I make a suggestion?' Again, as typically, it was a very simple one. This was the strategy: 'Energy conciousness has to be instilled. We will aid it with an electricity meter installed in each working area. We'll take a reading not every month, but every day. Should the Chief Engineer find that even a single unit more has been consumed, he should inform the General Manager.' A three per cent cut in each department was all Rai Bahadur demanded. At the individual-area level, they would hardly feel the effects of so small a deprivation, but, cumulatively, it would add up to a saving of five crore rupees.

He provided a concrete example from the system established at his own farm, where he had brought down consumption by one-fifth, simply by making each area-head responsible. The experiment succeeded at the macro level as well, as the hotel's Managers suddenly realized obvious truths. For example, bath water needed to be only hot enough for the highest individual need; it did not have to be so hot that it had always to be diluted with cold water.

The cut-costs-but-never-corners principle, however, did not get washed away by the new stringency; the baby did not get thrown out with the no longer scalding bath water. Guest facilities were improved not pruned on the simple logic that, since the same number of staff was looking after fewer guests, attention should be greater. More towels, more pampering.

He also told Bombay to persuade all the Oberoi Towers non-contractual guests to switch to the swankier The Oberoi. It would put to use existing facilities and push up the chain's income. Having revelled in the greater luxury, a lot of guests were seduced into asking for the more expensive hotel on their own the next time round. When Biki returned, recovered, in September 1991 he discovered that Dad and the hotels were both looking up.

Rai Bahadur continues in his own unhurried, unruffled way. Continues his policy of not letting worry crowd the brain. Continues to hitch his wagon to all the stars in his chain: budget, medium, super deluxe. One way or the other, he is still determined to have a hundred hotels. The king of the room boom still has not lost either his touch or his dream.

CHAPTER LVII

Sun-downer

The cows have come home. Roopwati, Ganga and Munni swish their tails as the smell of dust and dung rises from their shed. The hospitable wild almond in the courtyard stretches its branches to gather in the peacocks; they alight, a minute later, sweeping up their sequined skirts like socialites side-stepping puddles. The dusk fissions with a myriad-noted cacophony as parakeets, sparrows, the raucous class-monitor crows and our curious friend, the mynah-bird, squabble over roosting places. The partridge settles in the pear tree. Palms, lining the avenue to infinity, bow their fronds in a *huzoor* to advancing twilight.

The contractor hired to axe the decaying eucalyptus has called it a day, spreads his mat, and turns towards Mecca in a soundless spot-exercise of faith. Nearby, his Bihari hands knead their evening meal of *'sattu'* with rhythmic concentration. Across the massed bougainvillaea, the sandstone final resting place is aflame in the ochre light. Its flank of ashoka trees push their backs against the wall, reluctant to step out in defence of this monument to mortality.

Unchallenged, the shadows slip in. Rank upon rank of silent armies march towards the small farmhouse. They are again barred by the glass doors. Khayali has pattered in to draw the old-fashioned brocade drapes, exiles of a hotel renovation that replaced fussy Regency with uncluttered post-modern decor. The raw-silk shaded standard lamp, another refugee from a similar designer *putsch,* bathes a table piled with yellow files bearing the patriarch's monogram. Xeroxed newspaper clippings, their relevant paragraphs highlighted in neon pink, inform him of Madhavrao Scindia's imminent tourist policy and a new five-star hotel in Himachal still bereft of clientele. It is not one of his; our protagonist does not have to write out a prescription.

Muffling kilometres away from the clang of clashing political swords in the nation's capital, cocooned by a hundred greening acres, the Chairman sits upright in his chair, his podgy hands folded across his teddy bear tummy. He has brought the past up to the present and is in no hurry to avert his gaze from future, even if the twentieth century, with which he started life, prepares to consign itself to micro-filmed history.

'I have always used every minute I had because I knew that the next one may or may not be mine to do all I wanted,' he says.

As mind and memory tick almost unfalteringly, a *bidri* work clock marks the hours. Time, as punctual as a wake-up call, walks with measured tread across the room, perusing the framed milestones of his life. Mementoes cushion the loneliness of the long-distance hotelier who now sits virtually immobile, but who has not given away his running shoes. Indeed, he dons a pair of sneakers on his morning walk round the farm.

The 'trophies' symbolize the scores of awards that have come his way, from a scroll by a modest association of Punjabis to Hall of Fame citations from international federations of travel agents. Even more carefully polished are the inscribed salvers, scale- model hotels and great globes of silver that his employees around the world have presented to wish him many happy returns, year after year after year....

'I don't like it any more when my birthday comes round,' he says.

Tikki, in sharkskin prince-coat, chuckles from his photograph, in his right hand the whisky glass and cigarette that were the insignia of the 1950s man-about-town. On the table by his side, a dapper Biki stands against a European skyline. Alongside, the gracious Ishran Devi, her husband looking warmly into her eyes. On the wall, all the sons and daughters in a 1940s studio portrait: the young men in black Nehru jackets, the young women in white chiffon. Below it, the much larger family tumbling into great grandchildren, all of whom went *en masse* to New York in 1983 to share the pride of Big Daddy being honoured with the Man of the World Award, a portly Rai Bahadur still looking into the eyes of the still elegant Ishran Devi. Tikki is missing.

Rather belatedly, Rai Bahadur says, 'I think I should give less time to hotels and more time to my children, my grandchildren, their children. And my friends—I didn't have many, and of these not many are left. I think I should have a party just to meet them, not talk business.' Having said this, he immediately looks sceptical; he has never talked anything else. In his meticulous way, he has already drawn up the list for this great reunion. He adds, 'I don't feel as if I need to make up for lost time with the family or that I should take more active a part in the hotels than I'm doing. I have a strong feeling of happiness and satisfaction that Biki is able to manage and control the entire chain. I am leaving it in very good hands.'

He presses the buzzer at his side and Munir, gold braid a-glitter, appears. He asks for a copy of the fax message he sent that morning to his son recuperating in London from a six-month battle with a defiant gall-bladder. In it, he suggested a week at an English health resort, told him not to think at all about business. 'I've issued instructions to all our offices not to disturb Biki, but to direct all problems to me in his absence.' It is another matter that Biki, as much of a workaholic, sits in the Sloane Square house, constantly untangling business across the world.

During Biki's convalescence in London, the father had insisted on a daily health bulletin on the fax. 'The way he lectures me, one would think he's been mindful of his health all his life,' says the son with a wry smile as he replaces his Royal Doulton teacup on the coffee table with its antique Chinese bowl abloom with silk lotuses. 'Daddy didn't concede he had physical limitations till he was eighty-four, and that only because the stroke forced this reality on him. He never exercised, and ate irregularly. He never knew the meaning of leisure. Now, thank God, he's being very particular about his health.'

Rai Bahadur is finally making concessions to his age. 'I take a nap in the afternoon because my doctor insists I do. I don't think I could continue to rise at five in the morning and go to bed after eleven at night if I didn't.' The man whose only discipline was his work, has, in the last seven years, followed a spartan regimen. Regular walks and yoga. Precise mealtimes. No more of his favourite pork chops with apple sauce, or *paya,* though he sometimes sneaks in a *pakora* ostensibly ordered for a guest. The other weakness, *dahi bhalle,* continues to be eaten with a clear conscience and an unprotesting digestive tract.

He has actually condescended to ascend his bathroom scales every morning, and submits to their *diktat,* reducing his intake, increasing his exercise till the needle swings back to eighty. His bearers, as fussy as Executive Housekeepers, hand him pills from an Austrian enamelled silver case, pour out mixtures in a small glass of hand-cut crystal. He wrinkles his nose and says, 'I hate medicine; I never had to take it before.'

'But my health is fine,' he insists. 'My eyesight is not too good, but not bad enough to prevent me from reading my files and the papers. I hate wearing my hearing aid. I feel like throwing it away, and put it on only when I have to. All my vital organs are in perfect condition. My heart, the doctor tells me, is that of a man of forty or fifty.' The spirit is still willing, the gleam in the eye is not only of glaucoma.

1984 changed a lot. His mind may still be as clear as infra-red-treated water, his memory as sharp as a steak knife, he can still step in to offer the simple solution that saves crores, he is still part of corporate decision-making, but the galloping zest has gone. The stroke was only the effect, the cause was the death of Tikki, the prodigal son who ultimately never returned.

All his dreams now centre on Biki. The sense of dynasty is assured. Biki's son, Vikram, returned home recently after having made an impressive mark in Australia as art investment banker, and is being personally groomed in the business by Ratan Tata. Tikki's Arjun is training at the Savoy chain's headquarters in London. However, as Biki, ever the pragmatist, admits, 'You can plan a succession, but you can't always make it work.'

The night draws its blanket tighter around the farmhouse. The shadows push themselves against the plate glass; some slip in.

Mohan Singh Oberoi sits among the files and the photographs, and, through the hearing aid, filter the whispers and the whiplash of love and war long past.

Shiv Nath Singh, his *bête noir,* died in 1991. He spent his last years in an ashram. 'Perhaps his conscience worried him. Mine is clear,' says Rai Bahadur.

He permits himself only some self-satisfaction, no malice, over the thought of Shiv Nath losing his hotels and quarrelling even with the brother who had constantly bailed him out. He spent what was left of the rest of his life in penury in the ashram of Sathya Sai Baba; far, far away from the sharkskin dinner jackets, the silver-topped cane, the myriad lights of a ballroom, and a Rolls- Royce in beige and brown purring towards the Royal Calcutta Turf Club.

Ishran Devi's photograph dominates the room looking on in serene indulgence. It was a special kind of sadness when she died, an emptiness whose depths her husband had not plumbed when he was too busy pursuing his dreams. 'We never lost touch, not till the very end,' he says.

Rai Bahadur never believed in organized religion, never stepped into a place of worship. 'My faith was only in my work.' He believes in God, but does he credit him with his achievements? 'Only God knows,' he chuckles. 'I didn't ask for God's help. But if he extended it, I'm grateful.' He does not know what luck is all about. 'Yes, a lot came my way, but it was up to me to turn it to advantage. Some hotels dropped into my lap, but the success wasn't handed on a platter. 'The old ones were tumbledown ruins; my work made them what they became.'

He had left all the praying to his saintly wife. Now he repeats a three-line benediction every night: 'I pray that God will help me to be kind, that my mother, Tikki, and my wife go to heaven; and that I continue to have strength and good health.'

He is still very much the Chairman in name, deed and decision-making, but now he also takes cognizance of death. With a newfound submissiveness, Rai Bahadur, for the first time, is prepared to relinquish property without a fight. 'This body now belongs to God. He can take it when he chooses. I do not believe in *karma* or something beyond. This life is the most important. I strongly believe:

घर में दीये जलाकर मन्दिर में फिर जलाना'

(Light the candles in your home before you light them in the temple.)

The ultimate reality is tempered by the thought that he will depart, as always, from a room with a view—the tranquil, landscaped resting place he created adjacent to his farm and named after the mother to whom he owed so much.

Rai Bahadur soon lifts himself out of the grimness of the last huzza with a twinkling eye, 'I don't think J.R.D. Tata thought of creating such a paradise for himself.'

Loneliness? Yes, but then he always was a loner despite being in so highly social a business.

Sadness? Only at the death of those who should not have preceded him.

Regrets? None at all. 'The aim was to be the best and achieve it by never expecting my guests to settle for second best. Biki continues this, almost with a vengeance. My daughters manage their businesses admirably. My grandsons are steady professionals, holding their own. My company could not be in better hands.' The company, only the company. Now as always.

Rai Bahadur Mohan Singh Oberoi looks back over nine decades, inside thirty hotels in three tiers, across four continents—and rings for tea. It arrives, like the hospitality he has extended, on a silver platter. In a style befitting the man who has played host to the world.

Select Bibliography

Barr, Pat and Desmond, Ray. *Simla: A Hill Station in British India,* New York: Charles Scribner and Sons, 1978.

Buck, Edward. *Simla Past and Present* (1st edition 1904) Reprint—Simla: Minerva Book House, 1989.

Cotton, H.E.A. *Calcutta Old and New* (1st edition 1904) Reprint—Calcutta: General Printers & Publishers Pvt. Ltd., 1980.

Hobbs, Major H. *John Barleycorn Bahadur, Old Time Taverns in India,* Calcutta: H.Hobbs, 21 Old Court House Street, 1943.

Nelson, Nina. *The Mena House,* Mena House Hotel, 1987.

Pudney, John. *The Thomas Cook Story,* London: Michael Joseph, 1953.

Punjab Gazetteers, 1887-89.

Rolls, S.C. *Steel Chariots in the Desert,* Jonathan Cape, 1937.

Seth, Mesrov. *Armenians in India,* (1st edition 1937) Reprint—New Delhi: Oxford and IBH-Publishing Co., 1983.

Wild, Auguste. *Mixed Grill in Cairo* (Privately Printed) Bournemouth. Sydeham Ltd., 1952.

Archives of:
   The Times of India, Bombay.
   The Statesman, Calcutta.
   The Age, Melbourne.
   The National Library, Calcutta.

Appendix A

List of Hotels

HOTEL	LOCATION

In India

The Oberoi Towers	Bombay
The Oberoi	Bombay
The Oberoi Grand	Calcutta
The Oberoi	New Delhi
The Oberoi Maidens	Delhi
The Oberoi	Bhubaneswar
The Oberoi Bogmalo Beach	Goa
The Krishna Oberoi	Hyderabad
The Jass Oberoi	Khajuraho
The Trident (associate hotel)	Madras
The Oberoi Clarkes	Simla
The Oberoi Cecil	Simla
The Oberoi Palace	Srinagar
The Oberoi Palm Beach	Gopalpur-on-Sea
The Oberoi	Bangalore

Abroad

The Windsor	Melbourne, Australia
The Mena House Oberoi	Cairo, Egypt
The Aswan Oberoi	Aswan, Egypt
The Oberoi Shahryar &	Luxor/Aswan
The Oberoi Shehrazad	Luxor/Aswan
(Nile Cruisers)	

The Egoth Oberoi	El Arish, Egypt
The Oberoi	Bali, Indonesia
The Soaltee Oberoi	Kathmandu, Nepal
The Oberoi	Dammam, Saudi Arabia
The Dammam Hotel	Dammam, Saudi Arabia
The Medina Oberoi	Medina, Saudi Arabia
The Babylon Oberoi	Baghdad, Iraq
The Nineveh Oberoi	Mosul, Iraq
The Lanka Oberoi	Colombo, Sri Lanka
Queen's Hotel	Kandy, Sri Lanka

Hotels expected to be commissioned by 1994

In India

The Oberoi Mount Everest (under renovation)	Darjeeling

Abroad

The Oberoi	Mauritius
The Gresham Palace	Budapest, Hungary

Appendix B

Man of Honours

- 1943 The title of 'Rai Bahadur' conferred by the British Government.
- 1976 'Agastya Award' presented by the Travel Agents Association of India.
- 1976 'The Victory Pillar' the highest Indian hoteliering award from the Hotel and Catering Industry.
- 1977 'Udyog Patra' by the Government of India.
- 1978 'Escorts-NIF Man of the Year 1978 Award'.
- 1978 An international award presented by the Mayor of the City of Los Angeles in the United States.
- 1978 NEWSWEEK names M.S. Oberoi one of its elite 'Winners of 1978' who contributed to the enlargement of world business.
- 1981 American Society of Travel Agents (ASTA) 'Hall of Fame' confer highest distinction in the travel industry.
- 1983 'Man of the World' award at the International Hotel Convention in New York for the expertise and professionalism with which his name is associated worldwide. The first hotelier from a Third World country to receive this honour.
- 1984 Giants International award for his 'extraordinary efforts to achieve the highest standard in pursuing excellence'.
- 1985 'Order of The Republic—First Class' by the President of the Arab Republic of Egypt.
- 1986 IATA Hall of Fame Award.
- 1988 'Honorary Doctorate of Business Administration' conferred by The International Management Centre, Buckingham, England.

1991 'India Hotelier Hall of Fame Award', awarded for excellence and quality in the hotel and restaurant industry, initiated by the *Hotel and Food Services Review Magazine* in collaboration with the Western India Region Hotel Federation.

Index